A STAR IS TORN

A STAR IS TORN

ROBYN ARCHER & DIANA SIMMONDS

E. P. DUTTON NEW YORK

Published in the United States by E. P. Dutton,
a division of NAL Penguin Inc.,
2 Park Avenue, New York, N.Y. 10016.
Originally published in Great Britain.

Library of Congress Cataloging-in-Publication Data
Archer, Robyn, 1948–
A star is torn.
Bibliography: p.
Includes index.
1. Women entertainers—Biography.   2. Women
singers—Biography.   I. Simmonds, Diana.   II. Title.
PN1583.A85   1987   790.2′092′2 [B]   87-19653
ISBN: 0-525-48346-2

OBE

DESIGNED BY SUE LAMBLE

PICTURE RESEARCH BY MAGGIE COLBECK

10 9 8 7 6 5 4 3 2 1

First American Edition

This book is dedicated to the memory of
GLORIA DAWN, a great Aussie battler, and one of
the finest entertainers Australia has ever produced (RA)

and

to the memory of EVA MOTTLEY, a blazing talent
who could have been one of the finest black actresses
Britain has ever produced (DS)

Acknowledgements

The authors would like to thank the following for their generous and invaluable help: Cate Anderson; Rowena Balos; Maureen Barron; Maggie Colbeck; Rodney Fisher; Don Gettinger; Angelo Giahecchini; Bryan Hammond and The Gate Memorabilia Bookshop; Phillip Hedley; Michael Houldey; John Jeremy; Regis Lansac; Tony Locantro; Diana Manson; Susan Marshall; Mandy Merck; Helen Mills; Deborah Owen; Ursula Owen; Deborah Parry; Lyn Quayle; Michèle Roberts; Geoffrey Robertson; Annie Ross; Roy Robert Smith; Robyn Stacey; Penny Valentine; Katie Webb; Tom Willett; Val Wilmer.

Permission to reproduce the following songs has kindly been granted by the companies listed: 'A Coster Girl in Paris', Lee & Powell, © Francis Day and Hunter Ltd, by EMI Music Publishing Ltd, London WC2H 0LD; 'A Little of What You Fancy', Leigh & Arthurs, by EMI Music Publishing Ltd, London WC2H 0LD, Redwood Music, London W1X 2LR; 'Bill', Kern, Wodehouse & Hammerstein, © 1927 T.B. Harms Co, by Chappell Music Limited; 'God Bless the Child', Holiday & Herzog, © 1941 copyright renewed by Edward B. Marks Co, all rights reserved, Yale Music Corp Ltd, by Bron Organisation Ltd, London NW1 8BR; 'Honky Tonk Merry Go Round', Frank & Gardner, © Acuff-Rose Songs, by Acuff-Rose Music Ltd; 'Hymne à l'Amour, Piaf/Albert Monnot, © 1953 Editions Edimarton, France, by EMI Music Publishing Ltd, London WC2H 0LD, translation © Michèle Roberts, 1986; 'I'm a Bit of a Ruin', Bedford & Sullivan, © 1921 B. Feldman & Co Ltd, by EMI Music Publishing Ltd, London WC2H 0LD; 'I'm Gonna File My Claim', Newman-Darby, © 1954 Simon House Inc, U.S.A., by EMI Music Publishing Ltd, London WC2H 0LD; 'Kozmic Blues', Joplin & Mekler, © 1970 Strong Arm Music, all rights reserved, reproduced by permission of the publisher; 'La Belle Historie d'Amour', Piaf & Dumont, © 1961 Les Nouvelles Editions Meridian, by Southern Music Publishing Co Ltd, London WC2H 8LT, translation © Michèle Roberts, 1986; 'Lady Sings the Blues' words by Holiday and music by Nicholls, © 1956, 1972 by Northern Music Co, rights administered by MCA Music, a division of MCA Inc, New York, copyright renewed, used by permission, all rights reserved, reprinted by permission of MCA Music (Aust. Pty Ltd) reprinted by permission of MCA Music Ltd (UK); 'Les Blouses Blanches', Monnot & Rivegauche, © 1961 Les Nouvelles Editions Meridian, by Southern Music Publishing Co Ltd, London WC2H 8LT, translation © Michèle Roberts, 1986; 'My Man', Yvain & Arkell, © Editions Salabert, by Ascherberg, Hopwood & Crew Ltd; 'Mercedes Benz', Joplin, © 1970 Strong Arm Music, all rights reserved, reproduced

1870-1970

Introduction

Marie Lloyd 1870–1922 (52)

Bessie Smith 1894–1938 (44)

Helen Morgan 1900–1942 (42)

Jane Froman 1907–1980 (72)

Carmen Miranda 1909–1955 (46)

Billie Holiday 1915–1959 (44)

Edith Piaf 1915–1963 (48)

Judy Holliday 1921–1965 (44)

Judy Garland 1922–1968 (46)

Dinah Washington 1924–1963 (39)

Marilyn Monroe 1926–1962 (39)

Patsy Cline 1932–1963 (31)

Janis Joplin 1943–1970 (27)

Thirteen women; thirty-three husbands;
nine children (three of them were Judy Garland's)

Average age at death: 44

A STAR IS TORN

This book had its beginnings in a one-woman show that developed, with the collaboration of director Rodney Fisher, into a full-scale theatrical presentation called *A Star is Torn*. It premiered in Australia in 1979 and eventually found its way to London's West End Theatre where it enjoyed great success. The show, as primarily an entertainment, could only touch on stories, ideas, and themes which the book has allowed us to expand on and thus make relevant to a far wider audience.

The idea for the show, and for this book, began with the music of those women who, for me, epitomised the styles of Music Hall, Blues, Jazz, Country and Western, Chanteuse, Show Biz, Torch, Rock. As both listener and singer, my musical tastes were wide. Even in the days when a singer like Patsy Cline was looked down on outside the circles of strict Country and Western devotees, I found her style inspirational. When I heard Patsy swell out a note, yodel the middle of a phrase and glide on to the next, it was as unfashionably thrilling to me as the widely respected blues moaning of Bessie Smith, or the screams and growls of Janis Joplin. What I loved about them all was a sense of vocal abandon, a note from the teenage Judy Garland, or the tiny frame of Edith Piaf, that seemed to come from the middle of a deep well, never touching the sides, and leaving breath and power to spare; or the sorcery that Billie Holiday commanded in her phrasing and Marie Lloyd in her comic timing. They all took performing risks and brought them off wonderfully.

When I started to research beyond their music, into their lives, it came as a shock to find that they had all died too young. Marie Lloyd the eldest at fifty-two and Janis Joplin the youngest at twenty-seven, following working lives that were plagued by a degree of physical and spiritual misery that seemed inconsistent with their status as Stars. Similarly unexpected was the realisation that I could remove these idols of mine from the safe distance of past eras, and see them from first to last clearly in relation to my own experience. Marie Lloyd (at the turn of the century the most popular of the British Music Hall artists, who also toured the United States and

Canada) had performed in the East End music halls where my own great-grandmother sang as a young woman. From her I had learned my first songs at the age of four. Eighteen years later, as Adelaide's answer to Janis Joplin, I had felt my rock'n'roll heroine's death as a personal blow. Now with this book comes the opportunity to examine contradictions in their lives.

As any Hollywood waitress will tell you, Stardom can't be simply equated with Talent. Show business sets up individual performers as unique beings, separate from the rest of us, to be worshipped in isolation. Pin-ups celebrate this condition, biographies reinforce it, and public response makes the process concrete. Stars represent the pinnacle of popular culture; those who succeed in mirroring that image are rewarded. Those who refuse or challenge are viewed quite differently, and observers from the closest to the casually distant have interpreted such resistance as perverse. The feeling is that the suffering experienced by the renegades was of their own making, at best because of some tragic flaw, at worst because they were lushes, junkies and ballbreakers—causes unknown and irrelevant—who were never sufficiently grateful for the wonderful opportunities they'd been given. Thus the stage was set for these women to be misremembered and misrepresented, their real lives dismissed and forgotten. And for the most part, this is exactly what has happened.

This book is an attempt to reverse the process, to answer the question 'Who cares?' and 'So what?'. Its aim is to retrieve their genius and tragedy from the trashcan of nostalgia, minority cult and well-meaning patronisation; to celebrate that genius in the context of their struggle as women, and to illustrate how that burden, carried as it was at the sharp end of western capitalist society, makes them all as relevant to women today as if they were alive and kicking. Behind the images of isolated goddesses with feet of clay lie women like all of us, carrying the ambitions, prejudices and discrimination of their time and society. With the benefits of hindsight and feminism it is possible to set aside the obstacles between them and us, to offer the understanding and compassion they rarely experienced or were able to give themselves and, in so doing, to illuminate lives which are, as ever, in the process of being 'hidden from history'. Since the original publication of this book, Gloria Steinem's *Marilyn* has reinforced the way forward for feminist readings of famous lives, and we can only hope that more of the same will follow.

A dispassionate explanation of so many tragic deaths is that these were simply the normal percentage of women in entertainment who would have been ill, mad, addicts and dead at an early age, whatever the circumstances. Yet there is nothing normal about the exploitation that ruined their lives. The audiences that flocked to see them seemed healthy, intelligent and affluent—the kind of people who couldn't ignore an injured dog in the street. That same night, they would pay a small fortune to sit anonymously in the dark and witness the pathetic struggle of a profoundly distressed, often visibly ill human being, applaud her, cheer her on, and beg for more. Is it simply misplaced devotion, or is it inevitable that Stars should be so removed from real life that an audience feels unable to help and, thus relieved of responsibility, able to sit back and enjoy the catharsis its idol provides? Is it a similar dilemma to that of an outsider looking into a tight family circle, suspecting mistreatment but reticent or powerless to break in? And what about those within that circle? Are successful performers doomed to partners and associates who simply wish to bask in the glory and share in the profits, unwilling to call a halt even when the workhorse is obviously unwell and unhappy? How many lovers, friends or spouses had the guts to break a binding contract rather than see their loved one broken? How many were strong enough to stand up to the obstinate ego and show-must-go-on mentality of the trouper and simply stop them?

One of the tenets of the 'tragic flaw' school of thought is that these women were essentially weak, and should have been tougher; that if Ella Fitzgerald and Debbie Reynolds could survive, so could Billie and Judy. But the strength of this argument lies in a firm belief that the exploitation of one individual for the profit of another, especially in show business, is inevitable. A more humane approach would be to change the system that's causing the damage rather than demand harsh adaptation from those who might get hurt: one survivor more or less doesn't invalidate that need.

Central to a feminist reading of the available material is a reinterpretation of the way these women have been viewed in the past. It reveals that they were subject to pressures and discrimination different from those that governed the lives of their male counterparts. Fred Astaire, Gene Kelly, Donald O'Connor and Mickey Rooney all acknowledged Judy Garland as the greatest entertainer of them all, yet they were unable to fathom the contradictions of a society whose positive discrimination helped each of them outlive their colleague by decades. From birth they were taught that it was their right to go out and grab the world and its riches: fame, wealth, pleasure, women, wives, any toy they wanted was theirs to have, hold and control. At the same time Marie, Billie, Judy, Marilyn, Janis and millions of other ambitious young women were discovering something different; that the positive energy and physical attack vital to their performing lives were quite different from the qualities they would need to succeed in the more important role of wife and mother.

Aggression in the male and female are perceived in profoundly different ways. These perceptions, especially in the period we're dealing with, governed the style and quality of the lives of performers; and it is this difference that renders impossible a similar case for the men who are consistently offered up as comparable examples of the same condition. There is obviously a book in their stories too and it worth sampling their biographies if only to see how quickly a different pattern emerges. That Rudolph Valentino, Hank Williams, Charlie Parker, Lenny Bruce, Montgomery Clift, James Dean, Jimi Hendrix, and Elvis Presley, amongst others, were exploited by the business, suffered, and died too young is undeniable and pitiable; the points of similarity are obvious—Jimi's exploitation as a black stud in a white business, Monty Clift as homosexual victim of a macho Hollywood, Hank William's addiction as the result of physical illness, even Presley as slave to an image. But, with few exceptions, they were not thrown into terminal confusion by a central dichotomy in their lives. Instead of dying of frustration because of their powerlessness to control circumstances and events, it was the unlimited power that Stardom afforded them which led to all-consuming and fatal gluttony. When the women took drugs it was not in the spirit of all-girls-together camaraderie: their addictions were masked in the quasi-medical excuse which they hoped would cover the shame attached to that condition. In essence, the women died of deprivation, and the men of excess: the root cause of both was, and is, that society sees women and men differently.

Frances Gumm (Judy Garland) at forty-five . . .

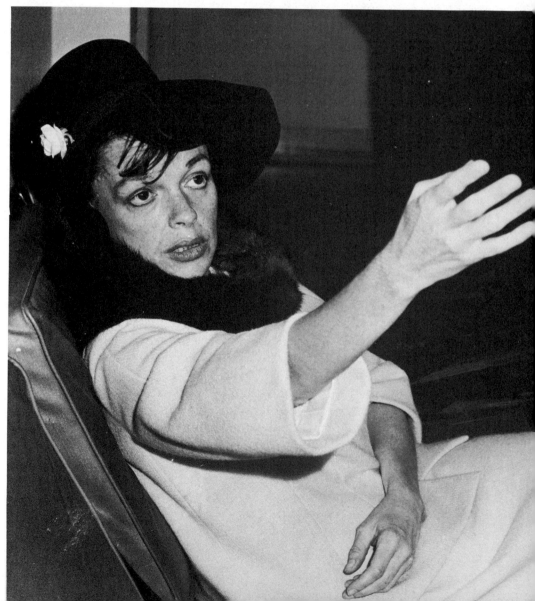

. . . and at five

In compiling this book we have tried to extract the lives of the individual women from a flood of fact, fancy, revenge and posthumous exploitation. Apart from Janis Joplin, who was able to avail herself of a growing, but already well-oiled, rock'n'roll media machine, and thus speak for herself on many widely broadcast occasions, the others were virtually silenced. This was partly to do with the times, but mostly to do with the accepted view that women had nothing to do with running their careers and nothing relevant to say on the matter. Interviews were often confined to moments of high drama (star in sunglasses, bursting into tears, nothing to say) or flippant facts on fashion and fad. We have quoted the women themselves

5

where possible, even second-hand via co-authors, but the most interesting pictures of their lives are still left to emerge from reading between the hundreds of thousands of lines that have been written about them.

In doing so, we have chosen to view them as women first, and as stars and phenomena second, in the hope that what will emerge are the similarities rather than the differences between their lives. The abstract notion of 'the star' is imperfectly and unsatisfactorily theorised elsewhere and, so far at least, serves mainly to bolster the tradition of separating women from one another. It seems that most theorists have failed to reconcile their own desires to view Stars as different from other people while at the same time trying to demystify the condition. Considering the origins of *A Star is Torn* it must be obvious that I do believe each of these women is possessed of an extraordinary and unique *talent*. What I don't believe is that any one of them was superhuman. When the particular system of her time and genre made each one famous, it did not automatically endow her with the larger-than-life strength she would need to survive, even though all of them, as their lives as 'ordinary women' show, were as strong and resilient as their upbringing demanded. That ambiguity is something the book tries to retain. At one moment we describe a woman confident enough to stand and deliver before an audience of thousands, brave enough to expose herself to the possibility of the most devastating abuse and criticism; the next we see that same woman cruelly unprotected and insecure. It was a contradiction they had to endure every day of their lives; and we maintain that not one was a deliberate suicide. Their deaths, even the 'accidental' ones, occurred as the result of long-term abuse which had more to do with trying to stay alive in a hostile environment than with killing themselves.

Most sections of the book deal with just one woman at a time, but in a way that we hope encourages connections to be made across cultures and generations between common issues like the central role of mother and daughter, early years of material deprivation, addictive propensities, the role of husband/lover/manager, the particulars of social environments and, always, the way each woman coped with the extra problem of 'being a woman'. Some sections link several women more directly with each other, and throughout we have tried to make comparisons with as many of their contemporaries as possible. What a book cannot do is to give you their singing, their performance, their energy, the lively and wry humour they all shared. For that you must go to the albums, the movies, the TV clips, any recorded media that have preserved, however imperfectly, some measure of the way these women worked, and worked very hard.

In the end the aim of the book is the same as that of the show. It celebrates their talent and laments their distress. It attributes much of that distress to causes that were clearly avoidable, and further laments the injustice of posthumous judgements that openly or by implication lay the blame solely on the victim. Finally it suggests that this kind of mistreat-

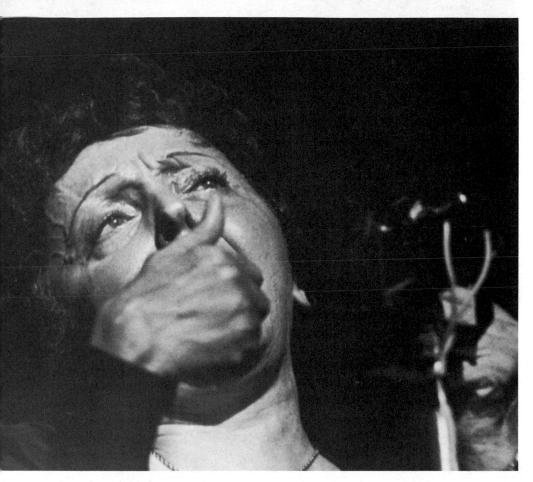

Edith Gassion
(La Môme Piaf)
in performance

ment, leading to similar fatalities, will continue to occur unless the process of reassessment which feminism has demanded elsewhere is applied to the business of entertainment and the position of women within it. The central dilemma in the lives of the women who comprise *A Star is Torn* relates to a common condition in all women, and we cannot afford to ignore the fact that Stardom, and the physical and material ideals embodied therein, is no less attractive to young women now than it was fifteen or a hundred and fifteen years ago. If we continue to enjoy and celebrate the talents and achievements of women like those in *A Star is Torn*, as I believe we should, we also need to be aware of the ultimate price those women paid to make that contribution.

Robyn Archer, 1987

Wishing you a Happy New Year

Marie Lloyd

8

**I'd like to go again
To Paris on the Seine
For Paris is a proper Pantomime,
And if they'd only shift the 'Ackney Road
And plant it over there . . .
Why I'd like to live in Paris all the time!**

'A Coster Girl in Paris', Lee and Powell

Marie Lloyd was born Matilda Alice Victoria Wood on 12 February 1870 in the East End of London. A legend in her own lifetime, mythologised since as one of the original working-class heroes, she was a poor lass who, as the eldest of ten children, worked alongside her parents from an early age to keep the family together. All true, but only half the story.

Marie's parents came from families of rural artisans who had joined a move to the industrial cities in the middle of the nineteenth century. John Wood was a maker of artificial flowers; it was a clean job for a craftsman who had aspirations towards bettering himself and his family. His wife Matilda shared his ambitions, and constantly urged her husband to claim his dues. With a growing family to feed Matilda at first assisted her husband at pittance wages but then began working independently at home, earning more in this way than she could from John's unappreciative employer. But John Wood was a man with prospects, and he no longer automatically expected his wife to be an equal earning partner. As the upper layer of the working class began to look towards the expanding middle class and its mores, John was the kind of man who would have preferred his wife to stay at home. For her part Matilda was far too practical. She met John's resistance with the undertaking that if he ever found her lacking in her domestic duties she would give up her paid work. He backed down and took a second job himself, becoming a popular local figure in his role as 'Brush' Wood, a waiter in one of the nearby music halls.

The changing times were mirrored in the Wood household. With the elevation of the family as the most desirable social unit, there was a new emphasis on symbols of respectability. Children were no longer merely members of the working team: there was school to consider; the home was the haven, and Matilda was noted for her meticulous housekeeping. Yet there were few luxuries and she practised typical self-sacrifice in keeping to a strict budget. In the absence of servants, the badge of the

9

middle class, the eldest girl was expected to look after the little ones, which suited 'young Tillie' because she disliked school. But her mother was illiterate, and intent on seeing that her children acquired at least the basics.

Tillie was always happier either at home with her mother or out in the neighbourhood where, with her already rumbustious nature, she began to get a taste for entertaining. She and her sisters were particularly fond of the elaborate funeral pageantry of the East End, and would often 'do' several funerals in one day, having a good cry at each, whilst enjoying the pomp and ceremony of the occasion. She also formed a troupe, the Fairy Bell Minstrels, who developed a repertoire including a well-liked temperance scene which ended with Tillie reciting solemnly, 'Throw down the bottle and never drink again.'

At a time when gin palaces, prostitution and their accompanying disease and decay were visible scourges in the East End, Matilda steered her daughter with a firm hand. As soon as Tillie left school, her mother insisted that any nonsense about the halls be set aside in favour of respectable employment. She helped Tillie secure a position first of all at a factory which fashioned babies' boots (her own family's old trade), then at feather-turning (akin to John Wood's trade), and finally at a bead-working factory; but Tillie remained stage-struck – and a dismal failure in gainful employment. Mrs Wood finally relented and then threw herself into coaching and encouraging Tillie with as much energy as she had previously devoted to her husband. Matilda insisted that if her daughter, by now known professionally as Bella Delmere, was going to perform, then she was going to do it properly.

The fancy name was shortlived, and in 1885, when Tillie was fifteen years old, records show that a 'Marie Lloyd' received fifteen shillings a week at the Star in Bermondsey. The qualities for which she soon became famous – a big clear voice, perfect timing in gesture and movement, and above all the desire and ability to make people laugh – were already apparent in the novice performer. Her rise was meteoric by any standards, and difficult to comprehend when the genre of which she became undisputed Queen has now disappeared. Getting a start was as difficult then as now, and while her mother could help with the costumes, Marie had no choice as a penniless beginner but to start boldly and pinch other singers' popular hits. In those days songs were commissioned and purchased for exclusive performance, and Marie was severely reprimanded by the offended artistes. But by the end of 1886 she was earning an astronomical £100 a week, and could well afford the proper accoutrements – the sharpest gowns any seamstress could devise, and her own material to perform.

There is no other woman in this book who had a similarly swift rise to fame. Overnight success is one of those show-business myths that is in fact extremely rare, yet Marie Lloyd became a Star in less than a year and remained at the top for over thirty years. Her success depended solely on that most ephemeral product – the strength of each performance – and so the secret of her allure remains elusive today. Recording was little more than an archival mechanism in her day, and unlike most of the other women in this book, was never a significant part of her career. Between 1903 and 1916 Marie recorded about a dozen songs, but they give scant indication of why she was so popular. Contemporary accounts and opinions, however, do give some oblique clues. At a time when bourgeois hypocrisy prevailed, Marie Lloyd was embarrassingly honest. When demure refinement was required of a lady, Marie was ostentatiously vulgar. No matter what her parents may have aspired to, Marie identified with the working class of the East End, and despite money and countless opportunities to associate with a 'better class' of person, she repeatedly thumbed her nose at polite society and remained true to what she saw as her natural audience – and they loved her for it.

In 1887, soon after her career was established, seventeen-year-old Marie married Percy Courtenay. A year later she gave birth to Marie Junior, her only child. Percy was considerably older than his wife and had all the charm of a man of leisure; what money he had came from the racetrack. Marie herself lived in high style. She enjoyed parties and companionship, and stinted herself of neither, but she was also noted for her fidelity to Matilda's example: although able to afford servants, Marie supervised the housework to what might now be considered an obsessive degree. Some of biographer Naomi Jacob's emphasis on Marie's domesticity may represent her desire to paint a picture of respectability to counteract the accounts of Marie's later decline. But it seems more than likely that Marie did cling to a notion of domestic order, not only to offset the hectic demands of her professional and private life but also to conform to and excel in those duties which came within woman's proper sphere. Motherhood was also high on Marie's list of priorities, and even when she was performing in as many as four halls a night, she always took her little girl with her, to maintain her 'proper care'. Consequently Marie Lloyd Jnr's own background was very like that of a majority of the women in this book: a strong, even larger-than-life mother, an unreliable, sometimes violent male presence, and a constantly changing environment. In all this Courtenay played out the classic reluctantly second-class role: he could not keep up with his wife's success nor reconcile himself to it. Another of Naomi Jacob's insistences is that Marie was never 'unfaithful' to her men, but once a thing was over, that was it, and she had few qualms about leaving. By 1893 the Courtenays were living apart. Percy retaliated by causing trouble over the custody of Marie Jnr, but Marie Snr fought him with equal energy and, after considerable unpleasantness, eventually won.

During the next few years, however, Marie and many of her colleagues would find themselves with more than just their private lives to worry

MARIE LLOYD.

CHRISTMAS ARRANGEMENTS:

PALACE,

METROPOLITAN,

AND

CAMBRIDGE.

PHOTO BY SCHLOSS, NEW YORK.

Grand Burlesque Tour, March 16, 1898.

SPECIALLY ENGAGED TO PLAY TITLE-RÔLE.

about. Many felt their very livelihoods were threatened when they came under public attack from the increasingly militant Purity Party. The history of Music Hall is as chequered as Marie's own; its origins and growth are well documented in Daniel Farson's *Marie Lloyd and Music Hall* – the prejudices against it were deeply embedded in the British class system. In the first half of the nineteenth century there were three areas of popular entertainment. At one end of the social scale the Penny Gaffs for the very poor (often young and female) audience, offering rough variety entertainment in squalid converted shops and stables where swearing, scatalogical humour and transvestite comedy were judged as 'lewd' by intruding middle-class observers. At the other end were the sumptuous and often notorious Song and Supper rooms where quality types drank and beheld entertainments of a similarly bawdy nature. Sex and blasphemy were also popular with the peers (and the Prince of Wales), MPs and gentlemen as they revelled in an atmosphere of naughty escapism, tobacco smoke and alcohol. Women were barred from attending, and it was not until 1860 that a woman first entertained in one of the more respectable of these establishments.

In between these two extremes were the taverns and Pleasure Gardens, most of which had a licence for entertainment. This might include singers, dancers, jugglers and comedians, but not 'plays', which were feared might inflame the lower classes and were thus the special privilege of the Drury Lane and Covent Garden theatres, both of which held the Royal Charter. Drama in the taverns had to be disguised as 'variety' by the insertion of background music or whole variety turns between scenes. Even then entrepreneurs risked arrest and fines for the illegal presentation of Shakespeare's dangerous realism. Eventually the people of the East End took to the streets in protest at their pitiful and ludicrous allowance of bowdlerised Bard; their banners demanded 'Freedom for the People's Amusement' and 'Workers Want Theatres'. In 1843 a new Act became law. But it carried with it the class prejudice of the lawmakers, and was to affect the concept of entertainment to the present day.

The Act permitted theatres to present plays in their entirety, but not to provide food and wine; places serving such fare could only stage 'entertainments'. This gave rise to the notion of 'legitimate' theatre versus the lower pleasure of a combination of food, drink and variety served up in halls newly acquired by taverns for that purpose. At a stroke Music Hall became the lesser art form, and was never again spoken of in the same breath as 'the theatre'. It was in these halls, however, that Marie Lloyd found her audience and the scope for developing her performing skills. From her first performance at The Eagle in London's City Road in 1885, to her last in Edmonton, then north of the city, Marie Lloyd played every one of the hundreds of notable halls in the United Kingdom.

She was clearly a remarkable performer and possessed of a great gift to

13

captivate and hold an audience. But the appeal of her particular repertoire cannot be underestimated. Biographers who have tried to sidestep
the issue of Marie's bawdy songs by dismissing them as one small part of
her career misunderstand the nature of popular entertainment. For the
public it is always thrilling to see and hear an articulation of the un-
acknowledged. In an age when it was unheard of for a woman even to
admit to the possibility of sexual pleasure, Marie was popularising songs
like:

> I never was a one to go and stint myself
> If I like a thing, I like it, that's enough.
> But there's lots of people say that if you like a thing a lot
> It'll grow on you and all that sort of stuff!
> Now, I like me drop of stout as well as anyone
> But a drop of stout's supposed to make you fat
> And there's many a lah di dah madam doesn't care to touch it
> 'Cos she mustn't spoil her figure, silly cat!
>
> I always hold in having it if you fancy it
> If you fancy it, that's understood!
> And suppose it makes you fat?
> I don't worry over that,
> 'Cos a little of what you fancy does you good!
>
> ('A Little of What You Fancy', Leigh and Arthurs)

It's not hard to see how Marie's audience would have understood that she
wasn't just singing about a particular kind of ale. The exuberant performance of such a song must have been a breath of fresh air in the
stifling climate of publicly acceptable morals. Marie's open and good-
natured boldness aren't to be confused with the crudity of what was later
to become 'blue' comedy, the sleazy snickering that still operates at the
core of a great deal of British humour. But to ignore her bawdiness, or to
downplay it, is to undermine an understanding of her success.

The continuing association of Music Hall with drink and East End low
life, particularly the then thriving and notorious docklands, made it the
obvious target for reformists of all kinds. In 1878 the Certificate of
Suitability Law had enforced the closure of two hundred halls which were
unable to comply with new strict fire regulations; the halls were constantly
under threat from temperance leagues which tried to outlaw the uni-
versally dreadful cheap gin, rightly known as 'mother's ruin'; and in
1894, with the formidable zeal of a certain Mrs Ormiston Chant in the
forefront, the Purity Party embarked on a campaign to purge the Empire
Theatre in Leicester Square, London, of the prostitutes who used its
promenade to their advantage. Like many progressive women of the day,
Mrs Chant was variously portrayed in the all-male press as a prune-faced

monster or a ridiculous Christian moralist. The prostitutes whose livelihoods were in jeopardy saw only middle-class privilege versus the lower orders. On the other hand, it was not in the interests of Mrs Chant's social peers to see prostitution abolished. Press and politicians alike defended the ladies of the Empire on liberal grounds: the necessity for prostitutes in an age when a gentleman was supposed to respect his wife and not force his animal desires on her was one of them.

Mrs Chant won the first round when canvas screens were erected to separate the bars from the promenade, thus concealing the undesirable strolling presence outside the Empire. But this had the effect of revealing a good deal about the toffs who patronised the bars, and one evening the Empire's audience, the young Winston Churchill among them, tore down the screens and paraded in triumph about the Square. Brass railings then replaced the canvas, but soon the municipal council reversed its decision altogether and the press dubbed Mrs Chant a right prude. Unperturbed by defeat and ridicule, she carried her action into the halls themselves, but those who might have benefited most from such campaigning were in the frontline of attack and were understandably unwilling to listen or understand. Mrs Chant conceded that she had no right to interfere with what people wanted for entertainment – if vulgarity was their taste then that was their business. But she pointed to the fact that chorus girls were unpaid or underpaid, and hoped that reform in the popular theatre might bring about a more equable distribution of the profits, as was currently being sought in factories. Mrs Chant was clearly not just a prude. She was a reformer of great energy and courage; part of that movement which would eventually bring about better conditions, including female suffrage, for all women. But such efforts were lost on women like Marie Lloyd. Despite Marie's concern for the underprivileged of the East End, and her willingness to join with lesser-paid performers in striking against bad managements, the energies of such a woman lay untapped by those who sought reform through an insistence on temperance and purity.

Marie's lifestyle, performance and repertoire seemed the very antithesis of such ideals, and there was no one to convince Marie that giving up her pleasures might eventually bring fulfilment and longevity. The mode of the purists was to attack rather than persuade, and Marie was a prime target. Yet her repertoire did not begin with the bawdy songs, nor was it ever entirely dominated by them. Her first hit was 'The Boy I Love is Up in the Gallery', sung with all throat-catching lilting sweetness; some songs were simply an excuse for a new costume, as in 'The Directoire Girl'. But songs like 'Oh Mr Porter', 'What's That For Eh?' or 'Twiggy Vous' all had the potential of being very rude indeed. Audiences adored them, and the Purity Party attacked with a vengeance.

In 1896 Mrs Chant had Marie up before the Licensing Authorities to answer charges of obscenity. There is a disagreement about the offending song; it might have been the one about the girl who 'sits among the lettuces and peas', or it could have been

What's that for eh? Oh tell me Ma!
If you won't tell me, I'll ask Pa!
But Ma said – oh it's nothing, shut your row!
Well – I've asked Johnny Jones see,
So I know now.

('What's That For Eh?', Lytton and LeBrunn)

Whichever it was, Marie delivered her songs to the committee without a single gesture and they were apparently convinced of her innocence. But, having been dismissed, she gave a rendition of 'Come Into The Garden Maud' that bubbled over with *double entendre*, shot them a line about it being 'all in the mind', and swept out. In October that year the Halls' licences were renewed and such threats were not experienced by them again. For Marie, however, the battle was not over, and her continuing refusal of middle-class mores would sour her life and career in the same way some sixteen years later.

For the moment, though, Marie was victorious and her professional status was unquestionable. Not only had she consolidated her popularity in the halls but she had appeared three years running in the prestigious Drury Lane theatre in pantomime. Now she ventured abroad for the first time, to South Africa in 1896, where she was an unwitting participant in the rising tide of British imperialist expansion (which would lead, just three years later, to the Boer War). When she landed at Cape Town, however, the famous Marie Lloyd was a welcome attraction, and she felt comfortable enough there to allow Marie Jnr her first stage appearance. In 1897 she travelled to the United States to find that her reputation as a somewhat scandalous woman had preceded her and that she was obliged to defend herself to the press:

I'll bet if I sang the songs of Solomon set to music I would be accused of making them bad, just because people at the halls want songs that are not quite dead marches and I give it to them. You take the Pit on a Saturday night or a Bank Holiday. You don't suppose they want Sunday School stuff do you? They want lively stuff with music they can learn quickly. Why, if I was to try to sing high moral songs they would fire ginger beer bottles and beer mugs at me . . .

(*Marie Lloyd and Music Hall*, Daniel Farson)

Some say that Marie was not so successful in the US, where her exclusively British humour and style were less well understood. Nevertheless, when she returned home she had an international reputation as one who was loved as much in New York, Johannesburg, Paris and Berlin as in her native London. And at this time Marie was pursuing a personal love interest in Alec Hurley.

Hurley was a coster comedian one year her junior, and most famous for the song 'The Lambeth Walk'. He soon became her constant companion, and by 1900 they were openly living together in Southampton Row: certainly several steps up from the East End, but also rakishly on the edge of Bloomsbury. Success and wealth gave her the confidence and wherewithal to live exactly as she pleased. Like the later stars of Country and Western music, who flaunted their new status with diamante bravado, Marie maintained a defiantly vulgar lifestyle that wore its origins like medals. She continued to prefer the winkles, whelks and kippers of the costers' barrows, and the large gatherings of mates, music hall colleagues, jockeys, boxers and racetrack types continued to dominate her social life and drain her purse.

Law reform during the nineteenth century had made divorce somewhat easier, but it was still uncommon and there was a stigma attached to

Marie with Alec Hurley

it. Marie remained officially married to Percy Courtenay until he filed for divorce in 1904. During that first decade of the new century Marie maintained her status as Queen of the Music Halls. She and Alec travelled to Australia in 1901 and made a very successful tour of theatres there as joint top of the bill. But it was Marie that audiences had heard about and come to see, and although she and Hurley married in 1906, it seems that he had long been relegated in his own mind at least to the position of Mr Marie Lloyd, and their relationship was disintegrating.

In 1907 Marie's participation in the Music Halls strike underlined for all time, and for all to see, her sympathy with the underdogs against the theatrical bourgeoisie. At the time the Halls were booming, and the artists began to demand better conditions and a bigger share of the proceeds – none of which directly affected Marie, whose salary and contracts were far removed from the standard pittance on offer to the rest. Nevertheless, she picketed, made speeches and played havoc with the scabs. As one Bella Elmore, a noted third-rater, crossed the picket line, deaf to all pleas, Marie reportedly yelled, 'Let her go in . . . she'll do more to help by playing than by stopping out!'

Eventually the managers agreed to strike out the offending 's' which often added three or four more shows to the workload of standard contract acts when appended to the word 'matinee'. For the performers it was a considerable gain, but Marie's focal role marked the point at which her combative style began to fall foul of those who should have been her professional peers – the owners, managers and other successful artistes who viewed her behaviour as an affront to their own hard-sought respectability.

In 1910 she managed to cap even this militant effrontery with a new outrage, when she met the dashing young jockey Bernard Dillon. He was twenty-two and King of the Turf; she was forty and still Queen of her domain. And thus began what many considered to be her last great indiscretion. In 1911 Dillon was involved in a betting scam and the ruling aristocracy of the Turf, the Jockey Club, took away his licence to ride. It was the end of his career and the end of his earning capacity; he began to drink heavily. Meanwhile, Alec Hurley had moved, publicly and noisily, to the inn Jack Straw's Castle in Hampstead where he too passed his time in heavy drinking. All in all Marie Lloyd was behaving in a way that offended polite society, and particularly the upper echelons of her own profession.

If Marie's critics had ever wished to burst the bubble of her extra-ordinary popularity they were handed an opportunity in 1912 when Edward Moss, Oswald Stoll and Walter de Frece were required to arrange a Royal Command Performance of Music Hall artists. It was the crowning moment for the theatre managers who had fought the law and reformist opinion to establish the respectability of their business. Indeed, Stoll had built the Coliseum with theatre rather than Music Hall in mind:

there were no bars, and he interspersed acts like George Robey with sprinklings of 'culture'. He had never invited Marie to perform there, and when the much-anticipated list of Royal Command performers was announced Marie's name was not on it, not even in the finale of one hundred and forty-two 'walk on' artists representing the profession. It was an astonishing snub, and Marie was deeply hurt. She was indisputably at the very top: the only other woman who commanded anything like her drawing power was Vesta Tilley, and the contrast in their fortunes in this instance highlights the prejudice harboured against Marie by the men who held the positions of increasing power at the time.

Although many considered her male impersonations 'daring', Vesta Tilley brought to the stage good taste in both costume and manner. She viewed with pity and contempt those young women who developed crushes on the elegant man/woman on stage, and privately her ambitions were satisfied by marriage to Walter de Frece and a place high on the bill for the Command Performance. It is said that Queen Mary and her entourage averted their eyes from the transvestite spectacle, but aspiring Tory MP Walter was nevertheless rewarded with a knighthood and Vesta eventually retired to write her memoirs as Lady de Frece.

Meanwhile, a short distance from the Palace Theatre where the Command Performance was establishing a long and enduring tradition of dreariness, Marie staged her own show at the London Pavilion. Loyal fans had returned their Command tickets and came to see Marie instead. She was billed as 'The Queen of Comedy' and she introduced new songs. Outside the posters bore strips which announced:

Every Performance by Marie Lloyd
is a Command Performance
By Order of the British Public

But no matter how faithful that public was, nor how successful her rival show had been, the snub by the cream of her profession was a bitter blow even for such a rebellious spirit. The following year Marie took up an offer to return to the United States. She and Bernard set sail on 13 October, straight into another nightmare. On arrival in New York she was immediately imprisoned on Ellis Island by immigration officials because she and Dillon were not married. More than a decade before, Marie had travelled freely to Australia in a similar *de facto* situation and had experienced no trouble. Now she was shocked and humiliated. She had long since been reconciled to the snobbery of first-class passengers on board ship, and always restricted her entertaining to shows for the steerage passengers, but imprisonment, brought about by a snooping reporter, was something else. Back in England the same public which had deplored Marie's exclusion from the Royal Command Performance similarly denounced American moral officialdom, and offered some small comfort to Marie who spoke with feeling to the press:

You call this a free country and yet there is not another country on earth that would expose a defenceless woman to such public ignominy, ridicule and humiliation. The same heartless ruling, if applied to grand opera singers and theatrical stars, would bar some of the greatest artists from your country . . .

(*Queen of the Music Halls*, W. MacQueen-Pope)

The class and cultural discrimination was not lost upon her. With passion she described the sickening feeling of looking out of her prison window to see the Statue of Liberty, knowing that if she had been a male star or even a woman 'of quality' she would not have been treated thus. In order to continue with the tour of the brave New World, Marie and Dillon had to comply with publicly imposed conditions, maintaining separate establishments and fulfilling the standards of propriety expected of the unwed.

Whilst in Canada Marie learned of Alec Hurley's death and she married Bernard Dillon shortly afterwards. Whether she would have thought twice about tying herself to a man who was already draining her purse for his own amusement if the pressures of the tour and considerable expense of separate living arrangements had not been present is hard to say. In the event, marry him she did, and in 1914 they returned home just as England went to war. Like every other trouper, Marie introduced topical wartime ditties into her repertoire and entertained troops and war workers. But at the end of the war official expressions of gratitude failed to mention her contribution to the war effort; and during it, Marie had to endure the humiliation of having her young husband first join the army and then desert. His 'cowardice' and then his violence towards her were much and publicly debated. It was obvious to everyone around her that Dillon's decline since forfeiting his livelihood was much more than she could cope with. In nine years together Marie and Bernard had gone through between £30,000 and £40,000, and the years had taken their toll of more than her finances. In 1920 Marie collapsed at her fiftieth birthday celebrations. Later in the year she was granted a legal separation from Dillon but only after he had extended his violence to her father. She was ill, tired and badly in need of rest, but her money was gone and she had to keep working. She kept up her professional standards, but she was drinking heavily and had lost the ebullience which had marked the performances of her prime. During the next eighteen months she collapsed several times but continued to reject any overtures of concern from her friends. She often needed advances on her salary and the period was spent in just keeping ahead of debt and impoverishment.

To many admirers, Marie represents that elusive but admired character 'the battler'. It is this quality that is usually held up to separate her from the 'neurotic' or 'troublemaking' types such as Judy Garland or Marilyn

Monroe. Thus to battle on and lose like Marie is somehow more admirable than battling on and losing like Marilyn or Judy. More than that, there has been a tendency to deny that her life was 'lost'; her tragedies were not nearly so widely broadcast in the much more limited media of the day. In the end she fulfilled her role as a good old stick and a trouper to the last. One night in Edmonton she completed 'I'm a Bit of a Ruin' to the usual appreciative response; it was one of her best-known songs:

You know I'm very fond of ruins
And ruins I like to scan,
You'd say I'm fond of ruins, hoo!
If you saw my old man.
Well I went into the country for a stroll the other day

21

'Cos I like to study hist'ry and the pubs along the way
I came across an abbey that was tumbled all to bits,
It seemed a relic of a bygone day,
A gentleman said 'what is this?'
I said 'Excuse me, sir. I'll tell you all about it if I may'.

I'm a bit of a ruin that Cromwell knocked about a bit
One of the ruins that Cromwell knocked about a bit
In the gay old days, there used to be some doin's,
No wonder that the poor old abbey fell to ruins.
Well those who study hist'ry sing and shout of it,
And you can bet your life there isn't a doubt of it,
'Cos outside the Cromwell Arms last Saturday night
I was one of the ruins that Cromwell knocked about a bit.

('I'm a Bit of a Ruin', Bedford and Sullivan)

Then she collapsed, and the laughing audience thought she had added a comical new piece of business to finish the act. Three days later she died at home; she was fifty-two.

What followed during the next few days set the seal on Marie's legendary status. Floral tributes of all shapes and sizes filled her house, covered the bier and followed the procession: a white horseshoe with whip, spurs and blue cap of flowers 'From her Jockey Pals'; a huge model stage with 'finis' in the card slot and a bunch of roses front and centre from her last agent and his wife; a birdcage of flowers with open door; a vast presentation from 'the Costermongers of Farringdon Road'; individual wreaths from every top star in the business; and countless other items from friends and anonymous followers, from the most intricate floral arrangement to the smallest bunch of violets. Millions mourned, tens of thousands lined the streets. It was more like a state funeral at which what is marked is not merely the death of an individual but of a symbol, and in this instance a symbol of *popular* culture.

Similarly the bodies of Edith Piaf, Billie Holiday and Judy Garland were to 'lie in state' whilst people, many of whom had never seen them alive, wept as they filed past. But such emotion counted for little where it really mattered. For Marie there was no revered old age, no memoirs, no honours. She was a national treasure to millions, yet accorded infinitely less care than any number of Old Ruins. Her performances were adored, but she was made to pay too high a price for remaining precisely the person who produced them. In the end no mountain of flowers, fine words or throngs lining the route could outweigh the disappointments of her professional life and the unhappiness that crowded her last ten years. In the contradiction of public idolatry and private misery Marie Lloyd stands at the beginning of this line of famous women whose lives proved less valuable than their talent to entertain.

24

**I'm sittin' and a-thinkin' of the days gone by
They filled my heart with pain
I'm too weak to stand, and too strong to cry
But I'm forgettin' it all in vain
Oh me, oh my
I wonder what will my end be?
Oh me, oh my
I wonder what will become of poor me?**

'Wasted Life Blues', Smith

When the Queen of the Music Halls died in 1922, Bessie Smith, the Empress of the Blues, was twenty-eight years old. In that year Bessie moved permanently to Philadelphia and caught the attention of New York record producers. The following year she began an historic recording career which would ensure her lasting fame.

Marie Lloyd was at the top for thirty years, Bessie Smith for six. Yet today, wherever records are sold, Bessie is recognised as one of the finest and best known of the classic blues singers. Marie Lloyd is virtually unknown outside Britain, and even then only to those with an interest in entertainment history and nostalgia. The reason for the difference lies in the development of the recording industry. When Marie was in her prime, records were used principally for archival preservation; by the time Bessie hit her stride they had become one of the principal avenues of popular culture. Though Bessie was born in 1894, she moved from the world of black vaudeville, not so unlike Marie's music halls, right to the heart of what would become this century's most widely available entertainment medium.

Bessie was not the first woman to record the blues: that distinction belonged to Mamie Smith (no relation), who filled in at the last minute for Sophie Tucker on 'Crazy Blues' in August 1920. But from 15 February 1923 when she made 'Downhearted Blues', to the last song of her final session, 'Down in the Dumps', in November 1933, Bessie Smith's performances were recorded and became synonymous with the blues, to be rediscovered by a future audience whose size and diversity were beyond the comprehension of those involved in the initial success.

Bessie is now regarded as one of the all-time entertainment greats, featuring prominently in the American *Who's Who* that ignores Billie Holiday and Judy Garland, and admired across a broad spectrum from jazz buffs to black feminists. But it was not always so. Black reform of the period echoed many of the strains of 'purity' to be found in the movement that so criticised Marie Lloyd, and Bessie's position was similar to Marie's.

She was a drinker and she loved to party; 'Gimme a Pigfoot and a Bottle of Beer' was a song she sang with feeling. She was a frequenter of the notorious 'Buffet flats', private high-class establishments where the bootleg booze was in steady supply along with opportunities to spectate or participate in any of the variety of sexual acts on the menu. Considered 'too black' by the producer of the show *Glorifying the Brownskin Girl*, which she auditioned for in 1912, Bessie herself always preferred dark-skinned women and men. She shunned 'dicty' (high-falutin') blacks, and rarely mixed it with sympathetic but patronising white liberal society. While performers like Josephine Baker, Ethel Waters, Alberta Hunter, Adelaide Hall, and later Billie Holiday and Ella Fitzgerald, revelled in their European triumphs, Bessie never left those American cities whose black population and environment she knew and identified with. Like Marie Lloyd, Bessie was a battler.

But for many early black feminists the hope of the race lay in its women and their educative role both within and outside the family. Speaking the year before Bessie's birth, black feminist Fannie Barrier Williams said:

> The home and social life of these people is in urgent need of the purifying power of religion ... the heart of every social evil and disorder among the colored people, especially of the rural south, is the lack of those inherent moral potencies of home and family ... The moral regeneration of a whole race of women is no idle sentiment – it is a serious business.

> (*Black Women in Nineteenth Century Life*, James Loewenberg and Ruth Bogin)

Consequently, the bold young thing who shimmied her knickers for all to see, and the mature woman bluesing and boozing away the best years of her life, must have appeared to black American feminists as Marie Lloyd had to their white British counterparts. Bessie, like Marie, remained suspicious of and aloof from such women who were educated, pro-temperance, and would have had them give up their high times for the greater good of womankind.

Even so, despite their open sexual and social defiance, both Bessie and Marie adhered to conventional ideas of mother and wife. Having no child of her own, Bessie adopted the son of one of her ex-chorus girls, and played the devoted mother to 'Snooks' no less than Marie had to Marie Junior. Both had husbands who beat them, and both turned to drink for consolation. But if Bessie Smith and Marie Lloyd shared conditions common to many women of the poorer classes (and indeed many of the wealthier ones), they differed greatly in the circumstances of their immediate environments. It is unlikely that Marie was unaware of Jack the Ripper, whose choice of target, the East End prostitutes, was not without its social significance; but the scope of his violence was nothing like that of the Ku Klux Klan who, at the time of Bessie's birth and in the immediate vicinity of her home in Chattanooga, Tennessee, were raping, torturing and lynching black men and women with the full sanction of local authorities.

Some thirty years after black Emancipation, when Bessie was born to Laura Smith and her Baptist preacher husband William, the South was ablaze with race hatred. It is not only Bessie's life but the lives of every black woman entertainer mentioned in this book that should be seen in this context. The musical line is clear: from Ma Rainey, the 'Mother' of the blues, to Bessie, the 'Empress'; from Bessie to Billie Holiday (and Lena Horne and Ella Fitzgerald); from Billie to Dinah Washington (whose idols were Bessie and Billie); from Dinah to Esther Phillips and to Nina Simone: these are just a few of the black women who have influenced popular singing in this century. But within that tradition is a series of multi-layered struggles – as women, as black women, as poor black women – and one of these was, and still is, racism. In 1894, particularly in the South, that struggle was being conducted amid unremitting barbarism.

Black militant and journalist Ida Wells Barnett painted a grim picture of the South in *Atrocities*, written in 1892 and addressed in part to British audiences while she was on a speaking tour in the year of Bessie's birth. She had been part owner of a Memphis newspaper, *Free Speech*, which had run an editorial which not only denounced a series of eight lynchings but also made a desperately courageous editorial assertion about the habitual lynching of black men for the 'rape' of white women:

> . . . If southern white men are not careful, they will over-reach themselves and public sentiment will have a reaction; a conclusion will then be reached which will be very damaging to the moral reputation of their women . . .
>
> (*Black Women in Nineteenth Century Life*, James Loewenberg and Ruth Bogin)

The effect was electric. Within days retaliatory editorials appeared in other papers, culminating in the *Evening Scimitar*'s recommendation that the editor of *Free Speech* be branded with a hot iron and castrated with tailor's shears. It was not merely hot rhetoric: a meeting was called at the Cotton Exchange, the seat of power in any southern rural centre, and, inspired by the *Scimitar*'s stirring words, the town's most influential and responsible citizens formed a party to carry out the recommendations. Fortunately the editor was long gone, and Ida, already in New York on business, had been warned not to return home. Her testimony is not only a frightening account of the public acceptability of such violence at the time of Bessie's birth but also illustrates that vigilante activity was not the exclusive domain of poor disenfranchised whites.

Atrocities actually cites Bessie's home town of Chattanooga as one in which the situation was slightly better. The city fathers had publicly denounced lynching, and one man accused of 'outrage' (rape) had been protected until his trial. The trial lasted only ten minutes; the man pleaded guilty even though he had in his possession letters from the white woman which indicated an entirely different relationship. He was sentenced to twenty-one years' imprisonment, but felt it was preferable to the certain death he faced upon acquittal and release beyond the protection of the law. Whether or not Chattanooga was really any easier for blacks in general, the Smith family's particular circumstances were difficult enough. Soon after Bessie's birth her father died, and the support of the six children fell to her mother Laura. When Bessie was eight or nine Laura died too, leaving the care of Tinnie, Lulu, Bessie, Clarence and Andrew to their eldest sister Viola. It wasn't long before Viola and Tinnie had children of their own; neither was married. Little else is known about them except that they became heavy drinkers, dependent finally on Bessie, and were still alive in the 1940s.

The absence of information about Bessie's family and their life in what she described as a 'ramshackle' cabin bears out Erlene Stetson's observation on women in the slave community:

> Tales of heroism centre almost exclusively on those who left and almost never on those who by sheer force of effort (morally, physically and otherwise) stayed because they would not/could not leave.

> (*But Some Of Us Are Brave*, Loria Hull, Patricia Scott and Barbara Smith)

It was still true at the end of the nineteenth century. Thus, next to nothing is known about Laura Smith but a great deal about one of her daughters: Bessie found her escape route and she left. From the time her mother died, Bessie started to sing on the streets for whatever coins she could pick up, and it wasn't long before she set her sights on a career in entertainment.

From the 1840s onwards, white entertainers had mimicked the style of the 'carefree simpleton negro' in a new craze for minstrel shows, throwing up some extraordinary performers in its long history – Sophie Tucker, for example, the daughter of Russian Jewish immigrants, began her career in 1908 as a blackface 'coon shouter'. Even the few black men who were employed in white minstrel shows were still blacking up with burnt cork into the 1950s when the National Association for the Advancement of Colored People pressed for reform. But from the 1860s the genuine article won increasing popularity, and by the time Bessie was busking on street corners black minstrelsy was a thriving if rough-and-tumble business. They were tent shows, the conditions were bad and the schedules gruelling, but to a young woman like Bessie it was paradise compared to the most common alternatives, domestic service or prostitution, both of which Billie Holiday endured before she was encouraged to sing for a living.

In 1912 Bessie's young brother Clarence was hired by Moses Stokes' Travelling Show, and he managed to get Bessie an audition too. It was the beginning of a ten-year vaudeville training during which Bessie established herself as a versatile performer who could dance and act as well as slay an audience with her huge voice. After her apprenticeship with the Stokes show she worked with many other companies, including one of Ma Rainey's – one-time leader of the famous 'Rainey and Rainey: Assassinators of the Blues'. Bessie also spent a lot of time at the 81 Theatre in Atlanta, where for ten dollars a week she did the shows – and trained the chorus line too, in the back yard of the theatre. Bessie's contemporary Alberta Hunter recalled that *she* was working as a domestic for six dollars a week when she heard the wild rumour that a theatre would pay ten. The 81 was part of the Theatre Owners' Booking Association (TOBA), variously known as Toby Time or Tough On Black Artists (or Asses), a circuit of venues which employed only black entertainers, and for which Bessie would draw thousands of paying customers.

Bessie, like Marie Lloyd, had everything a vaudeville performer needed to engage and delight a large audience: a commanding presence, a voice which could be both comic and moving, and an ability to use stage movement to great advantage. Sometimes she worked as a single with a band; sometimes in a show with other singers, a juggler, a comic dancer and chorus girls; sometimes she had her own show. There were times when she worked an extraordinary ten shows a day, seven days a week; but hard work was the name of the game that kept her in food, shelter and companionship. So she worked hard, played hard and came on as tough as the next pro when crossed. It was an apprenticeship that led her from the obscurity of busking on 9th Street to a broad popularity that was poised in 1923, when she was twenty-nine years old, to take her right to the top.

North America's 'roaring twenties' were remarkable years, especially in New York City where entertainment blossomed during Prohibition. Harlem, which had been almost entirely white in 1900, began to change character. Bessie's contemporary Ethel Waters described the scene just after the First World War:

> One hundred and twenty fifth Street was still a white boulevard, and we weren't welcome there. Coloured people could buy seats only in the peanut gallery in B.F. Keith's Alhambra Theatre, and none at all in the other white showhouses. My people were even barred from the burlesque houses on 125th Street, which marks high tide, I think, in white snobbishness.
>
> The most popular hangout for negro sporting men and big shots was Baron Wilkins famous night club, which also drew white trade from Downtown . . . But the ordinary working coloured people weren't wanted there and knew better than to try to get in.
>
> (*His Eye Is On The Sparrow*, Ethel Waters with Charles Samuel)

As the black population spread southwards during the 1920s, 125th

Street became its cultural centre. The Harlem Renaissance had begun, black entertainment flourished, but segregation was still a fact of life in New York City. The famous Cotton Club, for instance, featured black entertainers but was off-limits to all but the very few wealthy or privileged blacks who mixed with white society. The fashionable crowd, which included Helen Morgan, reigning star of the Broadway stage and night-club scene, could go slumming in Harlem for after-hours kicks, but few blacks could venture south to Broadway. Broadway musical shows which used blacks in the cast were either cast all black or kept black and white cast members strictly segregated backstage. Despite appearances among the Harlem chic, things had changed very little. If a black audience wanted to relax and enjoy black entertainment, it was only going to happen in the clubs which maintained an all black policy.

Meanwhile the recording industry, still in its infancy, had been trying to keep pace with developments. After the First World War it became obvious to the men in the music business that the large black urban communities in the north were a potential new market. Since Emancipation there had been several great waves of migration from south to north. Mythologised during slavery, the north had become a promised land as militants like Harriett Tubman spirited escapees away via the 'under-ground railway', a human network of resistance. But when they arrived in the north the cold facts were quickly apparent: most of the jobs went to European migrants who had been flooding to North America with similar hopes for a new life. They had numbered 1,200,000 in 1914, but the Great War brought a change for black Americans, when annual European immigration was reduced to 110,000 by 1918. Industry had been expanding to supply the war, and the labour needs in the north were now as great as they had been in the south when Africans were first dragged to America in chains to work the plantations and build the transportation and communication systems. By 1920 a third of the black American population had moved north.

For many who migrated in the hope of jobs and a new life, city existence was little better than what they had known in the rural south. Most were forced simply to trade one kind of subservience for another, albeit without the threat of sudden and violent death. But for the first time there was a large black population with a wage-earning capacity, and the men, both black and white, who owned the means of record production were only too anxious to supply its demands in return for enormous personal profit. Following the great success of Mamie Smith's 'Crazy Blues', many record companies acquired a 'race' catalogue of black artists intended for a black audience. Black Swan was the first black-owned label and was advertised as 'The Only Genuine Colored Record – Others Are Only Passing for Colored'. They recorded Ethel Waters, but were not interested in the much 'blacker' sound of Bessie Smith, who eventually signed with Columbia's 'race' division.

31

Black women had always been preservers and disseminators of culture, and the rough country blues were as much their domain as that of the men who later began to record them. But when the 'classic' blues singers recorded in the twenties, they were drawing attention to a blues form which was no longer a cultural extension of everyday life but the means to earn a living. Mamie Smith, Clara Smith, Ida Cox, Ethel Waters, Alberta Hunter, Victoria Spivey and Rosa Henderson were all part of a thriving business; and they all had the potential of a much wider urban appeal than the country blues singers.

Bessie's first record, 'Downhearted Blues', written by Alberta Hunter and Lovie Austin, sold 780,000 copies in its first six months. Sales like these meant immense profits for the company, but artist royalties were unheard of. Bessie's agreement was for a flat $125 a side. Even then Clarence Williams, black piano player and well-known cheat in charge of Columbia's 'race' records, tried to pocket half Bessie's fee by a contractual con, for which he earned a very nasty punch from the ever-pugilistic Bessie. The terms of the contract were resettled, guaranteed by an advance, and Bessie and her latest beau, ex-nightwatchman Jack Gee, raced off on the wings of prosperity to get married.

It was the beginning of Bessie's most successful years. Between 1923 and 1929 she recorded around one hundred and fifty songs for Columbia who, in addition to the sales at the time, have reissued her records and continue to profit to this day. When Janis Joplin was listening to Bessie Smith records in the sixties, the Empress's singing was as potent and influential as it had been forty years before. At the time, however, her total reimbursement amounted to a comparatively small $28,575 over the six years. In that time she had no choice but to keep up a heavy schedule of live performance. She toured east and south, with the westernmost limits of the route down from Chicago to St Louis and Kansas City. She had her own tent shows in the summer, and played TOBA theatres the rest of the time, never failing to pack the house.

Her first really big year was 1924 when, in addition to recording fees, she was commanding personal appearance money like the $1,500 she took from a week in Detroit, although out of that fee came all expenses, including the troupe's salaries. She was known to pay as little as possible, but had a reputation for generosity to those in need. In that first year she shared her success with Jack, who had given up his job to come along for the ride. And the following year the ride became a much more luxurious affair, commensurate with the status of the Empress of the Blues. As transport and accommodation were difficult or impossible for black performers in the South, Bessie invested in her own railroad car which travelled and housed the entire company. Now Bessie could feel at home on the road. She often cooked for the other artists, and when Jack did not accompany her, she pursued an offstage life of wild partying, drinking and affairs. When Jack was around, Bessie's life was much more sober in every respect.

By 1926 her popularity was well established and she was able to slacken the pace. Her instinct was to try to build a family around her. She brought her sisters and brothers to Philadelphia to live, adopted the little boy Snooks from her ex-chorine, and named him Jack Junior. But the chosen fruits of her labour were costly. Housing the family, plus a new Cadillac for Jack, contributed to a bill for the year that ran to $16,000. And their financial state wasn't the only shaky thing in the arrangement. Bessie's relationship with Jack was getting rougher. He always had pretensions about managing her, but it seems she never gave him that free hand – wisely, as he was always hopelessly disorganised. As the gap

widened between them, Bessie hit the booze, and Jack hit Bessie to keep her in line. The happy family she had tried to construct in the midst of popular success was not working out. Brother Clarence continued to manage most of her business on a live-it-up-today-forget-tomorrow basis; plans for economising were not his forte, particularly in areas like the Smith sisters' booze bill which was at times inordinately high.

Bessie and Jack

Unfortunately this economic expansion of Bessie's empire took place just at a time when New York, centre of the recording industry, experienced a waning in the blues market. The TOBA circuit registered 1927 as its most disastrous year of business. At first these downward trends were not reflected in Bessie's work, which continued to draw huge audiences and favourable press. As a blues singer she was still the greatest, even though she had continued to avoid the socialising and hype that even then seemed a requisite part of show business. Nor did she

33

seem interested in extending her audience overseas. In 1928 Josephine Baker, for instance, was playing her Casino de Paris show to the royal family of Denmark, the ex-King of Spain, the King of Sweden and the King of Siam. Ethel Waters would soon head for Paris and London too and, like Billie and Ella some years later, enjoy the welcome and respect that Europe offered. While a musical stage star like Ethel Waters seemed content to cultivate the friendship of white liberals like Carl Van Vechten, Bessie remained strictly black and, for the time being, strictly blues.

Van Vechten was a wealthy intellectual who kept a Harlem apartment,

Bessie in St
Louis Blues

famous for its parties, to which he invited talented and 'interesting' Afro-Americans for his equally liberal white friends to meet. His curiosity extended to the anthropology of the race, and though irrefutably racist in his patronisation, he befriended and assisted a number of the poets of the Harlem Renaissance and was a genuine admirer of Bessie's live performance. She eventually accepted one of many invitations he had extended to her, but she might have known that the one time she let down her guard to the white intelligentsia she'd create a mild disaster that would keep her in good stories for years afterwards.

Bessie arrived at the Van Vechten apartment accompanied by her niece and longtime companion Ruby Walker, and her dapper homosexual piano player Porter Grainger. She refused the proffered martinis and loudly demanded large gins, one of which went down her throat between each of six or seven songs. At the end, as Ruby and Porter tried to get her out, Van Vechten's ex-Russian ballet star wife, Fania Marinoff, tried to kiss Bessie goodbye. Bessie gave the small woman such a shove that she fell over; and with a mouthful of her favourite expletives, the

Empress departed to pass out in the waiting car. The evening would have been more than enough to reassure Bessie that her separatism was justified.

By the end of 1928 her relationship with Jack had deteriorated even further. Acquaintances and colleagues saw that Bessie was deeply depressed. Despite superstar status, lots of parties and a number of affairs, there was a sadness about the Empress that nothing or no one seemed able to cure. Bessie was thirty-five years old when *Variety* ran its famous headline of 30 October 1929: 'Wall Street Lays An Egg'. On Broadway there was a positive boom. Helen Morgan, for instance, had her busiest year ever as she starred in two musicals, worked the clubs late each night, played a big concert at the Palace, and made three movies. But Helen, like Marie Lloyd, was not principally a recording artist, and the record industry started feeling the effects of the crash almost immediately. One of these was to kill off the market for 'race' records. Despite her continued full houses in the South, Bessie's record sales began falling as buyers, both white and black, found themselves on breadlines. While white vaudevillians could turn to radio, or to Hollywood, where the talkies were already threatening many forms of live entertainment, black vaudeville was at an end. TOBA folded in 1930, and in that year Columbia was on the verge of bankruptcy. They dropped Bessie mid-contract, in November of 1931.

Biographer Chris Albertson has insisted, however, that it was not the waning of the great 'classic' blues that brought Bessie down. By 1931 she had already started to record pop songs like 'After You've Gone' and Irving Berlin's 'Alexander's Ragtime Band', and listening to them today gives a good insight into Bessie's versatility. In May of 1929 she had gone into an all black musical, *Pansy*, which laid almost as big an egg as Wall Street (although Bessie herself was well reviewed), and in July she made the seventeen-minute all black film, *St Louis Blues*. It was clear that even in 1929 Bessie had begun the process of transition that fashion demanded.

Bessie continued to earn a decent, if much reduced wage, and could afford to keep the apartment in Philadelphia. Her personal life was quite another matter. In 1929 she recorded 'Nobody Knows You When You're Down and Out', and the conviction in the performance has persuaded listeners ever since of its autobiographical nature:

Once I lived the life of a millionaire
Spendin' my money, I didn't care,
I took my friends out on a good time
Bought 'em bootleg liquor, champagne and wine.
Oh but when I was down so low,
Nobody wanted me around their door
If I get my hand on a dollar again
I'm gonna squeeze it till that eagle grins.

Nobody knows you, when you're down and out.
In my pocket, not a penny,
And my friends you know I ain't got any
But when I get on my feet again
I'm gonna reclaim my long lost friends
It's a cryin' shame, but there ain't no doubt,
Nobody knows you when you're down and out.

('Nobody Knows You When You're Down and Out', Cox and Allen)

That year Bessie discovered that Jack had used her money to finance a show starring another singer, Gertrude Saunders. Bessie applied her well-known fist treatment but could not separate Jack from his new woman for more than a few months. Jack retaliated with an act of sheer vengeance. Although he had never shown much interest in Jack Jnr, in 1930 he stole the boy away and put him in a home. It had the desired effect of making Bessie even more miserable than before, and she lost trace of her adopted son for two years.

In that time she took up with an old friend, Richard Morgan, a bootlegger from Chicago (and uncle of musician Lionel Hampton). Morgan was wealthy from his black-market trade and happy to supplement Bessie's income, now around $500–$700 a week, whenever the cost of high living soared at home. Even after Prohibition was repealed, and drinkers like Bessie continued to prefer the 'bad stuff', his income remained steady. Richard also had an old friend's tolerance for Bessie's lifestyle, and as such seems to have been a source of genuine love and support during two difficult years.

At the end of 1932, at the age of thirty-eight, she enjoyed a brief respite when she received a letter at last from Jack Jnr. At his request Bessie brought him back to live with her and Richard: it had been her leanest year so far, but the personal happiness of having her boy back was some compensation. This was coupled with top billing (something she had not enjoyed for some time) in a new show, *Hot Stuff*, in Philadelphia, and in 1933 her first New York appearance in two years. Things were starting to look up.

Always quick on the uptake, entrepreneurs had looked forward to the end of Prohibition, and Franklin D. Roosevelt's New Deal gave the entertainment business a brief spurt of optimism. It was a good time for Bessie too. She was commanding slightly higher fees again, her billing was improving, and wealthy young jazz enthusiast John Hammond had spotted her and interested the Okeh label in recording her. The record industry was only just beginning to feel its way again, but there was every reason for confidence. Bessie closed the year with a four-day Christmas show at the Harlem Opera House.

The following year brought harsher truths. At the Hotcha Club Bessie heard a new kid who was going by the name of Billie Halliday. Another youngster, Ella Fitzgerald, had made a stunning debut in the Harlem Opera House talent quest. While Mamie Smith was packin' 'em in and layin' 'em down with her pop songs down south, Bessie got a lukewarm reception. She now knew that the changes she had begun five years before would have to be followed through unless she wanted to see her career ended by the age of forty. Although 1935 signalled little hope for America at large, and the figure of unemployed would not fall below seven million until the next Great War did its bit for democracy and the economy, it presented a broad spectrum of fortunes for the women in this book. While Ella Fitzgerald was being coached in the trade by drummer Chick Webb, Billie Halliday was struggling to keep down a job. Actress Frances Farmer signed with Paramount Pictures just as Frances Gumm signed with MGM. While Helen Morgan hit the bottle and worked only infrequently, Marilyn Monroe had just begun her second

Bessie in the 30s

round of foster homes, and Edith Piaf was discovered in Paris by Louis Leplée. And in this year Bessie Smith began to rework her material in earnest. Richard Morgan was still there to help support her and her family, but Bessie's sisters were drinking even more heavily and their dependency was an increasing strain. In 1936, however, Bessie's persistence started paying off.

Billie Halliday had a dose of ptomaine poisoning, and Bessie replaced her at Connie's Inn, a famous Harlem jazz spot. With her new repertoire which included few if any blues, and swing hits like 'Pennies From Heaven', together with the much more sophisticated look of simple dresses, no wigs and no headgear, Bessie began to attract a new audience. Although she was not recording, she was still writing songs, and by 1937 John Hammond did have plans to record her; there was also a new film in the pipeline. She worked extensively in New York and Philadelphia, receiving good fees and good notices. Her comeback at forty-three years old was well under way, and despite the fact that Jack Jnr was getting restless and hard to handle, Bessie felt more assured about her future than at any time since 1929. In September of 1937 she accepted an offer to tour the South in a show called *Broadway Rastus*. In a fit of typical show business 'let's drive there tonight' adrenalin, Bessie persuaded Richard away from his card game to drive south with her overnight. They crashed on the way.

The circumstances of Bessie's death are examined in detail in Albertson's biography. He is the first to try to sort out the conflicting stories about what really happened, and still there are many things left unexplained. Morgan was at the wheel at the time of the crash, and Bessie was still alive, though critically injured and bleeding heavily, when an ambulance arrived. There is enough corroborating evidence to suggest that Edward Albee's play, *The Death of Bessie Smith*, sensationalised and distorted events in claiming that Bessie bled to death when the white hospital she was taken to wouldn't admit her. The nearest town, Clarksdale, had two hospitals, one for blacks, one for whites, and the local ambulance officers must have known which one to go to. The area of doubt lies rather in a third vehicle which collided with the already wrecked car of Richard Morgan and a truck involved in the accident. This third vehicle belonged to a doctor. His car was undamaged, he was unhurt and on hand to treat crash victims. Yet it seems that others may have been treated or taken to hospital before Bessie. Bessie was dead on arrival at the black hospital, and the truth about the incident remains in doubt.

Eight days later Philadelphia gave Bessie a huge send-off; ten thousand filed past the bier to pay final respects to the greatest blues singer of the era. It was Bessie's insurance policy that paid for the funeral. Richard Morgan was there along with the family; but Jack Gee, a cad to the end, not only stole all the publicity by wailing the loudest, but also took off with the money that had been raised to purchase Bessie's headstone.

Although he received royalties on a number of her songs for many years after her death, neither he nor Morgan nor Columbia ever did anything about Bessie's unmarked grave. It was only in the spate of publicity that surrounded the 1970 re-releases of her recordings that a black Philadelphian woman drew public attention to this neglect. The *Philadelphia Enquirer* called for donations and Bessie's one-time maid, Juanita Green, and one of Bessie's greatest fans, Janis Joplin (who would die in that same year), agreed to pay half, whatever the cost. The inscription read 'The Greatest Blues Singer in the World Will Never Stop Singing'.

What is known of Bessie Smith is reflected in the songs and recorded performances: they indicate an awesome power and an intriguing depth. She lived with enormous energy. Together with the nurturing of an extended family, she maintained a lusty appetite for eating, drinking and partying; an open enjoyment of the companionship and sensuality of both women and men; a creative talent that set her at the top of her profession, and the stamina and resilience to endure the harsh realities of the profession's dictates and vicissitudes. Her contemporaries have said that she sought not so much fame as acceptance; but she rarely got it, because it had to be acceptance on her terms and, as Marie Lloyd discovered, there were few who were willing to offer real friendship. Bessie was regarded by most as passionate and generous, but also as rough, crude and dangerous. She was highly competitive and she treated fellow performers, especially women, with suspicion. She fought hard with little help from the age of nine until, at thirty-six, she found a loyal friend in Richard Morgan. The tough shell was easily explained, and always betrayed by the yearning qualities of her singing and the extraordinary softness that the photographs reveal.

Bessie Smith is reported to have said that she was 'raised in a shithouse'. Had she remained in it, her life would have passed unnoticed, as did those of hundreds of thousands of her black women contemporaries. As it happened, her life points up one of the great paradoxes of popular entertainment. Of all the women in this book, Bessie was by far the most prolific songwriter and her songs were always personal-political in the most valuable way. And yet those songs would never have been heard had Bessie herself not escaped the particular socio-economic conditions she was singing about. Bessie had inherited a black female oral tradition, and her blues worked accordingly in both a private and public way. Sometimes they reflected particular working conditions, as in 'Washwoman's Blues'; sometimes more general situations, as in 'Backwater Blues', which she wrote after travelling through the 1927 Mississippi floods. Often they were more personal: 'Wasted Life Blues' (see p. 25), for instance, or the inspirational 'Young Woman's Blues' in which she concludes: 'I'm a young woman, and I ain't done runnin' around'. Like 'Hard Time Blues' which similarly asserts 'I'm a good woman, I can get a man any time', or 'Baby Doll' or 'I Ain't Gonna Play No Second Fiddle',

Bessie's own version of a woman's feelings were not crammed with the 'he's my good jelly-roll' clichés of the period. Even her laments were more articulate:

> It's all about a man who kicks and dogs me aroun'
> It's all about a man who kicks and dogs me aroun'
> And when I try to kill him,
> That's when my love for him come down.

('Please Help Me Get Him Off My Mind', Smith)

A perennial problem for women performers was their obligation to sing songs that men had written. In many cases men's versions of what women thought and felt were hopelessly misplaced. Even Bessie was subject to this problem; while her sexually explicit songs were positive and energetic, many of them, like many of Janis's songs much later, simply reiterated male clichés. Bessie's own lyrics were much more interesting.

It is this area of repertoire – the songs they wrote themselves – that is most telling about the women in this book. A singer is known as much for her repertoire as for her vocal style, and often for the lay audience the two are indistinguishable. The choice and composition of repertoire is as much the art of the singer as her vocal technique: that she chooses to sing certain songs, have certain songs written for her, and writes so few herself is as revealing as the way she sings. It would seem to be more than just coincidence that the five women in *A Star is Torn* who wrote their own songs were also the most sexually assertive and ambivalent. Piaf was like a female gigolo; Bessie, Billie, Janis and Judy Holliday all had affairs with women. Perhaps having the courage to write their own songs was an extension of the positive that surfaced elsewhere. Significantly, Judy Garland sketched out lyrics, and Marilyn Monroe wrote private poetry, but neither made that final leap of performing her own material.

Bessie wrote her own tunes too. While the blues were not the most intricate musical medium, there is enough variety within the given limitations of Bessie's blues to indicate that she knew how to put together the kind of song that suited her voice, but didn't always follow the twelve-bar musical cliché. Such tunes, designed to show off the huge rich voice, the earthy growl and the wry delivery, combined with the simple repetitions of her lyrics to produce perhaps the most accurate picture we have of Bessie Smith. They were folk songs of the first order. Perhaps the changes she was heading for when she died would have modified the choice and content of her songs, but the repertoire that does survive is firmly rooted, despite her fame, in the common experience of black women of her generation and background. In this sense her direct descendants are Nina Simone and, before her, almost contemporary with the Empress herself, Billie Holiday.

41

Them that's got shall have
Them that's not shall lose
So the bible says
And it still is news
Poppa may have, Momma may have
But God bless the child that's got his own
That's got his own

'God Bless The Child', Holiday and Herzog

In November 1933, a teenager calling herself Billie Halliday recorded the first two songs of her career, 'Riffin' thc Scotch' and 'My Mother's Son-in-Law' at the Okeh Studios, 55 Fifth Avenue. The band was led by Benny Goodman; the producer was John Hammond who, three days before, in the same studio, had put down four tracks with Bessie Smith as the beginning of her revival. No one could have suspected that 'Do Your Duty', 'Gimme a Pigfoot', 'Take Me For A Buggy Ride' and 'Down in the Dumps' would be the Empress's last recordings any more than they could have predicted that young Billie would go on to record over two hundred and fifty songs in the next twenty-five years, and leave a legacy to jazz as Bessie had to the classic blues.

Billie remains a gauge of jazz singing: new singers are still compared with her, as Janis Joplin was in the sixties. They sounded nothing alike, even Janis knew that; the comparison simply acknowledged certain qualities in the rock singer for which Billie had set the standard – playing havoc with phrasing, complete devotion to a song at the moment of performance, the ability to make even the most complex interpretation seem like second nature. Billie's recordings are enduring evidence of this genius; but clues to the life of the woman born Eleanora Fagan, in Baltimore, are less certain.

Billie's 'autobiography' *Lady Sings The Blues* was co-authored by William Dufty, whose sensationalised articles after her death have thrown doubts on the accuracy of the original work. The biopic based on the book begged even more questions, despite Diana Ross's respectful portrayal. But many of Billie's 'recollections' have been confirmed by John Jeremy's research for his BBC TV documentary *The Long Night of Lady Day*, and even in the remaining confusion of detail, date and place, there is a picture of unsettled and often unhappy childhood and adolescence. It was Billie's own lasting *impression*, and as such is important.

That Eleanora Fagan (later to be known as Billie Halliday, Billie Holiday and Lady Day) ever made it to late adolescence and that first recording session in 1933 was a feat in itself. As with Bessie, Edith Piaf and Marilyn Monroe, survival to that age with a sense of optimism intact was evidence of a powerful will to live. Billie usually gave her birthdate as 1915, except in the one instance when she might have been more inclined to tell the truth: her 1947 Alderson Reformatory admission documents give 1919 as her date of birth. And it is possible that the 1915 date had always been used effectively by the larger-than-average and well-developed young woman whenever she needed officially to be older than she really was. It is worth bearing in mind that she may have been younger than all accounts give, including this one and her own; the implications for her precocious talent and the experiences of rape and prostitution are obvious.

Billie also recalled that her mother, Sadie Fagan, was thirteen and her father fifteen when she was born, and they were still teenagers when they married three years later. This doesn't tally with their birth certificates and gravestones, but the truth of Billie's impression remains: that her parents were just a couple of kids when they had a kid of their own. Clarence Holiday was drafted into the army and the First World War. Sadie went north to Philadelphia and New York to find domestic work. When Clarence returned, his career as a trumpeter destroyed by the poison gas he'd inhaled in the European trenches, he took up the guitar and was soon on the road again as a musician. At whatever point of these proceedings Eleanora was born, the greater part of her young life was spent without her parents. Sadie left her with her grandmother, great-grandmother and Aunt Ida. Eleanora was fond of her great-grandmother, but the old woman was an invalid and could not protect her from the preference shown to Ida's own son. Billie's memory was of a hostile environment softened only by the times she spent looking after her great-grandmother and listening to tales of her youth as a slave when she was the backyard mistress of Irish plantation owner, Charles Fagan. But time off for story-telling was rare, and Eleanora was kept busy as the poor relation. As well as attending school, she supplemented the money her mother sent for her keep by scrubbing the front steps and bathrooms of Baltimore's well-to-do and running errands for the girls at a nearby whorehouse. She kept the latter occupation a secret from her guardians and it was in the welcoming surroundings of Alice Dean's that she heard her first Bessie Smith and Louis Armstrong records.

Early in the twenties Sadie returned with her savings and opened a boarding house in Baltimore. Eleanora was glad to leave her aunt's house where she had recently experienced the trauma of her great-grandmother's death. The new house brought her a brief period of happiness. Sadie and Clarence had divorced and both remarried. Eleanora liked her new stepfather, but had little time to get to know him. After the premature death of her second husband, Sadie did not marry again and seemed always to carry a torch for the itinerant Clarence. She was trying as best she could to provide respectability and a new life for her young daughter, but was thwarted on all sides. According to Billie, it was while they were at this house that she was raped by a neighbour, 'Mr Dick'. Under pretence of taking her to meet her mother, he took her instead to a nearby brothel and, assisted by one of the women, raped her. Alerted by another neighbour, Sadie arrived too late to prevent the outrage, but in time to have the attacker arrested. Billie's recollection of what followed has an unnerving contemporary ring to it:

> When we got there, instead of treating me and Mom like somebody who called the cops for help, they treated me like I'd killed somebody. They wouldn't let my mother take me home. Mr Dick was in his forties, and I was only ten. Maybe the police sergeant took one look at my breasts and limbs and figured my age from that. I don't know. Anyway I guess they had me figured for having enticed this old goat into the whorehouse or something. All I knew for sure is that they threw me into a cell. My mother cried and screamed and pleaded, but they just put her out of the jailhouse and turned me over to a fat white matron. When she saw I was still bleeding, she felt sorry for me and gave me a couple of glasses of milk. But nobody else did anything for me except give me filthy dirty looks and snigger to themselves.
>
> After a couple of days in a cell they dragged me into court. Mr Dick got sentenced five years. They sentenced me to a Catholic institution.

(*Lady Sings The Blues*, Billie Holiday and William Dufty)

Institutions, like beatings, were to become a part of Eleanora/Billie's life, and her memories of this one were all bad, including a punishment which entailed being locked in a room where a young girl's body had been laid out for burial. Exactly how long she spent in the reform school is unknown; by the original order she could have been held until she was twenty-one. Sadie managed to secure her release within two years, but it had been a bitterly unjust and profoundly terrifying experience. John Jeremy theorises that Billie's entanglement with Roman Catholicism, positively from her devout mother, negatively from the reformatory with its forced re-experience of death, and her later adoption of St Theresa as patron saint, encouraged concepts of martyrdom that not only persuaded her to accept her lot on earth, but also ruled out suicide as an escape. The tragedy of Billie's story is that the alternatives proved to be no less dangerous.

By the time her daughter was released Sadie had returned to New York. For Eleanora it was back to Aunt Ida and scrubbing the steps. But as soon as she completed fifth grade at school, she took the train to New York and joined her mother. Sadie found her a live-in position at

Florence Williams's boarding house, which young Eleanora instantly recognised, from her odd-jobbing around Alice Dean's in Baltimore, as a whorehouse. According to Billie, her mother was innocent of the fact that the comfortable residence was anything other than one whose female lodgers kept odd hours. It wasn't long before Eleanora swapped scrubbing brush, drudgery and pittance for twenty-dollar tricks and a bit of luxury: for the first time in her life she had someone to do *her* washing. But the relief was shortlived. She was badly hurt by one black punter and vowed she would take on no more black clients. It seemed that unlike white clients, who were only after a quickie before going home to wife and family, black men often expected something more of her, perhaps because she was the only black woman in that establishment. Unfortunately she caught the eye of a Harlem hot shot, Big Blue Rainier, and her refusal of him went down badly. Blue had excellent contacts within the Police Department and the next morning the brothel was raided and Eleanora arrested.

At Jefferson Market Court, despite her mother's pleas and assurances that she was not under age (which she may well have been), she was packed off to a city hospital by Magistrate Jean Hortense Norris, whose reputation amongst the girls contradicted her own platform that it took a woman to understand social problems. In the hospital where wayward women were treated for syphilis, Eleanora repelled advances from a warder by shoving her down a flight of stairs, in return for which Magistrate Norris sent her up the river for four months. She was learning early that a young black woman like herself stood no chance against the law, and she began to accept her sentences with docile resignation.

After her release, Eleanora and Sadie were back to the same old business of scratching for a living in the depths of the Depression. Billie says she ranged from turning tricks to hostessing in a casino; Sadie continued to work as a domestic. Little had changed since Bessie's time, and as Lena Horne said of her own mother:

> When my mother left my grandmother's house she went on the
> stage. Naturally she did, because a beautiful negro woman who
> wasn't trained and didn't want to be a prostitute had no other
> choice.

(*Lena*, Lena Horne and Richard Schickel)

Going on the stage was the last alternative for Eleanora. She had paid her dues as domestic and prostitute; now she found that the main chance wasn't going to be much easier by comparison. She would have to work long hours; and no matter how naturally gifted, learning songs and moulding performances would take time, effort and confidence. Given the experiences of the first fifteen years of her life it is remarkable that

FLASH

WEEKLY NEWSPICTURE MAGAZINE

10¢

MAY 3, 1937

anything remotely related to confidence could still be aroused. Billie tells a version of events in which she auditioned as a dancer but was so hopeless that the manager advised her to try singing instead, which she did, and got the job; yet at least one Baltimore elder recalls her singing in her hometown much earlier. It seems, however, that she was not convinced of her vocal abilities, a doubt which a number of contemporaries maintain she never quite lost.

John Chilton takes up his biography, *Billie's Blues*, at this point (avoiding the problems of dissecting the early years by omitting them). He quotes several musicians who remember Billie working around New

York as early as 1930; but the first strictly verifiable date in her performing life is John Hammond's review of 'Billie Halliday', published by *Melody Maker* in April 1933, the year of those first Okeh Studios recordings, also produced by Hammond, when she was at most eighteen years old. At this time Billie was gigging at a number of Harlem's most popular clubs – Monette's Supper Club, where Hammond heard her; Pod's and Jerry's; the Alhambra Grill, and the Hotcha Bar, where Bessie first heard her. In at least one of them Sadie worked the kitchen while Billie worked the audience, and as Sadie was still only in her thirties they often passed for sisters. They lived together, with Sadie keeping a watchful eye over her daughter, at the same time tolerating a sex, booze and jazz lifestyle that was not in accordance with her religious beliefs.

Billie's records from that first session with Hammond in 1933 drew minimal attention. She worked the clubs, appeared in two short films, and generally rode easy in times that otherwise might have been desperately hard. According to John Chilton's sources she drank steadily, smoked cigarettes and marijuana, but seemed to be well in control of their service to her good times. In April 1935 she made her debut at the Apollo where so many famous black artists got their start. She was a great success and was rebooked on the spot for a later date. When she returned in August she was billed as Billie *Holiday* for the first time. Meanwhile she had begun recording with pianist Teddy Wilson, perhaps her most successful accompanist. Session fees had dropped dramatically since Bessie's $125 a side ten years earlier, but the $75 a side (still no royalties) that Billie was paid, plus regular club work, were by 1936 enough to set herself and Sadie up with the latter's heart's desire – an apartment above a restaurant where Sadie cooked soul food. It was less a commercial venture than an open house for Billie's musical colleagues and steady succession of lovers.

But as smooth as it sounds, Billie still harboured a great deal of resentment and insecurity. Neither relative success nor Sadie's care and religion were enough to cancel out the worst memories of her childhood, her fear of being hounded by the police and a constant awareness of her second-class status. At the height of her fame the word 'nigger' was enough to precipitate inescapable depression. It was a despair not necessarily echoed by other black performers. Lena Horne and Ella Fitzgerald were at that time bent on careers that would see them performing and triumphing well into their sixties. Lena always attributed her personal strength to her Suffragette grandmother Cora Calhoun Horne, a militant Urban League and NAACP activist, whom she felt she unconsciously emulated; Ella had the benefits of her mentor Chick Webb. The hunchbacked white drummer and band leader had taken her into his home and taught her the ropes after seeing her win the Harlem Opera House talent quest. When he died aged thirty-two, Ella, a poor black girl with no less a bad start than Billie, had accumulated enough knowledge and confidence from this apprenticeship to lead the band herself for two years afterwards. There was no such professional influence in Billie's life. Her father could have provided the background but she didn't see him often enough. When they did meet, Clarence enjoyed being passed off as Billie's beau or brother. While he was around he was usually good for a handout, but, weakened by his wartime lung condition, Clarence Holiday died prematurely in 1937.

Billie did find a decent agent in Joe Glaser, with whom she maintained a stormy business relationship over many years. But her climb through the ranks during the thirties was a frustrating one. Billie's problems were not entirely to do with the disadvantages she suffered as a black woman. She also felt the rub of her own individualism. She didn't sound like anyone else and she didn't want to; refusing to compromise on style and repertoire led to the typical paradox of praise from enthusiasts who welcomed her originality, and difficulty in holding down a job in the early days before that genius was generally recognised. She was sacked early on in Chicago for 'singing too slow', yet she was rapidly becoming the jazz musician's favourite song stylist. She recorded exquisite versions of new songs, but they were invariably songs that publishers considered second rate. They wouldn't give Billie potential hits because they feared her idiosyncratic licence. She despised routine as being contrary to 'real singing' and this left her without a hit and often without a job. On the one hand she was sacked from New York's Onyx Club in 1936 because she was starting to get better notices than the resident band; on the other she left an enviable job with the Count Basie Orchestra in 1937 because she refused to sing more blues.

Racism had never been absent from either her life or her work, but its effects were intensified when she joined the all-white Artie Shaw band in 1938. On a tour of the South Billie was hospitalised with acute cystitis brought on by the lack of toilet facilities which a black woman might use in the clubs and halls where they played. This particular problem had been overcome in the black Basie band by the entire group entering the toilets together and avoiding misdemeanour charges by mass disobedience. But other problems arose when the Shaw band began to get dates in the fancier northern hotels. In one she was required to enter the building through a goods entrance, stay upstairs in a small room all evening and come down only for her numbers. Despite ecstatic reviews of the musical magic that Billie and Shaw's band were creating together, a white vocalist Helen Forrest was hired at this time. Billie shared the job with her until it became obvious from Billie's omission from the important live radio broadcast segments of the evening that Helen Forrest was the more acceptable front woman – and that there was no future for Billie with Shaw.

In 1939 she consolidated her career. Her success seemed paltry next to that of Ella Fitzgerald who had started her climb to international stardom with the release of the million seller 'A Tisket A Tasket', and who had begun to take the *Melody Maker* and *Downbeat* magazine polls every year, but Billie knew she had achieved recognition within the jazz circles that counted. John Hammond recommended her to Barney Josephson who had opened a revolutionary new club in January of 1939. Café Society, whose slogan was 'The wrong place for the right people', had an entertainment policy of encouraging promising new talent and a house policy of allowing black and white customers to sit together anywhere in the room. Not surprisingly it was the favourite workplace of many black artists of the time, among them Lena Horne and Billie, who stayed for nine months. On the strength of this residency she sailed into the forties with an esoteric but devoted following and the respect of the musicians she worked with. She wasn't making a fortune, but the price of the reefers she'd been smoking since the age of fifteen was not going to break the bank.

Considering Billie's unique style and approach, it's possible that even under better or different circumstances she may never have had Ella's hit record or Lena's popular success. Billie was as naturally adventurous in her choice of material as she was in her singing; and 'Strange Fruit' is a good example. She had been apprehensive about having the lyrics set as a song for her, but once premiered at Café Society, to a stunned audience, it was ever after her own:

Billie with Art Tatum, Oscar Pettiford and Sid Catlett at the first Esquire Jazz Concert, Metropolitan Opera House, 1944

Southern trees bear strange fruit
Blood on the leaves and blood at the root
Black body swinging in the Southern breeze
Strange fruit hanging from the poplar trees

Pastoral scene of the gallant South
The bulging eyes and the twisted mouth
Scent of magnolia sweet and fresh
Then the sudden smell of burning flesh

Here is a fruit for the crows to pluck
For the rain to gather, for the wind to suck
For the sun to rot, for the tree to drop
Here is a strange and bitter crop

('Strange Fruit', Allen)

To say the least, it wasn't hit single material; and while it and 'Some Other Spring', recorded in 1939, and 'God Bless The Child' and 'Gloomy Sunday', recorded in 1941, became identified with her and her performance, their interpretation was far too idiosyncratic – and certainly too sensitive – for any market wider than the expanding cult of jazz fans. Like Bessie, when Billie wrote lyrics she articulated sentiments that Tin Pan Alley rarely touched on:

Rich relations give a crust of bread and such
You can help yourself but don't take too much
Momma may have, poppa may have
But God bless the child that's got his own
That's got his own

('God Bless The Child', Holiday and Herzog)

Billie's one outstanding hit dwelt on a lingering sense of deprivation and the failure of the one thing her mother had tried to instil in her – the Catholic faith. The lyric is reminiscent of what Billie once said; 'You gotta have enough to eat, and a little love in your life, before you can hold still for anyone's damn sermon.'

Her 'Lady Sings The Blues' lyric had more pragmatic than aesthetic value, written as it was to coincide with the publication of her autobiography (the title of which had been changed by Dufty from the original *Bitter Crop*). But two of her ballads, 'Tell Me More' (for which she is also credited with the music) and 'Don't Explain', are more akin, in a jazz ballad medium which made them somewhat softer than the blues, to Bessie's positive sexuality. Given Billie's great talent for musical invention within existing tunes, it's difficult to believe she didn't contribute to the music of her collaborative songs as well. Yet there's little to indicate that she set any greater store in her talents as a songwriter than as a singer.

It wasn't just her low self-esteem that soured a career that looked so promising at the beginning of the forties. Then as now there are many reasons, and as many ways, of becoming a heroin user. Many of Billie's contemporaries felt that even though she heeded the words of the song 'Laughin' At Life' at every opportunity, her laughter barely concealed an almost permanent state of insecurity. One listen to the bitter-sweet rendition of the recorded version confirms it. When Edith Piaf sang 'Non, je ne regrette rien' every passionate vibrant word was believable; when Billie sang 'No Regrets' it was tinged with the kind of world-weariness that also said 'what good would it do?' Acquaintance with a user or a pusher, often one and the same, is and was one of the commonest ways to a habit. In 1941 Billie married Jimmy Monroe, a man she had known since 1937 and who had initiated her in the delights of opium. Neither Sadie nor Joe Glaser liked Monroe; and Sadie spoke her mind to Billie, who moved out and began experimenting with the harder stuff.

Billie always maintained that Monroe did not introduce her to heroin, but loyalty to her man was a trait that would always do her more harm than good. Later she was to testify in a federal court that Joe Guy, a boyfriend and known user, had nothing to do with heroin. Later still she said of John Levy, a *de facto* husband who inadvertently framed her on a drug charge: 'If he was to walk in the room this minute, I'd melt, he's my man and I love him.' She was also quoting almost verbatim from lyrics of the old Fanny Brice song 'My Man', which she'd first recorded in 1937. Marriage to Monroe did not last, but the habit did. By the mid-forties Billie's addiction was costing her around $500 a week and the effect on her work was obvious to everyone. Performances were uneven and she could not be relied upon even to show up, let alone on time. In 1945 she was dealt an additional blow when her mother died. Billie's regrets were enormous, as was her guilt that she had not been successful enough to give Sadie an easier time. Sadie Fagan had worked hard all her life and done her best to keep her kid on the straight and narrow. Nicknamed 'Duchess' by Billie's friend, saxophonist Lester Young, she was treated as such by the friends who dropped in and out of the always welcoming restaurant-apartment. Thereafter, without the considerable influence of Sadie's accommodating devoutness and moral strength, Billie's battle with drugs became a solitary and intolerable burden.

In 1946 she made her solo concert debut in the New York Town Hall and played a 'yes ma'am' maid in the movie *New Orleans* which also featured Louis Armstrong as a butler. At the time, the Second World War was just reaching the United States in the form of economic recession, which signalled widespread club closure and a subsequent gap in Billie's schedule. On Joe Glaser's advice she had herself admitted to a clinic for drug rehabilitation. Glaser was the kind of agent-entrepreneur who liked to think he took care of the whole person, not just the artist, and he believed that unless Billie took time to kick her habit she could consider her career already over. According to Billie, it was this period at the clinic that actually sealed her fate. Until that time she had not been aware of any kind of surveillance, but after leaving the clinic, cured, federal agents were just waiting an opportunity to jump. In 1947 they had their chance, and raided the hotel room she was sharing with

trumpeter, lover and heroin addict, Joe Guy: Billie was not in the room and managed to slip away, but she was arrested two weeks later. Having given testimony that set Guy free, she herself was sentenced to a year and a day at Alderson Reformatory. Her admission documents described the renowned jazz singer as 'inconsistent', with an abnormally low IQ, but did record in her favour that she 'had done housework and singing . . .'

Billie served her sentence quietly, taking increasing comfort in the Catholic mass and the intimate company of fellow inmates. For the most part the letters and phone calls which poured in from fans and well-wishers were kept from her. For all she knew, she had been abandoned. A warder later commented that she felt it strange that Billie had not sung a note whilst at Alderson. Billie was paroled after serving nine and a half months; ten days later those loyal fans had an opportunity to express

Satchmo and the Lady in the movie New Orleans

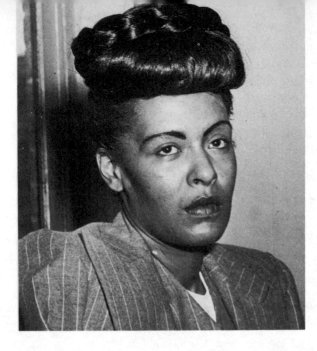

their faith and appreciation at a midnight concert in Carnegie Hall. It was sold out, the first of many occasions on which audiences felt they had a duty, as did Judy Garland's, to applaud more than just the act of singing. But, as always, the instant and vociferous feedback from an audience of thousands was not enough to drown out the ugly truth for long.

There was a law in New York, repealed in 1967, which prohibited anyone with a narcotics conviction from working in a place where liquor was sold. As night clubs sold liquor, and the New York clubs in particular set the pace in jazz, it was a severe blow to Billie's career. She tried on several occasions to appeal but was rejected. She had to face the fact that, to all intents and purposes, New York's intimate venues which were central to her art and profession, were closed to her – except that then, as now, such problems could sometimes be dealt with by passing large amounts of cash from hand to hand. Despite the ban, Billie almost immediately started a season at the Ebony Club. John Chilton suggests that police might have turned a blind eye to it in order to keep a relatively easy watch on the ex-offender. A more likely reason is that John H. Levy had become lover, manager and controller of the purse. His influence in certain circles was unquestionable. Joe Glaser, on the other hand, had no such pull, and no choice but to put Billie to work in other cities. For the rest of her life she worked north, south, east and west coast clubs, but save for one more stint at the Ebony, never again in New York clubs. In what was now her home town, she was forced on to the concert stage, which she always found a frightening and unsatisfactory medium.

In 1949 Billie divorced Jimmy Monroe and thereafter referred to Levy as her husband. Together they became regular targets for surveillance, and that year, when she was playing San Francisco's Café Society, their room was raided. As the police forced entry, Levy handed Billie a small package of opium to consign to the city's sewage system. She was caught white-handed. Her view of the incident was that she had no idea what was in the packet, and anyway, she did whatever Levy told her – that was her duty to her man. Subsequently she voluntarily submitted to tests and after two weeks was deemed clean and released. Levy escaped any charge whatsoever. But even in 1950 people around Billie suspected that she was back in the habit which was very much in evidence by the following year. It had become obvious that Levy had hopelessly mismanaged her earnings, and when confronted with a handful of unpaid bills he had no answers. Billie took up with another lover/manager, Louis McKay, whom she married in 1951. He advised that she stay on the West Coast and work solidly to clear the debts.

The fifties were as strange for Billie as the sixties would be for Judy Garland; on the debit side was a combination of general physical deterioration (specifically the weakening of the all-important voice) and professional unreliability because of that faltering health and the effects of addiction. In contrast, she was receiving the accolades of vast audiences. Billie appeared in Count Basie's Twenty Five Years in Show Business concert at Carnegie Hall and was greeted by thunderous ovations. In Europe she was treated like a proper celebrity, and her Royal Albert Hall concert in London was a triumph. Back home she did 'The Comeback Story' on television, and although she had never won a *Downbeat* poll, the magazine awarded her special recognition in 1954. With hindsight it can be seen as too little and too late.

In 1955 Ella Fitzgerald began recording the series of 'Songbooks' (Cole Porter, Rodgers and Hart, Gershwin) which would confirm her place in the century and boost her to another thirty years as successful as the previous twenty. Ella had begun only a few years after Billie, but in 1955 expectations for Ella's continuing success were as sure as the fears that Billie might not have long to go. She had been happier in Europe, but Glaser vetoed another tour; and in 1956, after another bust in Philadelphia, Billie once more had herself admitted to a clinic. This time the doctors tried for longer-term results by weaning her on substitutes. They produced disastrous side effects when she left the clinic. In order to stay away from heroin she took to alcohol until her consumption was up to two bottles of spirits a day. The transfer proved fatal.

Good performances from Billie were more difficult to come by, although even the observer who was appalled by the physical deterioration could still be caught up in the old magic. Technique, despite her command of it, had always been secondary to the high value she set on 'feeling'; and so the songs would always be charged with whatever the heart held at the time. There are enough illegal tapes made on portable machines smuggled into live performances and pirated on to record to testify to the full horror of what had happened to her voice over the years. But there are also studio albums like 'Lady in Satin', recorded in 1958, and even her 1959 appearance on British television's 'Chelsea at Nine', which still have ample quantities of voice, some of the top range gone, but always the full measure of brilliant phrasing and interpretation.

That her profession was content to applaud her past but ignore her living present was fully in evidence in the last year of Billie's life. The late fifties saw a boom in the big concert style, and jazz festivals were all the rage. Always uncomfortable in large venues, always suffering from first-night nerves – a terrible disadvantage for the one-off gig – Billie was acknowledged by the audience for the legend she had created and for the inspiration she'd provided for vocal jazz; but there were few thrills in the performance. After her appearance at the first Monterey jazz festival in 1958, musicians ignored her as she sat alone in the airport waiting for her flight out. She had separated from Louis McKay in 1957, and at home in New York she lived in her apartment with the name Eleanora Fagan on the bell. She watched cartoons on television and was rarely visited.

She worked as much as her failing health would allow, and returning from disappointing dates in Paris, Milan and London, she had a slap-up forty-fourth (fortieth?) birthday at home in New York. The friends who attended tried to persuade her to go into hospital but she refused. Among the guests was singer Annie Ross, who was one of the few people who continued to visit her on a regular basis. She had known Billie for some time, had filled in for her once at the Apollo, swanked it with her in Paris when they were both working there, and now came around to talk, to wash Billie's hair, to be quietly helpful. Billie also developed a close relationship with Alice Vrbny, a teacher of anthropology, who shared the apartment for some time with Billie, and who speaks of her now with the same gentle care and understanding that first cemented their friendship and Alice's idolisation of Lady Day.

Discussion of Billie's lesbianism has so far failed to grasp a much larger truth about her relationship with women in general. She acknowledged physical relationships with women while she was in prison, and a number of biographers and commentators have adopted the liberal jazzer's attitude about a woman of spirit who would have a go at anything. But that ignores a longer pattern of relationships in her life: her greatest friendships were with women. From Alice Deans and the girls in the Baltimore whorehouse, to Florence and the girls in New York, from her ex-slave great-grandmother to Sadie her mother and dearest intimate, from the women musicians she worked with, including harpist/pianist Corky Hale, who became a real road companion, to the other singers she befriended, Billie enjoyed the close companionship of women. By comparison her involvements with men bore the appearance of an habitual game. Except at the end, there was no time in her life when there was any doubt that she would play the game; and for all the lyrics like:

Some day he'll come along, the man I love
And he'll be big and strong, the man I love

('The Man I Love', G. and I. Gershwin)

there were also lyrics like:

I jumped out of the frying pan
and right into the fire.
I lost me a cheatin' man
and I got a no-count liar.
Swapped the old one for the new one
Now the new one's breakin' my heart
I jumped out of the frying pan
and right into the fire,
Lord, right into the fire.

('Riffin' the Scotch', Buck, Goodman, McDough)

Billie's penchant was for handsome men; her contemporaries also vouched for the fact that whomever she chose was bound to be the meanest bastard in the room. Billie knew she needed men; it was obvious from a very early age who pulled the strings, and became even more obvious in the entertainment business. She played the game as the rules demanded, and handed over the controls to whichever man was giving her black eyes at the time. And yet Earle Warren Zaidins, an attorney whom Billie met by chance and asked to look over a recording contract, said that she had 'a formidable grasp of the legal technicalities'. Later, when he became a top show-business lawyer, he held that he had learned what he knew of recording contracts from Billie Holiday.

Similarly it's difficult to imagine that Billie hadn't learned a great deal from her sexual experiences, yet on the surface the game of lover/husband/manager was played with monotonous regularity. Raped at ten (or younger), a prostitute at fourteen (or younger), she said herself that she had been 'scared to death' of sex. Cynicism might also have been expected. According to piano player Mal Waldron, Billie once began jotting down a new song when they were on a flight together; it was going to be 'the story of her life and she was going to put down all men'. The song never surfaced. Unlike the lows that Bessie went through because of Jack Gee, or Marie Lloyd because of Bernard Dillon, Billie always seemed happier with a new man and not too upset by the departure of the last. Her greatest male friendship was with Lester Young with whom she had no sexual relationship. Already a sensitive individual, the 'Pres' was made to suffer brutal racist treatment when he was drafted into the Second World War: it reduced him to alcoholism, silence and premature death. But people found it hard to believe that they had not been lovers. They made such sweet music together for so long; he even shared her and Sadie's apartment for some time. Stock response held that if he wasn't Billie's lover then he must have been homosexual. Both the Pres and Lady Day upset conventional stereotyping when they didn't automatically play out the recognised roles – or when they played all of them at various times.

Billie often expressed the desire to have children. Whether the childhood rape or some other factor prevented it is unknown, but Earle Zaidins confirms that she tried hard to adopt a child. Her drug offences automatically disqualified her. In the end, apart from the few stalwarts like Annie who was often on the road, Alice with whom Billie had quarrelled and parted, and Zaidins who was a busy man, Billie was on her own. Without family, and with only a few recently made friends looking in on her, she went into a coma on the afternoon of 31 May 1959. Admitted as Eleanora McKay, she was suffering from cirrhosis of the liver and cardiac failure.

Remarkably, she began to revive within a few days and was laughing with visitors and looking well. But she had been in hospital only two weeks when the police raided her room. Those around her in the last weeks are sure that the raid reversed her improving condition. The police officers who entered her room 'found' a small quantity of opium in her bedside table; no one knows whether it was planted or whether it was the misguided gift of a well-wisher. In either case, Billie could not have put it there, nor could she reach it to use it; she was confined to bed and constrained by drip apparatus. She was too ill to be removed from the hospital, so the arrest was made in the room and a man was stationed outside the door in case she tried to escape. She was finger-printed and photographed in bed. Three detectives questioned her. They confiscated flowers, record player, radio, chocolates and, most pathetic of all, the comic books which had been her staple reading matter all her life. Billie died a month later, still under police guard. The post mortem revealed that she had not been using hard drugs in the last few years of her life.

Had Billie not become a singer, had she for instance remained a domestic, her life, like that of Bessie Smith's mother and her own mother, would have passed unnoticed along with the anonymous lives of other black American women who did what they could to survive in a society that was hostile to their race and to their sex. As it was, Billie did become a singer, and her voice, rather than taking her away from life in that harsh environment, carried the environment with it. Billie was occasionally irked by the 'blues' tag, and some said she was never a blues singer. In fact, her own description of her stylistic ideals is still the most accurate: she wanted 'Bessie's feel' and 'Louis' style'. Both to the pedant and the casual listener there was a great difference between Billie and her idol and early influence, Bessie Smith. That doesn't alter the fact that 'blues' as a description of something felt, rather than as a particular category

Lady Day in London

within the clinical carve-up of certain musical styles, is a term that can be applied to most of the singers in this book.

> The blues ain't nothin' but a pain in the heart
> When you get a bad start
> When you and your man have to part
> I ain't gonna sit down and cry
> I know I won't die cos I love him
> Lady sings the blues, nothin' to hide, she tells her side,
> Now the world will know
> Just what the blues is all about.

('Lady Sings the Blues', Holiday and Nicholls)

Billie used the voice like a virtuoso instrumentalist. She always said she never sang the same song twice; what is heard in her singing is a constant readiness for improvisation. It was the reason she was so admired by musicians, and why jazz buffs chose her as their favourite vocalist. She didn't read music, but she had a faultless grasp of the chordal structure of the songs she sang and could choose at will and at feel which harmonic direction she might take at any point in the song, drifting in and out of the melody as it suited her interpretation. When she was handed songs that no one else was doing, songs for which publishers had few expectations, she could do wonders with them: 'What a Little Moonlight Can Do' and 'Miss Brown To You' were two such 'dogs'. What she lacked in range she made up for in tonal colour within the span of notes comfortably available to her. The use of multi-layered sound, breathiness, breaks in the voice, deliberate rasping, were techniques used in tandem with full sound to increase her musical vocabulary.

To assist the range of her expression even further, Billie used diction and rhythm in exactly the same flexible ways. She could take words at their street roundness, or she could smile them out from 'o' to 'ee' to punch in humour or cynicism or downright coldness. She could let a consonant blur for softness or bite it off at the end of a line and spit it out (a technique later taken up and extended by Dinah Washington). And her phrasing is still the most dangerous and exciting of any singer. Billie Holiday holds back on phrases so long it's impossible to guess how she's going to fit the rest into the remaining bars. When she finally lets out the secret, it's an improvisation as tasteful, as tasty, as any blues musician fitting the sweetest and sparest solo into twelve bars. If that remains an immeasurable pleasure on record, imagine the thrills she was creating live, when all those elements of surprise and variety were at her immediate command. The tension she could create in this way was enormous, and it turned her relatively limited voice into an instrument truly expressive of the range of that woman's experience.

In the great line of black women singers that really started with Bessie, came up through Billie, and went on to include Ella Fitzgerald, Sarah Vaughan, Carmen McCrae, Della Reese, Dakota Staton, Nancy Wilson, Dinah Washington and Natalie Cole, to name a few, Billie still stands out as the one who purposely exerts the least fabricated control in the interests of a song being very close to an expression of 'the real thing': unpredictable, spontaneous, and certainly never the same twice. While Ella remains the undisputed champ in the realm of range and vocal gymnastics, and her physical and vocal survival remains a cause for continuing celebration of the woman's stamina and development in maturity, she maintains the kind of distance, in her private life and in her singing, that Lena Horne once described:

I developed a certain kind of guile and toughness, a way of isolating myself from the audience. It is a means of not letting them get to you, not letting them see that they can hurt you. I suppose isolation of this kind is really just a form of disguised hostility. The image I have chosen to give them is of a woman they can't reach. And it has worked not because I am artful, but because they are usually so busy comparing me to their pre-conceived images of what a Negro woman should be like, and so surprised that I did not seem to fit it, that they never seem to notice that they are not getting me – someone they can touch and hurt – but just a singer.

(*Lena*, Lena Horne and Richard Schickel)

It was precisely the kind of guile and toughness that Billie did not have; and it was this quality of openness, so essential to what is recognised as Billie's style, that separated her from the other great black women vocal technicians, and aligned her with performers like Garland and Piaf who similarly kept nothing in reserve, and who were similarly hurt.

Quand un homme vient vers moi
Je vais toujours vers lui
Je vais vers je n'sais quoi
Je marche dans la nuit . . .

Je n'oublierai jamais,
Nous deux comme on s'aimait
Toutes les nuites, tous les jours
La Belle Histoire d'Amour *

'La Belle Histoire d'Amour', Piaf and Dumont

Edith Piaf's life was such a roller-coaster of tragi-comedy that it would have been far fetched as anything other than a true story. Her version of love, marriage, independence and passion had all the ingredients of *film noir* melodrama – a vehicle for Bette Davis or Joan Crawford – but was actually lived for real by one frail but remarkably strong woman.

She was born in Paris on 19 December 1915 to a sixteen-year-old dope addict and street singer named Anetta. The story goes that her father, Louis Alphonse Gassion, thirty-three years old but as fancy-free as his profession of wandering acrobat would suggest, did not quite manage to secure the services of a doctor or midwife in time because of the number of café-bars along the way. Today tourists and pilgrims are shown the plaque high on the wall outside 72 rue de Belleville where Edith was born, on the pavement, with the aid of a couple of passing policemen. It was a good story that both father and daughter were fond of. In truth, she was born at Tenon Hospital. The Piaf legend continues in this vein. In 1915 France was deep in the conflict which killed millions. Three who did survive were Marie Lloyd's jockey husband Bernard Dillon, who deserted rather than end up as cannon fodder; Clarence Holiday, sixteen-year-old father of Billie, who made it to the front line only to be gassed in the trenches and sent home; the third was Edith's father. Louis Alphonse Gassion survived, and in 1917 returned to Paris to resume life with a wife

*When a man comes towards me
 then towards him I go
 I go towards the unknown
 through the night I flow . . .

 I tell you I'll never forget
 how we loved each other, we two
 telling our fine story of love
 all the days, all the nights through

Michèle Roberts

63

and daughter he barely knew. Anetta had long since gone back to her itinerant street singing, leaving the young Edith with her maternal grandmother, once known as 'Aicha' and for a time, the keeper of a performing flea circus. Louis himself was soon back on his own round of semi-begging street performance and the 'family' lived in Belleville in this haphazard way until Anetta – now calling herself 'Line Marsa' – finally left for good.

Edith was about seven years old and the bitterness and insecurity of that time never entirely left her. When Anetta died of a drug overdose in 1945, Edith did not attend the funeral. Shortly after Anetta's departure, Zaza, one of Louis's three sisters, took pity on the malnourished child and this time she was taken to her paternal grandmother, in Bernay, Normandy. Grandmère Gassion was the cook at the local brothel, a busy establishment patronised by the regiment then garrisoned in the town. Edith suddenly found herself the centre of attention for no fewer than eight doting 'mothers'.

For a year Edith thrived, and even went to school for a while. It was during this time that one of Edith's favourite stories occurred when she suddenly became blind and was cured by a miracle visit to nearby Lisieux where the fabled Thérèse would be canonised a few years later. Whether it was severe conjunctivitis or a corneal inflammation is now lost to legend; nevertheless it gave Edith a lasting faith in St Thérèse and a very colourful anecdote that she never tired of telling.

Late in 1922 Louis 'bought' a caravan from Zaza (he never actually paid for it) and took Edith off on the first of many tours around that part of France and Belgium. From that point on she lived largely by her wits and what she learned in street-craft from Louis and other performers encountered on their daily round. Her spirited patriotic airs and folk songs were easily as popular as Louis' labours, and, in his view, her efforts were to be preferred. Edith's other recorded talent was to entice, with her fawn-like eyes and sad tales, the women who might be persuaded to share her father's bed, with the result that she spent a good deal of time waiting on the stairs outside their lodgings, or sharing the bed too. During her childhood any possibility of the emergence of a conventional young girl was subsumed of necessity in the swaggering urchin whose voice and pathos caused passers-by to reach into their pockets, but whose uncanny toughness also kept her from the variety of fates worse that that which finally befell her.

When she was sixteen she loosened ties with her father when he finally settled down with a young woman of twenty-two and had another child – Denise. Edith was on her own but for another urchin and her constant shadow – Momone. This young girl later claimed to be Piaf's sister and wrote a 'memoir' which stood for years as the authoritative biography. Simone Berteaut – Momone – was not related to Piaf but their sisterhood was of the cold and thrills of the city, where they might have bursting

GASSION
CONTORSIONISTE·ANTIPODISTE

bellies one night and be threatened with a vagrant's cell the next. In between, Edith sang wherever and whenever she could: the streets, bars, cafés, market places, barracks and halls. To Edith herself those few years were a time to be remembered with affection:

> My life when I was a kid might strike you as awful, but actually it was beautiful. I lived in Barbes, in Pigalle, in Clichy, in the chic sections of town, in the theatre districts, the streets where the whores hung out . . . I was hungry, I was cold. But I was also free . . . free not to get up in the morning, not to go to bed at night, free to get drunk if I liked, to dream . . . to hope.

(*Piaf*, Monique Lange)

Line Marsa, street singer and mother of Edith. Her desertion left the girl to a childhood of drumming up business for father Louis – 'it isn't a trick. The artist performs before your very eyes. No safety net, no sawdust, no shit!'

By the time she was eighteen the reality of being female caught up with Edith. Her relationship with a twenty-four-year-old (unemployed) builder known as 'little Louis' resulted in a pregnancy and a baby daughter, Ceçelle, born in 1934. Edith didn't know how to be a mother; moreover, she had very little relevant experience to call on or learn from. She tried taking the baby everywhere, remembering that her own parents had not. She cared for the child as best she could but she had little money and even less expertise. Baby Ceçelle died of meningitis in Tenon Hospital before her second birthday. The funeral was paid for by friends and neighbours, and, according to Edith, ten francs earned by taking a man upstairs to her room.

The dividing line between Edith's life as a street singer and the lives of her prostitute friends was a fine one; it depended on the state of the rent, her stomach and whether she felt like having a bed-warmer that night. In any event, like the other girls, she had to pay part of her earnings to the pimps for 'protection'. Earning a living was earning a living; having a good time, a drink and her freedom was something else. Notwithstanding, her affair with little Louis had been love, on both sides. He had tried to look after her, they had set up and played house for a while but he didn't like her out on the streets and she couldn't stand being cooped up in the dismal factories of Belleville. Love with little Louis did not last and he disappeared from her life.

Soon after the death of Ceçelle in 1935 came a second major turning point in her adult life, and the first of her career. Edith was just twenty when sometime nightclub performer-turned-owner Louis Leplée heard her singing on the corner of the rue Troyon and avenue MacMahon. After telling her that she was ruining her voice he invited her to audition the next day. Edith managed to oversleep the appointed time of the audition and whoever finally prompted her to bother to attend, she was an hour later than specified. Whatever misgivings Leplée felt about her tardiness were dispelled when she opened her mouth and sang her entire repertoire. He hired her, gave her four new songs to learn by Friday and sent her home with a new name and instructions to wear something simple and black. On the streets and in the cheap music halls she had been known variously as Tania, Denise, Huguette and undoubtedly other romantic inventions. To Leplée she was a tiny, bright-eyed, chirping sparrow – la Môme Moineau – Kid Sparrow. Unfortunately another long-since-forgotten singing scruff had already picked on the same idea, so they settled for the Parisian slang for sparrow, 'piaf'. Thus she became La Môme Piaf, with a nightclub date, new material to learn and an outfit to scramble together. The outfit bothered her more than the rest and she knitted furiously: on her opening night, the accidentally revealed half-finished sleeve provided a further delicious frisson for the chic audience who'd just heard the tiny creature belting her heart out in a way no one had ever before experienced.

After her initial discovery and (moderate) success Edith Piaf's career took in the long haul of years, clubs, tours, halls, highs, lows, hopes and disappointments. Despite being taken up, early on, as the quaint clown and darling of the intellectuals and cabaret set (including Jean Cocteau who remained a lifelong friend), like Marie Lloyd, Piaf's great success and base of support came from the loyal audiences who had seen her in the flesh. And in the early years they had plenty of opportunity as Edith toured the cinemas, dance halls, clubs and music halls of France, Belgium and Switzerland. Her repertoire then was that of the chansonière: whimsical, romantic, fervently patriotic, revolutionary and, above all, passionate. The chanson tradition of which she was a part had, like Marie Lloyd's music hall, and Judy Garland's vaudeville, always included songs other than love ballads. Edith sang about circus performers, carnivals, parties; and she brought to them all the stylised performance which was itself part of the art of the chanteuse. Her voice was nasal, her 'rrr' purposely exaggerated, her early style of volume and attack closely akin to the busking she'd done on her father's behalf. She gave to less private themes the same passion a love song demanded. In all, the combination was irresistible.

Piaf's name steadily climbed the bill, then in 1936 Louis Leplée was murdered and Edith's career took a tumble into the accompanying scandal. Leplée had been telling friends and anyone else listening in his bar of the amount of money he'd just made, in good hard cash, on the sale of an apartment. He was killed at his house the same night and neither the money nor the murderers ever came to light. What had been amusing and rather chic when alive became an unpleasant and sordid mess once murdered. Like everyone else attached to the club, Edith was hauled off by the gendarmes for questioning. To the press she was implicated by her association with Leplée, and for a while Edith found herself back in very small and provincial venues.

But vilified or lionised, in draughty village halls or chic Paris night-clubs, Edith's singing was fuelled by the experience of equally large doses of misery and happiness. Her appetite for love, life, drink, drugs and companionship manifested itself in an aura of raw energy. She went at everything with the same gusto and depth of feeling which she put into her songs; there were no half measures. Her voice and her grab for the best in life came from deep down in a gut which, while never forgetting the harsh youth, always managed to dredge up sparks of optimism. She had a childlike fervour and trust in the final triumph of right and love, even beyond death. Like Judy Garland, her lifelong inability to close herself off from experience, good or bad, gave her performances a particular vulnerability which extended, damagingly, into her own life. Likewise for Marilyn Monroe, the lack of defences or their deliberate deconstruction (when studying the Stanislavsky 'Method' for instance), quickly became dangerous to her mental and physical health. Yet these displays of raw humanity were hungrily consumed by audiences, and were made more perilous by the demands of the business. Work schedules and the lust for more and more product made no allowances for performers who, in giving their all to produce the towering emotions their audiences craved, were unable to retain the little for themselves necessary for a degree of personal safety.

In private, the lack of defences also extended to men. Society demanded that these dynamic, purposeful women acquire and defer to a male partner in order to fulfil the requirement of proper womanliness; yet the peculiar strains and stresses of their positions as women-out-of-place gave them no guidelines and little support in a role consisting entirely of contradictions. Edith Piaf gained and has retained since her death a reputation as something of a masochist, a woman who was happiest when her man had given her a good slapping around. It isn't borne out by the evidence. Edith's powerful personality was the source of the trouble. It was always in conflict with her 'natural' desire for the all-powerful hero of her songs and of popular romance, 'Mon Legionnaire' for instance. He was her soldier of fortune whose strength, wisdom and innate manliness would give her protection and true happiness. In practice, her own well-developed sense of survival and independence made such submissions short lived.

After the death of Louis Leplée Edith took up with songwriter Raymond Asso. He sought to mould and tame the twenty-one-year-old Piaf and teach her what he knew of performance and presentation. He was determined that she should better herself professionally, and he began the classic role of managing and hustling for bookings: he also had rules that dictated a woman's behaviour towards her lover, and the affair was tempestuous. In 1937 he succeeded in getting Edith a booking at the ABC Theatre in Paris. It was a considerable coup as her name had been somewhat soiled by the Leplée affair and bourgeois theatre manage-ments were reluctant to touch her. The one-woman show was a triumph and Edith put the scandal behind her once and for all.

Her pursuit of love objects was anything but conventionally feminine: her behaviour towards potential and new lovers owed much to the bucks, gangsters and pimps amongst whom she had grown up. As soon as she could afford it, and frequently when she couldn't, her men were courted fiercely, showered with gifts of clothes, money, jewellery, travel, enter-tainment and lavish attention. It was an irresistible and impossible show of sheer power. Some merely wilted and disappeared, but others, after first succumbing to the onslaught, eventually needed to reassert them-selves as Men. As Edith held almost every advantage which would normally have accrued to the male, some, including Asso, eventually began to work off their feelings of inadequacy in the classic method always available to the physically superior.

In August 1939 Raymond Asso was called up into the army, effectively ending their relationship as lovers. By Christmas of that year Edith was starring in Cocteau's *Le Bel Indifferent*. Playing opposite her was Paul Meurisse, with whom she had already embarked on a stormy affair. Class was the main difference between the two: Meurisse's family were respect-able bankers; he himself was familiar with and fond of the bourgeois comforts of Paris. Edith moved from the seedy hotel lodgings she had shared with Asso to a smart apartment and smart life with Meurisse. It was a combustible arrangement, as she enjoyed it all but did not moder-ate her ways in the slightest. Two years previously Edith had made her debut as an actress with a small part in a film, *La Garçonne*. According to some critics, she would always be a better singer than actor, but in the role Cocteau had written for her she was allowed to utilise her particular, intensely dramatic talents and was a huge success. So much so that when Meurisse received his call-up papers she was able to send a handwritten plea for postponement to the Minister of War and receive ten more days with her co-star and lover.

In 1940, despite the Occupation, Edith and Paris kept working. She starred in a forgettable film, *Montmartre-sur-Seine*, which told the story of a young girl who rose from being a florist's assistant to become a big star; it was not a success. The same year Edith met and hired Andrée Bigard, a woman who was to be her secretary and a source of stability for the next ten years. Edith was already famous but her lifestyle was just as haphazard and crazy as it had ever been. Andrée brought order to the chaos and imposed some administrative organisation on her business. Meanwhile when Edith was between lovers the erratic Momone still shared her life, and in 1942 all three moved into the third floor of Madame Billy's in the rue de Villejust (now rue Paul-Valery). It was full circle for Edith: Billy was the keeper of a successful brothel and Edith felt quite at home. With the connivance and encouragement of Momone, she entered into various schoolgirl escapades, including a black-market sale of Madame Billy's alligator shoes, but Madame Billy indulged her famous tenant much as Grandmère Gassion had done some twenty years before, and once again Edith thrived. She engaged in a series of passing affairs and a great deal of productive work. The war had given her a new kind of audience – French prisoners in both Germany and France with whom she posed for souvenir photographs after performances in the camps. Those same photos were later used to forge identity papers for the prisoners, who could then use them to attempt to escape. Not that Edith felt she was being a heroine; she simply threw herself into the effort as she always did. At all times and in all circumstances, she lived hard and fast, and Paul Meurisse and his influence were long gone.

Yet Piaf did not seek out weaker consorts whom she could dominate: the fact was that there were few who could equal her 'monster' personality. That description of her sometime secretary and long-time friend Charles Aznavour is echoed in the same wry but loving way in Liza Minnelli's recollection of her own mother. Judy Garland and Edith Piaf both grabbed at life with both hands, creating intense excitement and chaos as they did so. They asked too much because (in their different ways) they had received too little in the beginning. Each sought the perfect love, the perfect man, lasting security and the warmth to banish memories of childhood chills; but if either realised she was searching for an impossibility, nothing in her upbringing or environment could prompt her to consider an alternative. Edith, free of conventional moral strictures (although deeply religious and self-judgemental in her own way), took up and discarded lovers as easily as kicking off a pair of shoes. Her greatest delight, in the throes of a new love affair, was to play Svengali to the man in question. In that way she either launched or enhanced a number of careers. In 1944 a handsome young hick arrived in Paris from Marseilles, where his Italian immigrant parents had settled and where he had

already achieved some local success. Edith seized on Yves Montand with characteristic zeal and began to knock off the rough edges to reveal the star she saw he might become.

As occupied France carried on as well as it could under the circumstances, Edith herself had never been so busy. All songs had to be submitted to the Gestapo censor for approval, but with the aid of Andrée's discretion and organisational powers she was constantly in work. Where Edith entered into her clandestine war effort with nose-thumbing bravado (at one point she ostentatiously took a Jewish lover), Andrée's involvement was rather more thoughtful: the combination was highly effective. Edith's touring, arranged by Andrée, brought her in contact with hundreds of prisoners and provided a legitimate reason for travelling freely about France, and even into Germany, bearing messages and the precious photographs. Madame Billy, despite the proximity of Gestapo headquarters, was able to hide and shelter Jewish friends, as well as safeguard their valuables when they were forced to flee.

Meanwhile Edith was succeeding with Yves Montand rather better than she had perhaps intended. In 1945 they appeared together in a film, *Etoile sans Lumière*; Edith was the stellar attraction, Yves her satellite. Then she took him on tour. He preceded her on the bill and his unexpected popularity gave her real problems; having outgrown his place in her life, he soon departed, but Yves and Edith remained friends. Later that year Edith had trouble with another of her acolytes. Momone loved her 'sister' but was always jealous of her fame and adulation. On occasion she engaged in little tricks to discomfit Edith, and one day Andrée returned to Madame Billy's to discover that the Gestapo had arrested Edith for smuggling Jews. Andrée was able to prove that, in this instance anyway, the allegations were unfounded: her meticulously kept records of the singing tours showed the charges to be impossible. There seems to have been no further trouble from Momone, or from Nazi officialdom, through to the end of the war.

With the Liberation, Edith decided that it was time to try America. She had been touring with Les Compagnons de la Chanson, a nine-man folk group whose leader, Jean-Louis Jaubert, had become her lover. Edith, as always, was coaching the group, and in a spirit of professional guidance and camaraderie took the group with her. But when they opened at the Playhouse, a huge venue at Broadway and 48th Street, she found her generosity had backfired again. Their folksy harmonies were just what America wanted: indeed, one of the songs Edith had chosen for them against their wishes, 'Les Trois Cloches', was later released as 'Jimmy Brown' and became an enormous hit. Then when Edith walked on to do the second half, expectations on both sides of the stage were dashed. The young Charles Aznavour was part of Piaf's closest circle at the time, and in Michael Houldey's 1970 TV documentary *I Regret Nothing*, he recalled her reception:

71

They were expecting – you know – the woman that came from Paris with the fancy dresses and singing . . . 'C'est si bon' and things like that . . . in those days America wasn't ready for dramatic songs . . . I remember that when she used to explain the songs in English before to sing in French . . . and she say this is a story of a woman who died for love . . . some people used to laugh in the audience . . .

If they laughed at her introductions it was nervous laughter, accentuated by the presence of the unmoving black-clad figure who radiated the deepest emotions towards an audience whose feelings had hitherto been moved mainly by Betty Grable smiling cheekily over her shoulder in six million pin-up photos. Edith knew nothing of 'patter' or other American showbiz embellishments. On advice, she had employed an American actor to make a small précis before each song, and some of them were even translated into English for her. But nothing was right. Her natural style was direct and highly theatrical; her introductions limited to the name of composer, lyricist, and song title, in that order, and then straight into the song: the effect on record is still electric. The performance itself was deliberately vulnerable and entirely lacking in cynicism. It would be many years before an American concert audience was ready for this kind of undisguised passion. Edith Piaf booked her return passage to France having experienced a real failure.

Fortunately drama critic Virgil Thompson published an article in the

New York Times which suggested that American audiences would live to regret the lukewarm reception they had given this great artiste. Armed with this notice and fired by Edith's own desire to take up the challenge, her agent went to the Versailles Supper Club and secured a one-week engagement. Now, instead of going out to meet America on the vast concert stage, she had America come to her on her terms. The Versailles became her home from home for twelve weeks. Smart New York and Hollywood flocked in lines around the block to enter its intimate cabaret atmosphere. There in the dark, in smaller, safer numbers and with a drink to fortify them, the American audience were immersed in the real experience of a Piaf performance. Edith went, as ever, for the heart; and this time she won.

In New York she was feted by the famous who wanted to sit at her table, kiss her hand, be photographed with her, and generally be part of the entourage. It was here that she developed two of the great passions of her life. One was Marlene Dietrich. Of all the stars who came to pay homage, she and Edith enjoyed an instant regard for one another that lasted until Edith's death. The other was France's boxing hero and world middleweight champion, Marcel Cerdan, the only man who ever looked like staying the distance with Edith Piaf.

He was married, with children, but kept his family tucked away in the background. Piaf's relationship with him was adoring and for once on an equal footing. He was as famous as she and, more importantly, secure in himself and not overawed by her power. But in October 1949, hurrying at her instigation to rejoin her in New York, he was killed in a plane crash. She was left with a heavy burden of guilt, together with a new interest in the ouija board. When Momone was present at the sessions it seemed that Marcel would communicate with Edith. She became obsessed, and her friendship with Andrée Bigard deteriorated when the latter tried to wean her away from what she saw as a morbid and unhealthy fascination.

Edith had always been fond of melodramatic songs in which grand love affairs ended suddenly with the death of one of the lovers. Charles Aznavour later said that Edith was always asking him to write her songs that 'ended with a new way of dying'. Cerdan's death presented her with just such a situation. She wrote 'Hymne à l'Amour' for him, and Marguerite Monnot supplied the tune:

Le ciel bleu sur nous peut s'écrouler
Et la terre peut bien s'effondrer
Peu m'importe si tu m'aimes
Je me moque du monde entier
Tant qu'l'amour inondra mes matins
Que mon corps frémira sous tes mains
Peu m'importe les grands problèmes

73

Mon amour puis-que tu m'aimes

J'irais jusqu'au bout du monde
Je me ferais tendre en blonde
Si tu me le demandais
J'irais décrocher la lune
J'irais voler le fortune
Si tu me le demandais

Nous aurons pour nous l'éternité
Dans le bleu de toute l'immensité
Dans le ciel plus de problèmes
Dieu réunit ceux qui s'aiment.

('Hymmne à l'Amour', Piaf and Monnot)

The blue sky could tumble down upon us
The earth could collapse under our feet
A small matter as long as you love me
The problems of the world retreat

To the extent that my mornings are flooded with love
that my body trembles under your hands
problems are at one remove
my love, because you love me so

I'd go to the ends of the earth for you
I'd even go blonde
if you asked me to
Fetch down the moon
or steal for you
if you asked me to

Eternity will give our love a home
In the immense blue sky there's plenty of room
In heaven problems are few
God reunites those who love as we do.

Michèle Roberts

When Edith took to the stage with 'Hymne à l'Amour', it was no longer a case of anonymous passion or grief. Newspapers worldwide had reported Marcel Cerdan's death: everyone knew exactly what and whom she was singing about. This was the real thing, and the point at which Piaf turned from popular entertainer into popular legend. She toured, worked, recorded, partied, loved, lost and discarded in as reckless a fashion as ever; but now the performances, appearances and affairs took on a greater importance and drew more attention than ever before.

In 1951 she took up with Eddie Constantine, an expatriate American actor who was to come to prominence much later as the star of a series of continental Bond movie spin-offs; he was a rather raffish figure, very much the type that Edith liked. He starred with her in a seven-month run of *La Petite Lili* at the ABC theatre in Paris before she moved on yet again, this time to racing cyclists: first André Pousse and then Toto Gérardin.

Romantic crooner Jacques Pills was the next object of her affection, and she married him in New York in 1952 after a civil ceremony in Paris. It was a major event for Edith, who had considered herself to be Marcel Cerdan's widow in all but name. With Marlene Dietrich as witness, Piaf and Pills made their vows in the church where she had mourned Cerdan. It was a purposeful beginning and for a while it seemed that she might be happy. But it didn't last and their divorce became final in 1957.

In the early fifties Edith was involved in several car crashes. At thirty-eight she was already dependent on uppers for hyper-performance both on and off stage, and on downers for sleep. Since childhood she had kept up an ever-increasing intake of alcohol, and she regularly took painkillers to combat the aching discomfort of creeping arthritis. Now the injuries she sustained led her to morphine addiction, and in the opinion of one of her doctors the combination resulted in a woman who might already be classified as physiologically dead. But dead or alive, Piaf wasn't going to lie down. Her concerts were sell-outs, she triumphed in Carnegie Hall in

1956, she toured internationally, her records were hits, and her reputation soared to saint or plummeted to sinner according to what she was doing and who was watching her.

In 1957 she romanced handsome Greek composer Georges Moustaki. The affair itself was brief, but it resulted in Edith's greatest hit to date – 'Milord'. If there was ever need of a test case for the competing elements of lyrical content and physical delivery, this was the song. Moustaki's banal lyric, inviting a gloomy fellow in a café to forget the girl who's just jilted him and let the singer take him out to drown his sorrows, is no competition whatsoever for Piaf's nasal/guttural rendition of Marguerite Monnot's lusty tune, punctuated by the offbeat drum-crash which has become (like 'The Stripper' penned by Judy Garland's first husband David Rose) a universal leitmotif for painting the town red.

Monnot had been introduced to Piaf by Raymond Asso; trained as a classical pianist, she already had one hit with 'L'Etranger' and with Asso, 'Mon Legionnaire', first introduced by the great Marie Dubas. Simone Berteaut described Monnot as an absent-minded genius, always on call to take Edith's scraps of words and tunes and turn them into major hits. Whatever the truth of this picture, Marguerite ('La Guitte' to Piaf) was a longtime friend and collaborator until her death in 1961. As well as numerous hits with Edith, she went on to write the score of the hit musical *Irma La Douce*, with lyrics by Colette Renard. She also supplied the setting for one of Edith's most difficult dramatic songs, 'Les Blouses Blanches', the result of a collaboration late in her career with Michel Rivgauche who is credited with the lyric.

Ca fera bientôt huit années
Huit années qu'elle est internée
Oui! Internée avec fous,
Avec les fous!

Un grand traitsur les huit années
Tout comm'si rien n's'était passé!
Un'nuit elle ira leur voler
Leurs huit années!

Tiens! V'la main! Comm'le jour d'la rob'blanch'
Mais pourquoi qu'elle a mis tout's ces blous's blanch's?
Non'puis-que j'vous disque moi j'suis pas foll'!
Mais lachez-moi! J'suis pas foll!
J'suis pas foll! J'suis pas foll!

('Les Blouses Blanches', Rivegauche and Monnot)

Eight years have passed since she's been gone
Eight years ago, eight years so long
They locked her away in the bin
Oh yes– they locked her in

Eight years have been crossed off the list
Eight years that no longer exist
One night she'll count her costs
She'll steal back what she's lost

A hand waving. White dress. First Communion day?
Why these white canvas smocks that madwomen wear?
Why won't you believe me when I say
I'm not mad? Take your hands off me—
I'm not mad. I swear. I swear.

Michèle Roberts

In some ways Piaf's songs reverse the process seen in the repertoires of the other women in this book. It was the men writers who worked up the lyrics to her atypical dramatic songs; when she wrote her own, they expressed the unqualified pursuit and praise of love. Her international hit 'La Vie en Rose', written for and introduced by another singer, Marianne Michel, was in the same vein as 'Hymne à l'Amour'. Given a lifestyle which was devoted successfully to exactly that pursuit, those lyrics were no less honest for Piaf than 'Young Woman's Blues' was for Bessie Smith, or 'God Bless The Child' for Billie Holiday. Others would write 'interesting' songs for her as chanteuse, or hits for her as international popular singing star; for herself she wrote passionate love songs.

In 1958 Edith's attentions turned to another handsome young American. Douglas Davies was a painter, and for a few months they were inseparable. Later he too died in a plane crash, leaving only a handful of striking portraits of Piaf to be used as record-album covers. That year she was kept in hospital for some months. Rumours were rife but the cause was a secondary effect of her long-term addiction, a malfunction of the pancreas. Yet again the French press and public gloomily predicted her imminent death. Once more they were reprieved, and by December 1960 they were witnessing her one-woman triumph at the Paris Olympia.

Then in 1962, during a bitter winter that seriously affected her health, Edith met Theophanis Lambouskas. He was twenty-seven, gentle, handsome, working as a hairdresser, and he began, after their first casual meeting, to visit her regularly in hospital. As their relationship grew closer, it mattered much less to the press and the bourgeoisie that he might be a good companion than that he was twenty years her junior, and by far the most physically impressive of all her men. There was widespread muttering and head-shaking at her latest folly. Edith was ill and usually in pain, yet after Theo came along she seemed happy, and following an overwhelmingly sympathetic public response from a popular daily, she felt that she at least had the approval of her faithful public as she drove to the Town Hall to marry her new love. After a second, Greek Orthodox ceremony they were greeted and hailed by thousands of cheering women; Edith had once again cocked a snook at respectable sensibilities in a way that ordinary women clearly related to.

She responded to the cynics even more defiantly by introducing into her repertoire a new Francis Lai song which proclaimed her 'Right To Love'; and her husband, having changed his name on her advice to Theo Sarapo, joined her on stage and record in a duet, 'A Quoi ça Sert l'Amour?' In the one year of their marriage Edith recorded and performed almost as hard as ever, repeating her success at the Olympia and refusing to admit her illness and increasing frailty. Theo cared for her and protected her. She in turn did what she knew best, teaching him all she had learned of stagecraft, guiding him and advising him in his projected career in entertainment, which suddenly came to life with the addition of the magic name of Piaf. She bought him a train set and sat by while he played; he turned out and furnished her apartment. Then late in the autumn of 1963, at the age of forty-seven, she became ill in a way that even she seemed to acknowledge. Theo took her to the south of France, hoping that the sun and quiet might bring her back to health. Her resilience had always been extraordinary, and Theo simply believed her declaration that she would always recover.

Edith died on 14 October 1963, on the same day as her friend and admirer Jean Cocteau – a fact largely ignored by the press and public at the time, as all eyes turned, as usual, to Piaf. Like Marie Lloyd's, her funeral was virtually a state occasion with thousands of weeping men and women lining the streets, and flowers, messages and tokens from seemingly half the country. She who had craved love and affection all her life, who had fought for it indomitably in the only way she knew how, finally got more than anyone could quite comprehend. In 1983, twenty years after her death, a popular magazine published a readers' poll which had voted her France's woman of the century; and still in Père-Lachaise cemetery, while the tombs of Gertrude Stein, Colette and Oscar Wilde are bare, the plot whose inscription reads 'Madame Lambouskas (dite Edith Piaf), Theo Lambouskas, Louis et Ceçelle Gassion' is daily covered with fresh flowers.

Edith Piaf epitomises that enduring strand in western popular culture of women who dedicated their lives and work to men, and sang songs about how right that was. The implications for women have been enormous. Despite their own often bitter experiences in pursuit of the knight in shining armour, they continued to embark on paths of emotional and financial chaos, and at the same time sang about perfect 'love' as if they knew no more, as Janis Joplin sang, than when they were 'just girls'. All the while the lyrics belied their knowledge, but their voices embodied the resilience that kept them alive against the odds, and drew admirers in their millions. Nowhere is the combination more fascinating and dangerous than in the still-blazing star of Edith Piaf; and nowhere is it more enigmatic than in the now all-but-forgotten Helen Morgan.

Helen
Morgan

VOLUME 7   JANUARY 1, 1933   NUMBER 12

The
PLAYGOER
TRADE MARK

A Magazine for the Theatre

Why was I born? Why am I living?
What do I get? What am I giving?
Why do I want a thing I daren't hope for?
What can I hope for? I wish I knew

Why do I try to draw you near me?
Why do I cry? You never hear me
I'm a poor fool, but what can I do?
Why was I born to love you?

'Why Was I Born?', Kern and Hammerstein

First she popularised 'Bill (He's just my . . .)' in Jerome Kern and Oscar Hammerstein's *Showboat*; then it was 'Why Was I Born?' in their follow-up hit *Sweet Adeline*. With her pure soprano, and soft alabaster complexion, Helen Morgan won the hearts of New York theatre and nightclub patrons and became the darling of Broadway. These days she is as little known outside the United States as Marie Lloyd is outside the United Kingdom. And she would have been even less remembered had it not been for the sensationalised fifties biopic *The Helen Morgan Story*, starring Ann Blyth as an alcoholic goodtime girl who died of love just as the best ballads ordered.

In fact, Helen might just as well have been singing 'Why Was I Born?' to her mother, since Lulu Morgan was Helen's only life companion. If Edith Piaf's life was a study in the survival of a motherless child, Helen Morgan's was the story of a woman who never really broke away from her mother. And as mothers go, Lulu Morgan was a classic of her time. She had been deserted by her railroad-worker husband Tom after she told him she was pregnant. In Toronto, 1900, she had no choice but urgently to seek and secure employment. She got a job at a railroad canteen where she worked the eight-hour shift beginning at 6 a.m. up to and including the day Helen was born. She delivered the baby alone in their shanty on the wrong side of the tracks, and was back at work the next morning with the infant in a basket. Helen enjoyed four years of the canteen's convivial atmosphere and every bit of maternal attention that could be spared. Whether from exhaustion, ethic or inclination, Lulu had no occasional 'uncles' to share the shanty, and if baby Helen's life was secure her mother's was almost certainly an existence of mundane drudgery. Thus in 1905 when hard-drinking, good-time Tom reappeared, she was easily sold on his tales of reform and family. She upped sticks and went with him to Danville, Illinois, setting up house once again beside the railroad tracks. But the eight years that followed did not bear out Tom's good intentions; he was unable to stay off the whisky or in a job for very long and by the time Helen was twelve he was gone for good. This time the tight defensive unit formed by Lulu and Helen was to remain intact for the rest of their lives.

Having worked in one of the many factories that catered to Danville's farming trades, Lulu soon returned to another railroad canteen. She was described as spirited and independent, attractive and efficient, an ideal best friend for young Helen, who joined her mother as a workmate as soon as possible. In the canteen Helen was taught French-Canadian folk songs by the customers and ditties like 'The Camptown Races' by Lulu. It was here that the twelve-year-old was 'discovered' by Amy Leslie, ex-stage star-turned-journalist who was at the time engaged in researching the lives of the railroad wives. When she found the girl entertaining workers in the canteen with her folk songs, Miss Leslie was impressed to the extent of offering her an introduction to a club in Montreal. There was no need for Helen to persuade or cajole her mother, merely the need to keep up with the pace at which Lulu packed their bags for what had to be a chance for a better life for them both.

Helen's try-out at Jack Merceau's French Trocadero was no failure; nor did it lead to overnight fame and fortune, as later press reports would have had it. Helen and Lulu returned to the United States and the West Side of Chicago, where Helen attended school briefly before embarking on a series of jobs. Lulu was well aware of the uncertain possibilities of a singing career and encouraged Helen to fend for herself: unfortunately, she didn't reckon on her daughter's varied displays of unsuitability as factory fodder. Helen went through a dozen different jobs. She was fired from a gelatine factory when they found she couldn't stop eating the stuff; she was sacked from a Crackerjack factory for putting extra prizes in the boxes, and she resigned her position with the telephone company because bill-collecting made her too sad.

Meanwhile Helen had grown up to be a pretty young woman who won the title of 'Miss Illinois' in Chicago as well as 'Miss Mount Royal' in Canada. Part of her prize was a trip to New York, and once again Helen and Lulu made the best of the opportunity. Lulu got a job as a saleswoman at Gimbel's department store and Helen worked as an artist's model (strictly no nudes). Again it was only a small step, but this time it took Helen to within striking distance of Broadway and the nightclubs of New York. They arrived just in time for the Actors' Strike of 1919 and there were long periods when the occasional modelling fee and Lulu's wage from Gimbel's was all that stood between them and the poorhouse. On 16 January 1920, the 18th Amendment went into effect and Prohibition forced nightlife underground and even further beyond the pale than usual. But for the time being Helen kept her nose well above ground. She auditioned for a Ziegfeld musical, *Sally*. Jerome Kern had written some of the songs but the paths of singer and composer didn't cross in any significant way and Kern didn't recognise the potential of the woman he would later assist to stardom. While the show's leading lady Marilyn Miller (for whom Marilyn Monroe was named) signed a contract for $3,000 a week, plus – for the first time in show-business history – a percentage of the profits, Helen received a pittance to hoof and sing in the chorus line. When the show opened on 21 December 1920, they turned away six times the theatre's capacity, and *Sally* eventually ran for five hundred and seventy performances until February 1922. It was Helen's first steady job in show business.

As soon as the show finished Helen was offered work in Chicago's Café Montmartre. At twenty-two she remained a reserved young woman, content to spend most of her free time in her mother's company at home. But somehow the very innocence of her voice, its pleading quality and the pale Irish complexion which she rarely covered with make-up, were considered positive attributes in the less than savoury atmosphere of clubs, high-flyers and illegal hooch. When she returned to New York she went to work at the Backstage Club, a famous dive above a West 56th Street garage. It was run by Billy Rose, whom Tallulah Bankhead once described as 'animated slime' and to whom even the gentle Helen referred as a smelly little Napoleon 'because he's always got his right hand inside his shirt front feeling his left teat!' The club was closed within six months, and left Helen reliant on Lulu's income again.

Perhaps it was Helen's naïvete that made many people foster the myth of her overnight stardom. Someone who looked like a kid fresh out of charm school couldn't, in their eyes, have possibly come up through the hard-bitten ranks. Yet, more than any other woman in this book, Helen is truly representative of those whose tale was the hard grind upwards, ever dependent on the lucky break. In this case Amy Leslie came to the rescue again, and recommended Helen to George White, an entrepreneur famed for his revues, *George White's Scandals*. From the time she appeared in the 1925 *Scandals*, Helen's star was in the ascendant. In 1926 she went into another Broadway revue, *Americana*. It was here, as she sang 'Nobody Wants Me', another of the famous pleading ballads she was becoming famous for, that Jerome Kern sat in the audience and 'saw' her for the first time.

Meanwhile, Helen's moderate success on stage had led to even further involvement in the nightclub scene. Helen Morgan's 54th Street Club opened its peephole during 1926, and now Helen began what became her habitual routine throughout the twenties – finish the stage show, then rush to the club to deliver her torch songs sitting on top of the piano and clutching her trademark scarf.

Not that Helen had suddenly come into enough money to run her own club. Far from it. Bootleggers and gamblers put up money for clubs like these where they could (black) market their products or develop protection rackets behind a clean front, and they didn't come any cleaner than Helen Morgan, who gave the lasting impression of floating through

84

the entire era on a cloud of feather boas. Despite close association with the night-time world of gangland, she retained a certain homeliness rarely found in such circles. Later she hostessed several other clubs – 'The House of Morgan', or 'Chez Morgan', and 'Helen Morgan's Summer Home' – always successfully, and in a manner quite unlike that of her famous contemporary Texas Guinan, the 'Queen of the Nightclubs', whose rootin' tootin' personality and adopted first name revealed both her origins and her brash style.

As the two most prominent white women then operating in the urban wilderness of illegal booze joints, both Helen and Texas were targets for raid and arrest. For a while their most ardent pursuer was an ambitious district attorney, Mabel Walker Willebrandt, who later espoused Republicanism and friendship with movie magnate Louis B. Mayer. With shades of Marie Lloyd's Mrs Ormiston Chant, and Billie's magistrate Jean Norris, Mrs Willebrandt had been a staunch defender of women in Los Angeles. A militant teetotaller, she was now out to break New York's corrupt mayor Jimmy Walker, and the clubs were her principal target. Helen and Texas were repeatedly raided, and on one occasion, when their premises had been visited in their absence, they met (they were not known to be close friends) and went to the police station together to turn themselves in. To the chagrin of the lawmen, no one could find grounds to arrest them.

It's hard to believe that Helen wasn't in some way affected by this environment, yet nothing has so far indicated a desire on her part for the highs of the lowlife, or for a significant change in her lifestyle. Perhaps her involvement with racketeers is best understood in terms of simple opportunism bred of twenty years' struggle to make ends meet; a club in her name represented the chance to sing and to work as she pleased. Through all the notoriety Helen maintained the mien of a 'lady', and suffered genuine distress when in 1929 there was a threat that she might go to jail for a transgression of the Prohibition Act.

Texas Guinan, on the other hand, was a double-gaited gal if ever there was one. She mixed it with slick gangsters and pretty chorines alike, revelled in her infamy, and had the band strike up 'The Prisoner's Song' whenever the Feds arrived to cart her off in the paddywagon. It was she who persuaded her customers to part with thick wads of dollars for not very much in return and then had them rolling in the aisles with the derisive greeting 'Hello Suckers!' Texas also died young; her funeral was an event she might have staged herself for a laugh. There were backstage problems when the mortician discovered that her thrice-tucked chins had come loose during the embalming process. Meanwhile out front there was a riot amongst the seven thousand New Yorkers who had turned out to say goodbye. By comparison Helen gave an appearance of delicacy that verged on being fey, but it concealed a robust constitution and an appetite for work that would only become apparent when recognition and offers finally came rolling in.

Ever since Jerome Kern had seen her in *Americana*, he had been working to get a production of *Showboat* off the ground. He and Oscar Hammerstein had turned Edna Ferber's novel into a musical. They had a producer in the great Ziegfeld, and now Kern felt that he had found the right singer to play the tragic mulatto heroine, Julie Dozier. Despite the Harlem Renaissance, and the inclusion of fifty black artists in the chorus, it was further evidence of racial segregation in New York that Kern never considered using one of the many black women stars (Ethel Waters, Alberta Hunter, Adelaide Hall, to name a few) in the role. Why the whiter-than-white Helen should have so captured his imagination is anyone's guess; it can only have been Helen's persona as the original torch singer – a white woman who sang the bluesy laments and longing of unrequited loves in an idiom otherwise associated with black singers. Listening now to her recordings it's hard to fathom even that musical connection. But the fact remains that before *Showboat* Helen Morgan had been a moderately successful club singer and Broadway stage personality. The role of Julie Dozier took her through unknown quantities of Max Factor's 'Egyptian-tint' skin make-up and turned her into a major star.

Showboat opened in Washington in 1927; Helen was twenty-seven years old. By the time it reached New York just before Christmas, it bore all the signs of a hit and went on to be a critical and popular triumph. Critic Robert Garland (for whom Judy is said to have been named) called it 'an American masterpiece'. Helen's personal success was somewhat dampened when 'Chez Morgan' was raided on 30 December, and its hostess booked, fingerprinted and locked up until 5.30 a.m. when she was released on $1,000 bail. Her joint was wrecked by the dry agents. Although shaken by the experience, which included arraignment on New Year's Eve, there was a great deal to celebrate: *Showboat* and Helen Morgan were the toast of Broadway. There was also a hint of romance between her and Oscar Hammerstein, although friends believed his marriage prevented him from allowing the affair to go further than a warm friendship. Meanwhile Helen continued to live with Lulu, as each night she took command of the New Amsterdam Theatre stage to sing the hit show's hit song:

> He's just my Bill, an ordinary man
> He hasn't got a thing that I can brag about
> And yet to be upon his knee
> So comfy and roomy, seems natural to me
> Oh I can't explain, it's surely not his brain
> That makes me thrill
> I love him because he's – I don't know
> Because he's just my Bill

('Bill', Kern, Wodehouse and Hammerstein)

Jerome Kern and P.G. Wodehouse had written it in 1917 and had been waiting for the right singer ever since. Now, ten years later, slotted into *Showboat*, it became Helen's signature tune.

Showboat's initial run on Broadway lasted five hundred and seventy-two performances. This meant a weekly schedule of six evening and two matinee shows, but even then, in 1929 Helen also starred in the movie *Applause* and worked each night into the early hours at one or other of her successive establishments. In the meantime, Kern and Hammerstein set to work tailoring a new musical around Helen's particular talents. They wrote a new hit song in the torch idiom, 'Why Was I Born?', and the resulting show, *Sweet Adeline*, opened to a reception as enthusiastic as that which had greeted *Showboat*. If there was any truth in the Hammerstein/Morgan rumour, the lyric he penned for her was as unwittingly cruel as Arthur Miller's *The Misfits* for Marilyn Monroe, or Judy Garland's role in *I Could Go On Singing*: all were too close to the bone.

> Spending these lonely evenings
> With nothing to do but to live in dreams that I make up
> All by myself
> Dreaming that you're beside me
> I picture the prettiest stories only to wake up
> All by myself
> What is the good of me by myself?

('Why Was I Born?', Kern and Hammerstein)

On the other hand, it may well have been simply a case of Helen's image, and a lyric and melody crafted by professionals to fit it. For the star, the authors, and the audience, it was important simply that the song was a hit; and *Sweet Adeline*, after two hundred and thirty-four performances, seemed destined to 'run and run'. What no one counted on was the general intervention of the long-term effects of Depression: the show closed much earlier than anyone had predicted, and Helen found herself, with the exception of one headlining season at The Palace, saddled with a twelve-week 'rest'. Not that she didn't need it. She had been working at a furious pace and, in addition, had managed to get herself entangled with yet another irretrievably married man.

Arthur Loew was much Helen's senior, and head of the famous chain of theatres. While she continued to sing about ordinary uncomplicated Bills and Joes, Helen sought extraordinary and talented men. Or perhaps she was doing what was expected of any star; perhaps it was convenient that they were unobtainable. She remained relatively well off, even though she had thrown a good deal of her money away in spontaneous moments of abandon. Her generosity, like Marie Lloyd's, was legendary. The sight of down-and-outs triggered off memories of her own youth, and she was always a soft touch for unemployed colleagues. Even so, she managed, unlike Judy Garland and Billie Holiday, to provide for her mother to her own satisfaction: she bought Lulu a chicken farm upstate, in addition to the brownstone they shared in Brooklyn Heights. Helen still seemed happiest at home with Lulu, pursuing their hobby of doll-making, and confiding in no other.

Apart from Loew, Helen had one other good friend in Florenz Ziegfeld. When his 1932 revival of *Showboat* opened on Broadway in May, a new star was born in Paul Robeson, and Helen's name appeared above the name of the producer and the show: it was a first, and a testimony to her success. When he died in July, Helen lost her professional mentor, friend and adviser, and became deeply depressed. Always partial to a drink, the consumption of several ponies of brandy before the show now became a ritual in which her leading man, George Blackwood, found himself a reluctant partner. When the show went on tour later that year, Blackwood, although discreetly lodged in an adjoining room, became Helen's lover, and experienced some of her more eccentric and spirited behaviour; it also revealed a darker side both in her nature and in her capacity for alcohol. In the early stages it seemed not to affect her performance – although some said she wasn't as good when sober – and certainly nothing reached the press or was noted by critics who might have been the first to jump on a Drunken Star story. There were several evictions from hotels disenchanted by their noisy all-night partying, but the only story that made the papers concerned a lion cub. 'Princess' was a Christmas gift from Blackwood to Helen, and she shared their rooms until the day she got bored, tore the place apart and frightened witless an unsuspecting maid. George Blackwood departed for Hollywood soon after Princess was banished to a zoo.

Meanwhile *Showboat* had degenerated into a dilapidated shadow of its former brilliance. Altogether Helen played in its various manifestations for nine years on and off. While the show never toured the South because of problems of housing and transporting the black chorus, and because of the subject of miscegenation which the book dared to highlight, elsewhere it continued to play to rapturous receptions. By 1933, however, *Showboat* was looking more like burlesque than the Great Ziegfeld's first-rate theatrical production. Helen hit the bottle even harder, and seemed to gain more comfort from her seemingly irreconcilable interests in Christian Science and the sensational evangelist Aimee Semple McPherson (who could count Marilyn Monroe's grandmother among her thousands of devotees) than from the occasional visits that Arthur Loew continued to pay while she was on tour. Later in 1933 Helen embarked on a trip to Europe. Lulu accompanied her on the voyage, and on the return journey Arthur Loew was also among the passengers. On their arrival in New York, Loew went out of her life for good. Helen later said that he had asked her to give up her nightclub work because of the low male company she kept there, and because of her drinking.

Two weeks after her return, Helen went out on the town with one Maurice Mashke and they 'got hitched', apparently living together as husband and wife for only a few weeks before separating. She continued to work on and off for the next few years in clubs, movies and on the stage, but she was starting to get bad reviews, and her divorce from Mashke in 1936 made the papers. In that year Helen played Julie Dozier in the movie version of *Showboat*. Given her huge success in the stage

With first husband Maurice Mashke

versions to date, it was predictable that she should have been chosen to play her famous role on screen. It was more surprising that when the film was remade after Helen's death in the forties and Lena Horne lost the role to Ava Gardner, who didn't even have La Morgan's distinction of an outstanding voice. In 1936 it was just about all Helen Morgan did have; the woman who played Julie Dozier was tired, puffy and lacking in the former brilliance of her stage presence.

Whether life had lived up to her expectations is hard to say. She was thirty-six years old, had a severe drink problem, and was a has-been in the best sense – she *had been* a very big star. The watery-eyed passivity of her performance had served to popularise a particular kind of song which, at that time, could have been interpreted as a personal achievement plan by many young women:

There's a saying old says that love is blind
Still we're often told 'Seek and ye shall find'
So I'm going to seek a certain lad I've had in mind
Looking everywhere, haven't found him yet
He's the big affair I cannot forget
Only man I think of with regret
I'd like to add his initial to my monogram
Tell me where is the shepherd for this lost lamb?

There's a somebody I'm longing to see
I hope that he turns out to be
Someone to watch over me
I'm a little lamb who's lost in the woods
I know I should always be good
To one who'd watch over me

Though he may not be the man
Some girls think of as handsome
To my heart he carries the key

Won't you tell him please to put on some speed
Follow my lead, Oh how I need
Someone to watch over me

('Someone to Watch Over Me', G. and I. Gershwin)

Helen's own quest through two married men, a few months with an actor, a few weeks with her first husband and one real live 'Bill' in the form of car dealer Lloyd Johnson, to whom she was married for the last three months of her life, never seemed particularly desperate. She always had her 'someone' in Lulu. The problem was more one of adjusting to social expectations; and as the giggles from her fellow performers proved early on, it was not expected that a Star should be content to spend her spare time with her mum.

But it would be foolish to assume that every song was sung straight from the heart. Apart from material written specifically for them or by them, most of these women had a third area of repertoire in which they sang and recorded 'standards', the classics of popular music, and contributed to the establishment of others. 'Someone to Watch Over Me', for instance, was first introduced by Gertrude Lawrence and reinterpreted by Helen Morgan. The combination of a pleasurable musical challenge and appealingly romantic lyrics has proved durable and endlessly attractive to certain singers and audiences. The reinterpretation of classics is an established part of most popular art forms, a means by which newcomers seek to prove that not only can they follow in the footsteps of their idols, but also come up with a new slant. There are commercial reasons too. In show business one of the basic beliefs is that what worked once will work again, and again. And it's not just the songs that benefit from repackaging, but the underlying content too. A song like 'Someone to Watch Over Me' expressed hopes that were repeatedly destroyed for women; but couched in a pretty tune and a convincing performance, the myth lives on. Alison Moyet's 1985 revival of 'That Old Devil Called Love' (recorded by Billie forty years earlier) is a good example.

Although a few of the women in this book escaped the influence of such songs – Marie Lloyd because she was before their time, Edith Piaf because she dabbled only minimally in American songs, and Janis Joplin because she was part of a cultural revolution that rejected them stylistically – most ballad, middle-of-the-road, even jazz singers have used such songs from the twenties to the present day. Given Bessie's revamping of her material at the time of her death, it's likely that even she would have chosen from this classic group of 'men' songs within the standards repertoire: 'Someone to Watch Over Me', 'The Man I Love', 'Trouble is a Man', 'The Man That Got Away', 'Can't Help Lovin' That Man of Mine', 'Stormy Weather' and 'My Man'. The last of these had been introduced early in the century by Fanny Brice, whose comic genius had made the song much more appealing than subsequent versions – and there have been hundreds, including reworkings by Lena, Ella, Della Reese, Sarah Vaughan, Jane Froman, Judy Garland and, most interesting because of its hopeless irony, Billie Holiday:

It cost me a lot
But there's one thing I've got
It's my man

Cold and wet, tired you bet
All of this I'll soon forget
With my man

He's not much on looks
No hero out of books
But I love him

Two or three girls has he
That he likes as well as me
But I love him

I don't know why I should
He isn't true, he beats me too
What can I do?

Oh my man I love him so
He'll never know
All my life is just despair

But I don't care
When he takes me in his arms
The world is bright all right

What's the difference if I say
I'll go away
When I know I'll come back

On my knees some day
For whatever my man is
I am his for ever more

('My Man', Yvain and Arkell)

For every woman in this book, that indefinable 'whatever' turned out to be a trial and a curse at one time or another. The men they pursued were often strong on looks and charisma, but 'he beats me too' was a frequent refrain in life as much as on stage. Contrary to the song, however, when it got to that point they unromantically and sensibly dropped or divorced them as fast as they could. As for everything in the world being bright once they were safely in the arms of their men, those men more often than not mismanaged their worlds (their workloads, earnings, investments, health) time and again, and in many cases exacerbated the worst problems. Still they continued to conjure up the lie for themselves and for their audience, because a song like that, their command and reinterpretation of it, their ability to move an audience with it, was proof of their place in the line of great performers since Fanny Brice herself. These were the kinds of songs that made hit records and so these were the songs they sang, all the time reinforcing the myth for millions of popular music fans for decades afterwards. When the 'someone to watch over me' didn't come up to scratch, ordinary women could shrug their shoulders philosophically and have Helen Morgan soothe their disillusion with the rueful admission 'can't help lovin' that man o' mine'.

But Helen's reality was her work and her mother. She had seen Lulu's 'Bill' fade into sour memory; as soon as she was able, she had reversed that state, taking care of her mother's material needs to the best of her ability. That fame, public adulation and spasmodic fortune could not be the precursor to her own happy-ever-after must have been unthinkable; the eventual realisation that she too might be wrong was a bitter one and a revelation shared by many mothers and daughters, not just the famous. Millions were forced to come to terms with the dream of Bill being just that. Fantasy, reverie and the peculiarly delicious sentiments of the songs became a part of getting on with what they had. As it happened, Helen's mother remained a loyal and trusting friend who lived quietly in her daughter's shadow, and finally buried her when Helen died at the age of forty of cirrhosis of the liver.

With Edith Piaf (and Jimi Hendrix) as the notable exceptions, an

extraordinarily high proportion of the performers (men and women) mentioned in this book were raised by a deserted or divorced mother or, in the few cases of continuing marriage, a mother who ruled the roost. And showbiz mothers have earned a reputation for being ruthless, pushy, scheming, domineering, cruel, unnatural, and, most damning of all, parasitic bitches living vicariously through the fame and riches of their children – taking and basking in the luxury and limelight they had so desperately desired for themselves but were unable to attain because they had neither the talent nor the looks. But the truth is neither so simple nor so pitiless.

The American mothers, in particular, were of a generation whose living memory contained the fear and uncertainty of being the children of immigrants or refugees, or of living in communities which saw an influx of such people. Their goal was that their children should be educated: their sons would enter a profession, their daughters must become fit to marry such men, and a tiny number might even make that leap themselves. For those like Lulu Morgan whose working lives had been spent in penury and humiliation, their consuming desire was that their children should achieve a reasonable degree of dignity and comfort; and those women who perceived and understood the possibility of the Rainbow's End being in Hollywood and Show Business sought what was best for their offspring. The results were both tragic and brilliant, quite in keeping with the bizarre manifestations of the American Dream of which they in turn became a part.

The mother of Frances Farmer was just such a woman. Lillian van Ornum fought through and survived a frustrating youth and unsatisfactory marriages, then encouraged her youngest daughter to climb the very highest peak of success – only to see her daughter take a long hard look at Hollywood and refuse everything Lillian had ever hoped for. Lillian's reaction was violent and cruel, but years later her victim was nevertheless able to perceive the root of the bitterness. But Lillian (whose image as selfish and heartless bitch has been perpetuated in both the Hollywood biopic *Frances*, and in the feminist alternative *Committed*) has suffered the uncomprehending condemnation of every other observer. Frances's own picture of her mother in the memoir *Will There Really Be A Morning?* is that of an extraordinary woman.

It wasn't that Frances didn't want to be one of the chosen with a place in the Californian sun; but, like Judy Holliday and Marilyn Monroe, she wanted to do it with her brain and self-respect intact. She refused to be merely the beautiful blonde with a lovely body, the vacant sex symbol. All Lillian demanded was that Frances behave like a normal grateful American girl and *be* a movie star. It was beyond her comprehension that, like her own young self, Frances might want more from life. It was the cruellest twist for both that they were mother and daughter. As Hollywood tried to straitjacket both her talent and the very independence she'd acquired from her mother, Frances lashed out with drink, abuse, and any other behaviour which might express her revolt. After several rampages that resulted in arrest, Frances was committed to an asylum and to her mother's legal guardianship at the age of twenty-seven. To Lillian, incarceration was the severest punishment she could inflict and one which her own husband had tried on her years before. Frances was returned to asylum, rest home and sanatorium three times in the next eleven years. She was partially lobotomised to keep her quiet, and was finally released to her aged parents who, having spent years separated, wanted her home to take care of them. Fearing that, as before, she would be recommitted for the slightest misdemeanour, Frances was their obedient slave until she discovered that her 'competency' had been restored some years before by a letter from her father to the hospital authorities. Within a year she married as a means of escape, moved her parents to the care of their other children, left her husband, and bought a one-way ticket to the furthest destination she could afford – Eureka, California.

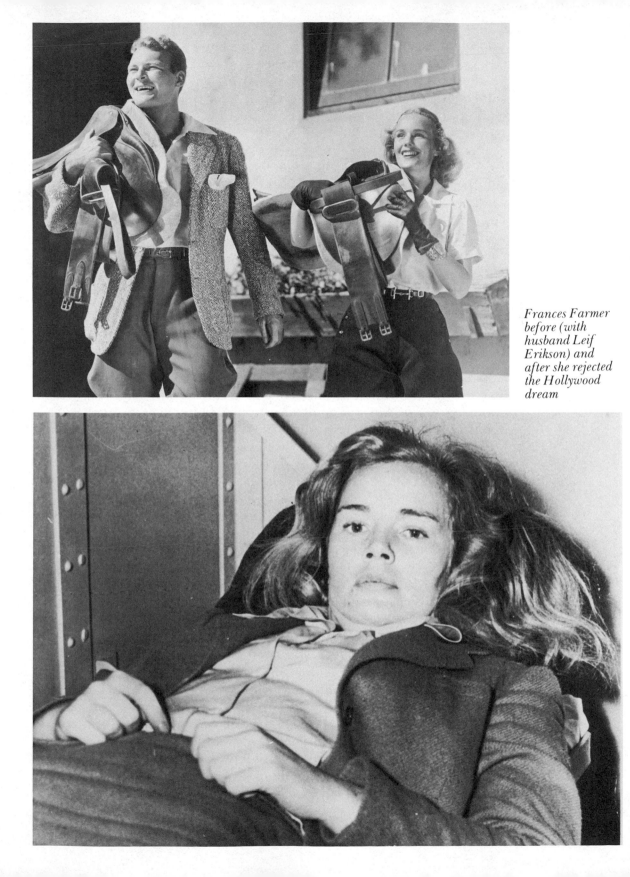

*Frances Farmer
before (with
husband Leif
Erikson) and
after she rejected
the Hollywood
dream*

Frances Farmer lived to work again, in a limited fashion, and to tell the tale (in *Will There Really Be A Morning?*). Like Doris Day, she was marginally better off than those who died early, but her life was all but ruined. And Frances had been punished for quite simple reasons: her mother really believed she was mad not to want to be a famous movie star, and no one else disagreed with her. When Frances signed a seven-year contract with Paramount on her twenty-first birthday, 19 September 1935, it was everything a girl should have wanted. Just six days before, on another studio lot, a twelve-year-old Frances, already known as Judy Garland, auditioned for MGM and was rewarded with a similar contract. For both mothers, Lillian Farmer and Ethel Gumm, those documents were American womanhood's highest honour. If, in that great democracy, Everywoman's son could grow up to be president, then her daughter could be a movie star, or perhaps even First Lady.

The times were bursting with ambitious mothers. Those of Doris Kappelhof, Frances Gumm and Joe Yule Jnr all adopted Lillian's pioneer spirit as they took off across America in their jalopies as the first step towards creating Doris Day, Judy Garland and Mickey Rooney. Nell Carter Yule left her single-handed home-cooked chicken-and-hot-biscuit restaurant in Kansas City and drove west, camping in a tent along the way with five-year-old Joe Jnr. Ethel Gumm drove the sixty miles from Lancaster to Los Angeles and back again day after day in order to have her Baby Frances audition. Alma Sophia Kappelhof packed Doris and her young dancing partner and his mother into their car, together with the money they'd won in a talent quest, and drove a thousand miles from Cincinnati to California to seek their fortunes.

All these mothers suffered the economic deprivation of the Great Depression. They budgeted and saved, struggling all the while to shore up marriages which failed and left them emotionally stranded. But throughout their lives they never allowed their ingenuity and spirits to be entirely dissipated. They invested their energies and hopes in placing the right bet on the right offspring, and they finally and, in their eyes, rightly, won. But the victories were shortlived. For the female offspring there were fundamental contradictions involved in the dual requirement of being both strong and submissive – to support their men, and to defer to them. Survival itself in one way or another depended on their fortitude: each grew up in the twin shadow of her mother's obvious autonomy *and* her search for the one true strong man. Ironically but understandably, no other achievement quite matched reproduction and the skills of home-making. No matter how much a girl was encouraged to explore, exploit and develop her own talents, somewhere along the line, if she wanted to feel *really* whole, she would have to find a man, develop her housekeeping abilities and bear children of her own. Without a child to justify herself, Marilyn Monroe would embark on spasmodic attempts to create houses beautiful; when Judy's contempt for her own inability to keep husband, family and career in equilibrium grew too strong, her recourse was to take to the scouring pads or frantically cook herself into a state of grace.

The mothers had no such complications. The Land of the Free rewarded those who worked hardest, so it was said, and these mothers – to a woman – worked hardest. And these, in summary, were their rewards. Lulu Morgan saw her daughter die of alcoholic poisoning at the age of forty; Lillian van Ornum lived a life constantly embattled with her daughter; Alma Kappelhof's daughter retired hurt, an almost total recluse, by the age of fifty; Nell Carter Yule's son drifted into debt, alcoholism and a severe personality crisis. And Ethel Gumm lived to bear Judy Garland's resentment and alienation but was, perhaps thankfully, spared the full horror of her youngest daughter's final years.

Judy Garland with her mother Ethel and the father of MGM, Louis B. Mayer

**That great beginning has seen the final inning
Don't know what happened,
It's all a crazy game . . .**

'The Man That Got Away', Arlen and Gershwin

Memories of Judy Garland seem to be as diverse as her astonishing career which spanned four decades. Some recall only the pitiful creature of her last years. For others she is forever Dorothy in the Land of Oz. She has been written about by fans, colleagues, ex-husbands, ex-lovers, one-night-stands, journalists, psychologists, and in the definitive 600-plus-page epic by Gerold Frank. Few of the private memories, and none of the published accounts, seem willing to extract a simple story of addiction which began in her early teens and lasted until her death thirty-five years later. In all that time, Judy Garland's dependence on a depressant-stimulant cycle was never effectively tackled and its cumulative effect brought about her premature death. Hospitalisation and psychoanalysis failed to reveal the source of Judy's conflict, and the treatment she received was always of the band aid kind.

Popular opinion argues that because they choose such a lifestyle, the famous have no right to complain about risk or loss; that in the course of human suffering there have been more tortured lives. In Garland's case that isn't at all obvious, and right from the start she had little choice. Her parents' marriage was already in trouble when she was conceived; they didn't want a third child, but if it had to be, they fervently hoped for a boy they could call Frank Junior. When Baby Frances arrived, she was a source of temporary harmony between Frank and Ethel Gumm, and a centre of attention for the whole family.

Like Lillian van Ornum and Lulu Morgan, Ethel's struggles began young. She was born in 1896 in northern Michigan, one of four daughters and four sons of John Milne, a Scottish engineer and hardline atheist, and his Irish wife, Eva Fitzpatrick. In 1911 they moved to Superior where John ran one of the town's movie houses for a while. Money was scarce, so Ethel, with a number of her siblings, turned to entertaining as the best chance of making a living. Later diagnosed as having the same hyper-thyroid condition as her husband Frank, Ethel was always energetic. But she was also efficient and resourceful, and in 1913, at seventeen, she became resident pianist at the Savoy, Superior's first purpose-built movie theatre. By that time about half the vaudeville theatres in Superior had disappeared as film gradually ousted variety acts, but the Savoy's programme still consisted of live vaudeville, a four piece 'orchestra', a short and a main feature. Between the reels of film a live song, illustrated with hand-tinted slide photographs, kept the audience amused. At the Savoy that job fell to Frank Gumm; it was probably not the career he had envisioned when he'd dropped out of college after his first year.

Like Ernest Farmer, Frank was a Southern boy, and the 'educated' partner in the eventual marriage. He was one of three sons of a wealthy Murfreesboro family. The town, fifty miles south-east of Nashville, Tennessee, sported a grammar school from which Frank had graduated with a good academic and musical record. His charm and tenor voice brought youthful success and a swift exit from college, but greater fortune did not come his way. He was twenty-eight, gallant and outgoing, but no further advanced in his profession when he met Ethel. He was much impressed by her energy and vitality and they married in 1914. Later they moved to Grand Rapids, Minnesota, with the intention of setting up regular family life. Naturally it meant that Ethel, talented or not, gave her own ambitions a back seat in deference to Frank's position as head of their household.

He became manager of Grand Rapids' movie theatre and the Gumms were welcomed into the community. They performed together at the theatre and took an active part in local life. By 1920 they had purchased a half share in the theatre and moved their family of two daughters to a larger rented house. But the picture of happy family life was deceptive. Ethel already suspected that Frank wasn't the all-American husband she thought she had married. For his part, if this true son of Dixie had acknowledged his homosexuality, even to himself, it's more than likely he'd trusted that marriage to a good woman would straighten him out.

Frank's work with the church choir slowly became the source of disbelieving gossip. Meanwhile he went on with his life and work as a good citizen and responsible young husband, with the growing burden of rumour threatening them both. In that atmosphere Ethel became pregnant for the third time. Acknowledging the difficulties between them, Ethel allowed herself to be persuaded that a medical friend of his, one hundred and fifty miles away in Minneapolis, might be the answer to this particular problem. But in 1921 the weight of illegality, immorality and considerable danger involved in an abortion caused Frank's friend to back out, and their third child was born on 19 June 1922. She was bright, precocious, delicate and, according to her sisters, 'spoiled rotten'. This had something to do with 'mysterious' illnesses which twice threatened her infant life, but more to do with her own inclination to demand attention at all times. From her first performance, Christmas 1924, at Frank Gumm's New Grand Theatre, 'Little Miss Leather Lungs' was acclaimed by her audience; and the two-and-a-half-year-old lapped it up.

During the next few years Frank became a reporter for the *Grand Rapids Independent* as well as being engaged with the theatre, church and other civic duties; Ethel continued to play the piano and also manage her full-time work as housewife and mother. They were both equally absorbed in promoting 'The Gumm Sisters with Baby Frances'. They even made a few appearances together in nearby towns. But by 1926 Frank's – and therefore his family's – standing in Grand Rapids had been wrecked by his homosexual activities. It soon became obvious that the Gumms had no future in the town. It was a major turning point for Ethel. The assumptions that every 'decent' young woman made about marriage were not true for her; it was plain that she had failed, and her only course must

Mary Jane, Virginia and Frances, mistakenly billed as 'The Glum Sisters'

have seemed equally clear – to care for her children come what may.

In the summer of 1926 the Gumm sisters went on the road for three months of one-night stands. It was a face-saving preliminary to their final departure from Grand Rapids. They spent a short time in Los Angeles and hoped to settle there. But, unable to find a theatre, they ended up in Lancaster, a desert town sixty miles from the metropolis, where Frank opened another movie house. Ethel's energies were channelled into the three girls, first as a trio, then just Baby Frances. There were endless round trips to Los Angeles as she worked her way through the ranks of the Meglin Kiddies, countless auditions, and performances even further afield if it seemed like a good opportunity – to Chicago for instance, for a booking at the World's Fair. Frances knew nothing of her father's homosexuality nor of the façade that Ethel kept up. Frances's sisters denied that their mother was the real 'wicked witch of the west', as Judy Garland would later call her. Judy painted her early childhood in Grand Rapids as idyllic, and blamed her mother entirely for its disruption. She remembered Ethel as cruel and vindictive, although others have interpreted actual incidents – Ethel's method of dealing with Frances's chronic bouts of hay fever, for instance – quite differently. Despite the exhaustion of running family life and piano playing, Ethel would put Babe in the car and drive up into the hills where the air was clearer and where she would drive around all night whilst the child slept (and whilst she was able to avoid some of the truth of her marriage). Judy later saw this as some kind of perverse punishment and could never be convinced that Ethel's intentions were good.

As Ethel's alienation from Frank deepened, she began to place more and more hope in her remarkably talented youngest child, and this marked the beginning of Babe's discontent. Separation from her father came to be associated with having to sing and to please her mother; she began to hate the interminable chase for auditions and even performing itself, especially solo. She believed that people were not interested in *her*, only in her voice, which increasingly became the focus not only of her earning power and fame, but also, predictably, of her vulnerability.

In 1931 she had further cause to stoke what would prove to be a long-nurtured grudge against her mother when she caught Ethel with her one known indiscretion, William Gilmore. Frances was horrified but still too young to understand the true nature of her parents' troubles. Lancaster was even smaller and more straitlaced than Grand Rapids, so when Frank found himself unable to curtail or conceal his homosexual activities his departure in 1934 was swift. He took over the Lomita Theatre, closer to Los Angeles, but this time his family did not join him. By 1935, Ethel and her daughters had settled in Los Angeles and Frank visited whenever possible.

At twelve years old, Frances was already perched on the edge of a yawning chasm of doubt and misgiving. She adored her father, longed to be with him, and could not understand Ethel's animosity towards him. At the same time, although she expressed 'normal' desires for completing school, of becoming a nurse, and eventually a wife and mother, Frances – already known professionally as Judy Garland – was only too aware that her family and public saw her as something very special and not 'normal' at all. In September of the first year of permanent residence in Los Angeles Judy was, unusually, accompanied by Frank to MGM for an audition (Ethel had not been at home when the peremptory summons came). The voice was all, and it was agreed that its possessor, although in MGM's opinion showing no other movie potential, should be signed up immediately.

Just over a month later, on the evening of one of her first radio broadcasts under the MGM banner, Frank Gumm checked into hospital with what he thought was a minor upset, then died suddenly of spinal meningitis. It was the worst thing that had ever happened to Judy, and as much as she was thrilled by her contract with Hollywood's biggest studio, it was ever after linked with an irreparable loss for which she blamed her mother. Whatever Judy's circumstances from that point on, she would have had to go through a very painful process of re-appraising her early years and establishing some comprehension of her mother's position if she were ever to enjoy and fulfil her life. Had she been allowed to confront the truth (like Frances Farmer) she might at least have come to understand her mother's vicarious ambitions, and even made her peace. But the truth was denied her, first by the family's avoidance of it, and later, when she dared to ask, by outright denial from one of her father's closest friends. So she was destined to harbour a hatred towards her mother which would fester into neurosis or addiction no matter what she did.

Judy began the next phase of her life in dire conflict; and the career she embarked on could not have exacerbated it more. When Judy signed with MGM she was told she was fat, ugly and that only by a great deal of hard work would she become acceptable in Hollywood's terms. Neither Ethel nor Judy, nor anyone else at the time, would have thought to question the relative standards of acceptability between Hollywood and real life; and indeed for most there was no difference. Judy was made to diet, to take 'slimming pills', encouraged to smoke and drink coffee without milk, all to get her weight down. She was thirteen years old.

Judy might have expected someone, at the very least her own mother, to be concerned about such treatment; but such was Louis B. Mayer's hegemony, and so significant was the achievement of securing the MGM deal, that it is doubtful whether Mrs Gumm could have exercised judgement independent of either her ambition for Judy, her fear of the alternative, or her awe of Mayer himself. The head of MGM was in effect the head of Hollywood. That meant, in turn, being one of the most influential men in America as well as, for some years, the highest paid. Louis B. had little time for Art or smut; he demanded high profits and even higher morality. In a canteen revamped to hold the 'family' together (and to cut down on afternoon absenteeism) most of the kids were fed chicken soup made to his special recipe: nourishing but not fattening. In Judy's case it was often the only *real* food she was allowed. Mayer's character was that of the late-Victorian despotic patriarch, standing aloof from the licentious goings-on of the early film community; he kept his own two daughters in a state resembling unveiled purdah. His disdain for loose women was as energetic as his championing of 'good' wives and mothers. He would punch a man for insulting a woman, yet he could also reduce the young Elizabeth Taylor's mother to tears with a tirade in which the mildest epithet was 'whore'. His temper was violent and his command of abuse total. If he ever appeared to be losing an argument he would collapse and his victim would not hear the end of the reproach. Few employees, including the biggest stars, escaped. Thus, when Mayer said that Judy was too fat, Ethel saw to it that she lost weight, and by the prescribed methods.

The denial of pleasure was not only confined to the intestinal tract. Although instigated in 1935 when ex-child star Jackie Coogan turned twenty-one and found himself broke and dependent on his wife Betty Grable, the Coogan Act did not become law as the Child Actors' Bill until May 1940. This bill allowed the courts to set aside fifty per cent of a child performer's earnings in a trust fund for future security. In the meantime, Judy's financial and contractual affairs were handled by her mother (sometimes with the aid of experts recommended by the studio) until she was eighteen. And it was only at nineteen that Judy was finally allowed a serious relationship, in the form of marriage. Until then her passions were ruthlessly vetted, and she was only permitted dates that were good for publicity. The binding of her breasts at the age of sixteen for her role as Dorothy in *The Wizard of Oz* is an appropriate symbol for young Judy's state of constant restraint at MGM.

In 1938 MGM teamed her for the first time with Mickey Rooney, who had fulfilled *his* mother's every expectation and was climbing the ladder to America's box office number one by 1940. With *Thoroughbreds Don't Cry* Judy and Mickey began a partnership which made them as famous a pair as Rogers and Astaire and, in the Andy Hardy movies, epitomised everything Louis B. Mayer wished for America. They sparkled with the clean-cut, fresh-faced, innocent enthusiasm that was supposed to represent the most wholesome and desirable aspects of young white America. To do so meant delaying their adulthood as long as possible. At all times Mickey was to be seen to be living up to the shining example of the boy Andy Hardy; for Judy, the lucrative little girl image was prolonged by a fatal denial of personal independence and growth both on and off screen. To the public it seemed that the kids were just having fun. Happily for the pair they became close friends. They filmed together, larked together, were seen together, made personal appearances together, were famous

Mickey and Judy speeding to success in Babes in Arms *and (below) with Louis B. at a look-but-don't-eat birthday party*

and successful together. And their studio schedules handed out equally tough treatment. One poster advertised their teamwork at a *Wizard of Oz* premiere as an 'unforgettable entertainment (5 shows daily)', and this kind of publicity work could go on for as many days in a row in as many cities as the movie opened. Judy and Mickey danced, sang and got their show on the road with a sustained energy which in retrospect could only have come from speed.

A great deal has been said about the studio's involvement and complicity in the use of drugs, but a lot of that debate misses the point. To deplore the practice and condemn the society and its popular culture machinery for allowing it to go on, it is not necessary to insist that the studio moguls were acting with conscious ill-will. Uppers and downers were regarded then as wonder compounds; they kept the kids (and adults) high for performance and put them to sleep quickly after a gruelling day's work. If shooting ran late, Mickey and Judy might sleep in the studio hospital instead of going home, blissed out with a hefty dose of Seconal and instantly to hand for the next morning's pre-dawn start. Even during a short break in shooting a tired kid might be knocked out with one pill and revived (with increasing difficulty) with another. There was no thought of addiction and no questions were asked in the early years. Blame must be attached, however, to the studio's conscious act of refusal to intervene when it became clear that the drugs were causing real damage. By the time Judy went tripping along the Yellow Brick Road, it was obvious to some that she was in trouble. Margaret Hamilton, the Wicked Witch of the West, and musical director Roger Edens both tried to intercede on Judy's behalf. Producer Arthur Freed said that his hands were tied, and the protest went no further. From then, Judy was never free from addiction.

But if Judy and Mickey suffered similar exploitation at the hands of MGM and its head, why was she so very bitter about it, while Mickey could afford to be so magnanimous? Although he found himself in a number of physical, psychological and financial dilemmas not dissimilar to Judy's, including a mid-life crisis of career and identity, he finally emerged as a durable star and survivor. His astonishing Broadway comeback at the age of sixty occurred when Judy had already been dead ten years. The answer lies somewhere in the fact that just beneath the glittering surface they were fundamentally apart, on separate courses governed by their gender and the times.

For a start, it simply was different for boys in those days. While in recent years the casting couch has become a threat to the career prospects of young men as it always has for young women, in those days it was hardly so. At no time was Mickey ever in the position of every young woman on the studio lot: faced with possible termination or stagnation of her career unless she complied with the sexual demands of the studio potentates, should those all-powerful figures deign to notice her. Mickey was actually a likely beneficiary of such predatory behaviour. Then again, wearing his 'show must go on' blinkers, he was able to respect Mayer because no matter what Mayer did it was for the good of *the* business, and in the end that was what really mattered.

Secondly, by the time they started working together, Judy's ego had already been under prolonged assault while Mickey's was being bolstered to an unprecedented degree. As little kids in vaudeville, both Mickey and Judy enjoyed performing. And from the moment Mickey Rooney arrived in Hollywood as the six-year-old tyke, then as a thirteen-year-old on the road to success (when he first met Judy at Ma Lawlor's School for Professional Children), and later in the character of Andy Hardy, Mickey was encouraged to maintain that joy. Louis B. Mayer fostered in Mickey the image of independent boyhood. He made some mistakes, sometimes he was unhappy, but he was in control of his life in a way that was forbidden to Judy. Andy Hardy was an active and acceptably aggressive youngblood, aided and abetted in his pursuit of girls, career, indeed anything he really wanted. It would be a betrayal of everything America stood for not to go after it with all he had, providing he remained within the bounds of God, Truth, and the Law, or at least wasn't caught out.

Judy, on the other hand, was playing roles which served only to reinforce the impression she was given of herself. Throughout the fourteen Andy Hardys, whilst Andy/Mickey was head over heels in love with a blonde bombshell, he failed to see the goodhearted, faithful but not-nearly-as-glamorous Judy-next-door. She would never win him by looks, always by personality or talent, and only in the last reel. Hollywood's values did not make that a winning ability. While Mickey was publicly saddled with Andy Hardy purity, he actually led a life of unbridled adolescent sex, backed up by all the cash and flash a boy could possibly need to date the long line of studio starlets, like Lana Turner and Ava Gardner, who rarely turned down an invitation from the country's number one box office star.

Thus, despite the habitual pairing of Judy with Mickey as the movie audience's archetypal youngsters with all the world similarly before them, reality was rooted in what must have been for Judy an unbearably bitter difference in their lifestyles. Mickey described himself at the time:

> I had done plenty. I had to do more. If I proved myself in twelve different ways, I'd have to prove myself in a thirteenth. I must have inherited in some gene a drive that pushed me harder and harder. The more successful I was, the more successful I had to become. I'd acted, sung, danced, drunk, gambled. I'd met President Roosevelt and Henry Ford. My face was postered all over America. What was there left for me to do? Try marriage, that was where this drive pushed me next.

(*I.E. An Autobiography*, Mickey Rooney)

In terms of objective experience, Mickey Rooney is the closest possible male parallel to Judy Garland and, as such, to the line of 'torn' women stars. Yet a confession like the above could have just as easily have come from Elvis Presley. Like Presley, Rooney was a small boy playing with big toys; Gluttony was their birthright. They gluttonised food, drugs, money, friendship, lovers, possessions. It was something that few of the women, except Piaf and Dinah Washington, were inclined or permitted to share. Writing in the early sixties, Mickey Rooney was still able to attribute his confidence and self-assertion to inheritance rather than to something that was being perpetually encouraged in him.

Similarly, others were able to ignore Judy's environment and attribute her problems entirely to her own inherent lack of fortitude. MGM producer Dore Schary for instance:

> It is ridiculous to believe that the studio ruined her – it didn't ruin other young stars such as Elizabeth Taylor, June Allyson, Jane Powell, Debbie Reynolds, Ava Gardner. L.B. adored Garland and it is nonsensical to think that he would have recommended drugs or forced her to work. Heavens and hells on earth are personal accomplishments or punishments. The tides in Judy's life were not calm ones but others have swum even rougher ones – Judy was not a strong swimmer and she couldn't make it to the shore.

> (*Heydays*, Dore Schary)

Unlike Judy, however, none of those young stars were obliged to carry the lead weights of her particular servitude, of having Mayer call her 'my little hunchback'. And none of them ever delivered the goods in such a compelling way.

Judy became reliant on uppers and downers ostensibly because her work was too strenuous. Anxiety had begun to produce insomnia as well, and so the pills were already having a secondary effect – it was harder to get to sleep, and harder to wake up again. But in her particularly insecure state, even if her work schedule had been eased – and it never was – it can be assumed that the pills also provided an out from any number of deep-seated problems. What was required was a programme of therapy that might expose those conflicts to her, and someone strong enough both to see her through withdrawal from the drugs and to defend her wellbeing against the men who contractually owned her. Throughout her life there were brief periods when that caring strength became available, and there were temporary periods of respite from the drug regime. But the causes of Judy's disturbance remained, and as soon as the assistance in the weaning process lacked faith and strength, the addiction took hold just as quickly again.

Meanwhile money became an added anxiety. By 1941 the nineteen-year-old 'child' star was only too aware that her voice was responsible for living up to her mother's expectation, and for the upkeep of a household commensurate with Ethel's perception of their status. Judy was also meal-ticket for a live-in family then consisting of grandmother Eva, a divorced sister and her child, and Ethel and Bill Gilmore (whom Ethel had married in 1939 on the anniversary of Frank Gumm's death). But it was Ethel and Bill who 'managed' her income and MGM who sought always to maximise profits from their increasingly popular star. As Judy's life off-camera grew more complex, her on-camera status became clearer than ever. Although she never made it to box office number one (reflected in her 1940 salary of $2,000 a week versus Mickey's $5,000), she and Bette Davis were the only women in the Top Ten for a decade. But if so many people adored her, why did she feel so tired and unhappy? Her principal quest in the years immediately following the Yellow Brick Road was for someone who would be at her side and on her side, someone who might stand up to Ethel and MGM on her behalf.

Her first choice was David Rose, a good Jewish boy, and a composer much in favour at the studio. Judy very soon found out that he was more interested in his giant train set than in his wife. He also tended to stay up all night writing. Judy's filming schedules were hardly compatible; and as she tried to keep his hours, but still stick to the studio grind, she found herself even more dependent on pills. Judy's battle with Ethel and the studio in winning approval for this marriage had been a hard one. Everyone interested in Judy's colossal earning power believed that her saleable image would be destroyed once she married. But eventually grudging approval was given. Not so for her first pregnancy. White veils and weddings were one thing, but sex and childbirth were beyond reasonable limits. Judy was twenty when she had her first abortion. It brought home to her her fundamental powerlessness: ruled at the studio by Mayer, ruled even in her marital home by Mayer's minion Ethel, she still had no control over career, earnings, or even her body.

The marriage with David Rose lasted about eight months, and they were divorced after eighteen. By 1943 her finances, centring around investments made by Ethel and Gilmore, were a hopeless mess. The process of dieting and its exacerbation of her chronic insomnia were dangerously out of control. When she tried to abstain from the pills, she suffered anxiety crises; these were treated with painkilling shots. Now Judy sought help. Through the assistance of producer Joe Mankiewicz (whom Mayer duly suspended then sacked for his interference) she secretly began therapy with Dr Ernst Simmel. She was not yet twenty-one.

The next focus of Judy's quest for someone to watch over her was Tyrone Power. He was a devastatingly handsome matinee idol, and was also married. His overwhelming desire to give and receive love made him irresistible to both men and women; like his father he resisted neither throughout his life. Judy fell in love, and if Power's own letters are to be believed, so did he. Their relationship has since been played down by

*Mr and Mrs
Vincente Minnelli
on their wedding
day*

biographers, but it would seem that it was of great importance to both and lasted almost a year. But Tyrone's unwillingness to hurt anyone often translated into weakness and indecision in adversity. When Judy became pregnant he swore he wanted the child, but when his wife Annabella refused an easy divorce, Judy was eventually persuaded to Mexico for her second abortion. The legend goes that she never quite 'got over' her romantic hero.

Her next try was a hero of a different kind. The popular concept of Vincente Minnelli's role in Judy's life is expressed in all its glorious chauvinism by Gerold Frank, who calls him 'the man with whom she would have her first child and who would play an important role in helping make a woman of Judy'. By this Frank meant that not only did Minnelli allow and encourage her to play more mature roles at MGM but, by giving her the benefit of his tastes in art, porcelain and architecture, that she also somehow began to glean the rudiments of homemaking, and to lust after motherhood. Minnelli was the first to challenge her drug taking. On a romantic trip to his home town, New York, Judy threw her pills into the river. He was deeply touched: Judy was pill-free and very soon pregnant. In most accounts Minnelli is painted as a rather self-absorbed intellectual and professional, but nevertheless a good catch; and it's true that he did go to great lengths to help Judy out of the deadly cycles of all too easily available 'medication'. But Jan Bauer, in her study of women and alcoholism, points out that in very few cases do husbands stick with their alcoholic wives the way wives stay with their alcoholic husbands; and there are many reasons to suggest – indeed Minnelli suggests it himself in his autobiography – that he simply could not go the whole way with her. It was too hard, he was not strong enough.

The reaction to this noble but unsuccessful attempt to help her has been to point to *her* terrors and weaknesses, to say that *she* simply had more problems than any man could be expected to deal with. So many critics have drawn attention to Judy's identification with the character of Norman Maine in *A Star Is Born* yet have failed to realise that for Judy, unlike Maine, there was never a spouse prepared to do anything, including give up his own career, to save her. Vincente did indeed do more than most, was more patient and enduring than most. But it was unthinkable that he should give up his career at MGM to take full-time care of Judy when she needed it, as Esther Blodgett would do for Norman Maine. The fact is that there was never anyone who would see Judy right the way through, and Minnelli came closest, perhaps because it was still early enough for a real cure to be possible.

In March 1946, Judy's first child was born. Liza was loved and needed, but she brought a new strain to Judy's already overloaded schedule. The combined pressures of movie-making and motherhood, and marriage to a man who was very busy himself, added to the mountain of insecurity she still laboured under. Judy went back on the pills – Benzedrine to put her to sleep, amphetamines to wake her up and keep her 'up' all day. In November of that year, MGM replaced her contract yet again with a more lucrative one. The money was welcome, but increased her sense of responsibility to the studio. Although Ethel had by this time divorced Bill Gilmore, together they had so mismanaged Judy's earnings that she had less than nothing to show for her first decade at MGM. Now, just as she began to break free from Ethel through marriage and a child, her servitude was transferred to the studio.

One of the constant threats was the suspension system. Persistent failure to comply with the shooting schedules brought suspension, during which there was neither payment nor the freedom to work anywhere else. When the pills got the better of her and she could either not wake up or the depression they produced kept her from work, Judy was suspended. After directing her in *The Pirate*, Vincente persuaded Judy into a California sanatorium. From there she went into a sanatorium on the east coast, and for the second time became pill-free. But still she could not reconcile her role as America's number one female box office draw with that of wife to busy Vincente and mother to beautiful baby Liza. No one was able to suggest that her ideal was unrealistic, or that she could still be a good wife and mother even if she didn't conform to the role norm.

Despite MGM's agreement that she should not report back to the studio until doctors agreed that she was ready, the pressure on Judy to resume work and salary was enormous. Each day off the set meant approximately $1,000 in lost earnings, and even with Vincente's steady income their Hollywood lifestyle and lack of proper financial management meant gigantic bills. It was also a time when her identity as a 'proper' wife, mother and woman was in turmoil: to be kept from the one thing she knew she did supremely well was a further burden, and she could not be persuaded to take more than the minimum rest. Soon, feeling good again, her relationship with both Vincente and Liza better than ever Judy returned to MGM and got through *Easter Parade* with Fred Astaire in forty days and with few hitches. The success of the team encouraged the studio to press on immediately with another vehicle for them, *The Berkeleys of Broadway*. But good health meant that she had also begun to resume her normal weight, and that was bad for the cameras. She went back on amphetamines to diet, and almost at once her intake was out of control. She failed to turn up for the shoot and on 12 July 1948 she was suspended again.

Vincente, still working for MGM, now began to buckle under the strain. When life became unbearable together, Judy now had another house to go to, and although it's hard to tell at whose instigation this arrangement had been made, the net result was ever-soaring bills and alienation for Judy. For the next two years, 1948–49, there were only brief respites from an almost permanent sense of crisis. Judy was offered large lump sums for two brief appearances in *Words and Music*. With the help and loving attention of her then manager Carleton Alsop and his (fifth) wife Sylvia Sidney, she got through *The Good Old Summertime*, although it was yet another juvenile role for this twice-married mother.

Now MGM bought *Annie Get Your Gun* as a vehicle for her. Judy was ill, insomniac, pill-dependent, estranged from her husband, and believed that she was not taking proper care of her young daughter. She and director Busby Berkeley did not get on, and with the $3 million production riding on her head, her skin started to break out, her hair to fall out, and then she was plagued by migraine headaches. She had developed an enormous tolerance to barbiturates and amphetamines, and attempted withdrawal resulted in physical agony. Dr Pobirs, her supervising physician, brought in a specialist who, according to Gerold Frank, gave her a series of six shock treatments to quieten her down to a point at which a minimal amount of medication would 'keep her calm enough to function'. Given what is now known about shock treatment, it's a wonder that Judy ever functioned again in any capacity. It was the spring of 1949; she was twenty-six.

She returned to the set in late March, presumably 'calmed down', but unable to work properly. On 10 May 1949 Judy was suspended again.

Two weeks later she entered hospital. Her liver, heart and blood were in reasonable condition, but she was suffering from acute fatigue and malnutrition, weighing only ninety pounds. According to Gerold Frank her own assessment of her condition, as confided to a Dr Rose, went like this:

> She was in a low mood. She could not sleep; she could not work; she felt she wanted to die; she could not control her temper and would fly into tantrums at what she realised was the slightest provocation, so that the most minute episode, word, concern, development, was inflated to catastrophic proportions. She was abysmally discouraged; her years of analysis had not helped her, she said; she had no respect for psychiatrists, she had seen more than a dozen of them, and they all failed her.

(*Judy*, Gerold Frank)

After some weeks under Rose's care, Judy was pill-free again. Rose had misgivings, but she was discharged and reunited with Minnelli. Indeed, she had made such a brilliant recovery that MGM asked her to do *Summer Stock*. That she had been fired from *Annie Get Your Gun* was already history and besides, they had merely borrowed Betty Hutton from Paramount and made it anyway. Judy was overweight but wanted to work, and went ahead without consulting Rose. Even though he was present on the set, she acquired pills by subterfuge. Once again close relationships became strained, and in the always volatile case of Judy and her mother, broke down completely. After a terrible fight, Ethel was banished from Judy's house and forbidden access to her granddaughter Liza. Like Frances Farmer's mother, Ethel didn't really understand what she'd done wrong. Never aware of the magnitude of Judy's bitterness, Ethel was hurt by what she saw as her daughter's callous ingratitude. She took herself off to Dallas and another daughter, Jimmy. With typical resolution Ethel started working her way into the community and a job as manager of a movie theatre.

By the end of *Summer Stock* Judy was heavily back into the pills and losing weight. When she was recalled to shoot the 'Get Happy' finale sequence she looked like a different person. As Hollywood's interest was in appearance rather than good health, Judy was congratulated on her stunning weight loss. Riding high, in more ways than one, she went straight into *Royal Wedding*. She was now taking paraldehyde, prescribed 'for people who had taken so much liquor or amphetamines that they needed an especially powerful sedative', as Gerold Frank noted. Judy couldn't make it to the set for the first day's shoot and was suspended by telegram. In response she cut her throat, not seriously enough to require stitches, but enough for Vincente to get hysterical and have her removed to her Sunset Boulevard residence. Ethel rushed back from Dallas; Judy refused to see her. The papers had a field day.

In fifteen years Judy had made a total of twenty-eight movies for MGM. Not one had lost money, not even those which had gone over budget because of her absenteeism; in fact they had grossed millions of dollars. MGM had often made shows of sympathy and goodwill, but only when the situation became truly impossible had they ever conceded time off, and then only with an eye to how quickly she could be returned to work. Judy was a commodity and had been treated as such. Having exacerbated her problems over so many years by adding to the pressures already on her, they now gave up. The stories of Judy's final break with MGM vary. Some say she was unceremoniously fired; others that she wanted out, and the studio gladly assented. They had paid her $40,000 hospital bill and now waived the balance of a $9,000 personal loan which she had taken out at that time. Whatever the truth of Judy's departure, it could still be summed up by one observation that Mayer's racehorses

On stage and screen Judy often assumed the guise of the old vaudevillian. 'Miss Showbiz' liked to think she had been 'born in a trunk'

received better treatment than Judy did.

On 28 September 1950 her contract, still with two years to go, was abrogated. The second phase of her life had ended in chaos, and at twenty-eight Judy Garland was a has-been. She went to New York to ride out the newspaper storm and to consider what to do with the rest of her life. She had a stack of private debts and owed $60,000 in back taxes from 1948–49, for which she was already paying monthly instalments. Her only income was her monthly MGM staff pension cheque of $171. It was at this time that Judy was introduced to the two elements that would change life as she had known it – one was the offer of a season at the London Palladium for her adoring British fans; the other was Sid Luft.

Luft was tough and charming, a successful racetrack punter and physically not unlike Frank Gumm. He was different from the other men Judy had known in that he seemed to have everything under control. During this early stage of the romance, and without the pressure of a work schedule, Judy remained *relatively* pill-free. Her return to the concert stage cannot be underestimated. She had performed only rarely before a live audience in the fifteen MGM years, and her return to the medium required a great deal of hard work and even more courage. Once there, Judy was a natural. Her Palladium season was an enormous success, and on returning to the States Sid had the idea of Judy's re-opening the Palace Theatre, New York, in a revival of the two-a-day vaudeville it had once been so famous for.

At the Palace Judy's repertoire would include songs which had become associated with her through her movies: songs like 'Over The Rainbow', 'The Trolley Song', 'The Atchison, Topeka and the Santa Fe'. The live performance albums, both from the Palace and later from Carnegie Hall, show that these songs were just as popular as any of the ballads or 'blues', like 'The Man That Got Away', that audiences later identified with Judy's much-publicised string of heartaches, affairs and divorces. She also had from MGM and her work with Roger Edens experience of the effectiveness of tailor-made preambles. When the studio had requested an entertainment for Clark Gable's birthday on 1 February 1937, Edens drew on a monologue by Carmel Myers to write a preamble for 'You Made Me Love You'. The spoken piece in which a star-struck fan bumps into Gable at a premiere and is won over by his 'niceness' and 'ordinariness' brought Gable to tears – and the young Judy to 'overnight' success. The item was included in *Broadway Melody of 1938*, Judy's first major appearance for MGM.

Now Edens repeated the process for her and constructed a medley for the Palace debut. He had taken her under his wing at MGM, and in him she had someone whom she trusted to give expression to her more assertive side. Show business was a passion they shared, and in that context he wrote well for her. He blended the signature songs of some of the Palace greats (Sophie Tucker's 'Some of These Days', Fanny Brice's 'My

Man', Eva Tanguay's blustering 'I Don't Care') in a series of exciting musical segues, but framed the medley with a prologue and an epilogue which allowed Judy to express her admiration for the idols of the tradition she had been raised in, and the one which she proceeded to return to in complete, record-breaking triumph. That run of nineteen weeks at the Palace established her for all time as one of the great performers of the century. In the ad libs, asides and everyday mayhem she injected into the precisely orchestrated show, she also won herself a following and reputation that stayed with her beyond the grave. 'Miss Show Business' was no Hollywood has-been and her particular line of dry humour was even drawn into the performance by Edens, as in the opening, half-spoken, half sung introduction:

> It's lovely seeing you . . .
> But the first thing I must do . . .
> Is give an interview to the press.
> To tell of them of the struggling,
> Of the long and ceaseless juggling
> Every time I . . . get into this dress!
> Call the Mirror! Call the News!
> You can see I've still got 90 lbs to lose . . .

It was a self-deprecation that could work wonderfully when it genuinely came from her. When she made *I Could Go On Singing* in 1962, the movie required her to play a middle-aged singer plagued by emotional problems, alcohol and a foul temper. It was a brave act of self-exposure – like Marilyn Monroe's in *The Misfits*, Billie's with 'Strange Fruit', Marie Lloyd's rueful 'I'm a Bit of a Ruin' and Piaf's tragic 'Les Blouses Blanches'. None was delivered at a safe distance, and none set out to win popular success by conforming to a female stereotype. Such performances were admissions of complexity, of ageing, of conflict; and in Judy's case also reflected a wry brand of humour that most of these women shared. As the singer in *I Could Go On Singing*, drunk and very late for her concert, walks through the audience with a fur coat slung over her shoulder, a man calls out 'Where'd ya get the coat?' 'I shot it' she cracks back, and all is forgiven. The script could have been taken from life, on many occasions.

Meanwhile, as Judy laid the foundations of this extraordinary concert career, things were not always as happy as the song and gags suggested. In November 1951, she fell from the Palace stage: the diagnosis was nervous exhaustion. In fact she was suffering from a course of 'thyroid pills' prescribed as a weight reducer by one Dr Salmon who at that time had dozens of New York socialites on various pill habits. Sid persuaded Judy to drop the doctor and the pills. She did and became pregnant again.

Following the Palace engagement, Judy gave concerts in Los Angeles,

receiving a rapturous welcome home from a Hollywood that had previously spurned her. Sid's management was helping to clear the debts, and Judy's concert comeback was an undeniable success, but still the spectres of her early life were there to haunt her. She remained estranged from her mother, and when Ethel turned up at the theatre she was civilly greeted by Luft but Judy refused to see her. In May 1952, the *Mirror* broke the story of wealthy daughter's cruel neglect of poor mother, and pointed out that while Judy earned $25,000 for her week's work in Los Angeles, Ethel was holding down a $61 a week clerk's job in Santa Monica. In November, Judy's second child, Lorna, was born. Judy

117

refused to let Ethel see the baby. Almost immediately, Sid and Judy began work on *A Star is Born* – it was their idea, their production company, their *other* baby. And the responsibilities were enormous. Despite Sid's warnings, Judy began to procure pills from the movie's production assistant, who thought he was doing her a favour. She was soon back on Seconal and Dexedrine. On 5 January 1953, Ethel was found dead of heart failure in her company car park. If the newspapers had revelled in Judy's exit from MGM two years before, this was an outright carnival. For Judy, shocked and stricken with guilt, it was the end of any hopes for a resolution of the conflicts she felt about her own life and her *raison d'être* in show business.

During the making of *A Star is Born* the newspapers kept up their taunts. Most were inclined to blame Judy for delays on the production. Sid managed to keep her at her floor medication – six grains of Seconal for sleep and Dexamyl to revive; even more admirable was his support immediately after the shoot was completed. They hired a cabin in the country and, with Sid's unflinching help, Judy cold turkeyed. This, and the triumph, against popular expectation, of their co-production on the movie, served to cement their relationship.

In 1954 Judy was nominated for an Oscar as Best Actress for her role in *A Star is Born*, and forty-eight hours before the awards ceremony she gave birth, with some problems, to her third child, Joey. She was odds-on favourite for the award. Drug-free, happy with Luft, she could be pleased with her new career as concert performer, and now she was ready to be rewarded and recognised by the motion picture industry for her unique contribution both as a child star and as a woman who had returned to co-produce and star in what is now considered a cinema classic.

With a TV crew at her bedside to record the moment of triumph, Judy and Sid heard that Grace Kelly had won for her performance in *A Country Girl*. The TV crew packed up and left without a word of condolence. Winning the Oscar might have sustained Judy's period of buoyancy, even if it might not have solved all the problems. Denied her profession's highest honour, she swiftly declined into a state of physical and financial horror. *A Star is Born* had been hacked to a 'commercial' length in the edit, and it was not grossing as well as expected, despite rave reviews for Judy. The deal with Warner Brothers looked shaky, and Sid's management was starting to come apart at the seams. Although Judy's tempestuous relationship with him was possibly the most successful she had with any man, and his punter-gambler personality kept her fascinated, he was not, in the end, the answer she sought. The closet pill-taker became a closet drinker.

These habits took their well-remembered effect on her concert performance. Still she opted to return to the scenes of her greatest and most recent triumphs – the Palladium and the Palace. Both dates were gravely uneconomical, and Sid knew it. Still he wasn't able, either as husband or manager, to say 'no'; her need was too great. At the same time they were living well beyond their means, and when they left for London it was only because Sid, having signed bad cheques to the tune of $15,000, had that very day collected an unexpected $30,000 insurance on a horse that had broken its leg. Once again, and as ever, the family fortunes rested on Judy Garland's vocal chords. When they returned to the US they were hundreds of thousands of dollars in debt. Judy was very fat, and seemed

With Sid Luft (l)
and Milton Berle

to be swelling up. She continued to perform. Sometimes it was great, sometimes it was terrible, sometimes she couldn't make it at all. At the end of 1959 she was admitted to hospital in a toxic state and not expected to live. Doctors said that even if she survived the crisis she would be permanently out of action. She had cirrhosis of the liver, which was enlarged to four times its normal size.

But she did survive. When she came out of hospital on 5 January 1960, she had lost thirty pounds and was told, apparently to her great relief, that she would never work again. Judy spent the next five months recuperating. At the end of this period she begged Sid to let her go to London again. Again he could not refuse, and he borrowed heavily for her further rehabilitation. At this stage she was free of most of her drugs except Ritalin. According to her doctors her addiction was by now incurable (she was thirty-eight) and they reckoned on the current Ritalin

119

dosage as the minimum she would need for the rest of her life.

Europe was as good for her as ever, and she was soon champing at the bit to get back on stage. She performed in London and Paris; and in Germany she turned out for John F. Kennedy's campaign and to sing for US servicemen. As Judy began to sing herself back to some kind of confidence and optimism, Sid started to initiate a few business plans of his own. These included handing Judy's management over to the exciting new team of Creative Management Services. Sid was genuinely pleased to think that Judy would be one of twelve on a very exclusive book that included Henry Fonda, Rock Hudson, Gregory Peck, Marilyn Monroe and Richard Burton. The management was Freddie Fields and David Begelman. Begelman's story can now be read in the book *Indecent Exposure*; but at the time Hollywood was taken in by his remarkable perfidy. His career was one of almost schizoid fraudulent behaviour, and he managed to outwit, among legions, Cliff Robertson, Martin Ritt and the entire Columbia organisation in a master plan of embezzlement. Almost as soon as he handed over Judy's business, Sid began to clash with Creative Management as he felt they were trying to squeeze him out altogether. He soon initiated a lawsuit against them, and it was still simmering at the time of Judy's death. Nearly ten years after the events in question, Sid Luft began stirring the pot again, contributing to an investigation which eventually came to the boil in the late seventies. In the end, the revelation that Begelman had embezzled some $300,000 of Judy's money turned out to be a relatively small potato in his extraordinary history of cooking the books.

For Judy it was disastrous, coinciding with and contributing to a number of factors that turned the last phase of her life into a nightmare. Creative Management had her working a very heavy schedule. By April 1961 she was on ten Ritalin a day instead of the recommended three; and there were bad nights both on stage and off. Even so, Judy invariably pulled out all the stops. On 23 April 1961 she played before a packed-to-overflowing Carnegie Hall. By now Judy's rapport with the audience was central to the show. They laughed and broke into songs with applause and cheering: they interjected, and she responded until they were hanging on every word and note. The live double album won two Grammy awards; and with Mort Lindsay's superb big band-orchestra sound, it is still perhaps the most direct way into the essence of Garland's performance style. With chuckles interpolated throughout her monologues, introductions and the 'verses' of which she was so fond (written *colle voce* introductions often dropped by other singers), she represented to her audience everything good about American entertainment: a unique combination of great notes, wonderful timing, the desire to share a laugh, and enough energy to go on all night.

Following the Palace, Carnegie Hall was the second great triumph of her concert career. But the pill problem was by now totally out of control.

The Lufts with
Liza and Lorna

As had been the case for the past thirty years, no one was attempting to do any more than string one day or week into the next. They, and she, had long since given up on any long-term solution. Again Judy seemed on the road to certain disaster; and even then she achieved more than just the remarkable feat of keeping her head above water. Her last seven years included two more great movie appearances (*I Could Go On Singing* and *Judgment at Nuremburg*), a multitude of concerts and, in 1963, her own prime-time networked TV show for CBS. The stated plan was for thirteen shows, to be put together by some of CBS's top names, featuring a glittering guest star each week and with Judy in the role of all-singing, dancing, conquering host. She approached the series with high hopes but from the very beginning there were signs that might have indicated that someone had miscalculated the best way to use Judy's unique abilities. She was initially introduced to CBS executives at a cocktail party. She sang the standard 'Call Me Irresponsible' and the executives who were about to gamble millions of dollars on a woman with a notorious reputation for unreliability did not find it nearly as funny as her assigned team of writers. A couple of gems they had dreamed up for a jokey dialogue sequence required Judy to react with amusement to: 'Say, aren't you Judy

Garland? What's a nice old lady like you doing on television?' And 'Are you the real Judy Garland? I thought she died years ago!' Judy was forty-one. Before the last of the series had been screened it had become obvious that the shows were not the smash hits required by ratings-hungry executives. 'The Judy Garland Show' had been scheduled to compete with NBC's 'Bonanza'. Not even her best in the series could put a dent in the popular western's ratings, and just before CBS announced that her show had been dropped, Judy announced that she would be taking a rest from television. The scandals continued.

The years between 1961–69 also included a $50,000 blackmail payment for photos of her naked, having her stomach pumped out in a London hospital; permanent indebtedness to the Inland Revenue Service, at one stage to the tune of $400,000; the suicide of her eldest sister Suzy; being booed from the stage in Melbourne and London (in both cases 'medicated' out of control); affairs with Glenn Ford and Tom Green, among others; marriage to actor Mark Herron, and to disco manager Mickey Deans; and estrangement from her eldest daughter.

The pattern of Ethel and Judy had virtually repeated itself in Judy's relationship with Liza. From the time she was four, Liza had been leading a split life between her gentle, over-indulgent father, and her erratic, compulsive but nevertheless passionate and very special mother. By the time she was thirteen Liza was taking responsibility for her mother, dealing with suicide attempts, tantrums, siblings and a predictable degree of professional criticism (Judy at first claimed that Lorna had all the talent). There was a period of banishment for Judy, just as there had been for Ethel. But there was one vast difference in that Liza was able, very early on, to acknowledge her love for her mother, achieve some degree of understanding of the 'monster' behaviour, and celebrate her indebtedness to Judy as a unique performer and mentor in Liza's chosen profession.

For Judy the crises were many and varied. At one stage a doctor managed a successful switch of her Seconal for the less harmful (under the circumstances) Valium by filling the Seconal capsules with the other drug, but the subterfuge did not last and Judy resumed the Seconal regime and added vodka to it again. The combination of liquor and barbiturate was synergistic; each reinforced the effects of the other to produce overdose. It was what the same doctor maintained had killed Marilyn Monroe in that year, 1962.

Immediately after the Melbourne concert debacle, when an emaciated and incoherent Judy was booed from the stage, Judy fled with husband Mark Herron to Hong Kong. She was recuperating well until a typhoon hit the island. Cooped up in a swaying high-rise hotel, Judy read a review of the concert in *Time* magazine. She overdosed, this time into a serious coma, and at one point stopped breathing. She weighed seventy pounds and should have died but didn't. With her life in chaos, her health in ruins, Judy continued to perform because she had nothing to live on. None of the men she attached herself to at this time could afford even to support her, let alone assist in overcoming her financial difficulties. Back in the US there were some dozen legal cases pending against her; they involved separate sums totalling hundreds of thousands of dollars. She still owed similar amounts to the IRS.

But in 1967 Sid Luft came to Judy with a proposition. He explained that he had formed a company called Group V which was designed specifically to stop a recurrence of bad management and continuing debts; it would benefit not only Judy but her three children as well. Group V was structured to administer Judy's career, give everyone enough to live on, and to set up a trust fund for future security. To Judy the arrangement sounded like an end to a nightmare, explained as it was by Sid as she was quite literally on her way to begin yet another tour. He presented her with the appropriate page of the contract and she signed it.

What Judy had so gratefully signed was a document that bound her not just to Sid, but to three of his acquaintances. One of them, Raymond Filliberti, already had a police record for fraud. Rather than being a contract for the benefit of his ex-wife and their children, it was a classic vehicle for the exploitation of the artist as commodity, pure and simple. Group V owned Garland as a performer and owned all her creative output from the time of her unwitting signature. Their ownership specified 'any and all the incidents, dialogue, characters, action, material, ideas and other literary, dramatic and musical material written, composed, submitted, added, improvised, interpolated and invented by Garland' as well as rights to 'sell, lease, stage or transmit any of it, by whatever means known or not yet invented'. The contract (like many then and now) forbade her to talk about any aspect of her business without their authorisation. In writing and in reality she had no more civil rights than Lassie – and public outcry would have saved him from most of the indignities which befell Judy. Much later she was given the fifteen pages that went with the one Sid had presented for signature. She then found that Group V did not even include herself or her children. She was, in essence, the consortium's chattel.

And yet the notion persisted that somehow these problems were all of Judy's making. The reflections of contemporaries are particularly telling – especially in the case of Doris Day who, before the activities of Group V came to light, made this comparison between herself and her husband, and Sid and Judy:

Sid Luft's relationship with Judy was about the same as Marty's and mine. Sid was Judy's manager and became involved in her pictures to the extent that Marty was involved in mine – but I never felt that Judy had as much confidence in Sid as I did in Marty. Perhaps that was attributable to Judy's nature. She was a terribly confused, unhappy woman who drank excessively and Sid's job was more to keep Judy out of harm's way, than to work on her career.

(*Doris Day: Her Own Story*, A.E. Hotchner)

Given that Doris had often expressed her admiration for Judy's no-bullshit attitude and its value in a place like Hollywood, she might have done better to take a few clues from Judy's suspicions of Sid; but she too was a product of the dream factory and she also believed that her man was watching over her. When Marty Melcher, Doris's second husband, died suddenly in 1968, she found that she was in a financial hole as vast as Judy's, and similar in kind. Since the forties Melcher had been working with high-flying investment lawyer Jerome Rosenthal. Not only were twenty years' earnings squandered by bad deals and poor investment, but Doris was already contracted for work, such as *The Doris Day Show* for television, for which she would never receive a penny. Rosenthal scored other victims, among them Kirk Douglas and Dorothy Dandridge, who committed suicide soon after her financial ruin had been revealed to her. In scale, Doris Day's case was a giant. Terry, her son by her first marriage, went in to bat for her and she was finally awarded what was then (in the early 1970s) the highest ever damages compensation in the US courts – some $22 million, the amount which Rosenthal and Marty Melcher were reckoned to have disposed of in Doris's long career. As soon as she had fulfilled her contractual commitments, Doris Day retired 'torn' but at least alive to live in peaceful seclusion, away from twenty years' hard labour and disillusion.

Judy Garland had no such luck, no such child who could at that time make repair, even though it was to Liza that the job of posthumous debt-clearing eventually fell. In 1968 Judy discovered that in May of that year she had been 'sold', to clear Sid's debt, to Howard Harper and Leon J. Greenspan. Judy found out in the middle of a season at the New Jersey Arts Centre, and she refused to leave her hotel room until Sid signed a guarantee that *she*, not any management, would be paid for her performance. Guarantee of cash payment was scrawled by Sid on a sheet of hotel stationery. Judy went on, but collapsed on stage two nights later and wound up in hospital in a state of exhaustion. To the press and the disappointed public it was Judy on the pills or the booze or just plain irresponsible again. The fact was that she was just about crushed by the strain of giving her incandescent all each night, knowing that not only were her fees attached by the IRS but that in her efforts to bring that problem under control she had also brought about a situation where she was working for a group of men who were bent on paying neither her nor her back taxes. She didn't even have the satisfaction of being able to throw herself off a bridge: the Group V contract also included, at Clause

17, a stipulation that failure on her part to give the Corporation notice of her death within twenty-four hours of its commencement would mean that her estate was liable for any losses incurred by the Corporation as a result.

Judy was legally bound to silence over the fact that Harper and Greenspan had been 'sold, assigned, transferred and set over' the rights to both a coal mine and 'all rights, title and interest in Judy Garland' for the 'exclusive use of her services' for the sum of 'ONE ($1) DOLLAR'. When the specified ninety days of this assignment were up, and Luft and Filliberti were still unable to repay the actual $18,000 they owed, Harper and Greenspan filed a summons in a New York court. They 'wanted either their money or Judy Garland'. Not surprising then that when Judy stood on a stage and began to sing 'Smile – tho' your heart is breaking', she sounded as if she was bleeding inside; that when she reached for 'Somewhere over the rainbow . . .' the voice might crack and not quite make it. She was forty-six years old, her furniture and possessions were impounded by the Harper-Greenspan assignment and she and her children were living a precarious existence. She had no home, no cash and, in law, no right to either. She was contracted to perform, but knew that if she did no money would accrue to her. Whichever way she turned she was faced by demands. Even that of 'we love you Judy' from fans was merely a further pressure to deliver of herself. Her isolation and desperate loneliness made her easy prey; the comfort and boost offered by lovers resulted in the kind of brief liaison which would normally be quietly forgotten by both parties – unless one happened to be notoriously famous and the other could make money out of it.

Later in 1968 things began to look up when she became involved with a younger man she had known for some time: Mickey Deans was then manager of a fashionable New York disco. In the winter, in an attempt to earn cash to live on, Judy set up a season at London's Talk of the Town. Apart from it being her favourite working town, she also believed (or hoped) that the Harper-Greenspan contract would not apply outside the United States. When she flew into London, however, she was served with a writ to prevent her appearance at the venue. For the first time the Group V story began to emerge in public. On 30 December, in arbitration of the writ, Mr Justice Magarry said: 'This transaction is one to which I would not enjoin a dog . . . certainly I would not enjoin Miss Garland . . .' He dismissed the case, declared that 'this woman has a right to earn a living', and ordered Harper and Greenspan to pay the considerable court costs.

Judy did appear at the Talk of the Town but the tension and terrors had taken their toll, and she performed erratically. The engagement was not the success she had so hoped for. For his part, Mickey Deans did what he could, within his own limitations; he cared for her, but he didn't really know her nor understand what it meant to be around her. In her own eyes Judy had already lived two ordinary lifetimes, she was mortally weary, but still making plans to go on singing. Most of 1969 was spent in her beloved London. Mickey had plans for a chain of movie theatres in the United States in her name; there were brief returns there, and a couple of nostalgic appearances that had audiences horrified by her appearance but on their feet in admiration. In the end Judy died 'quietly' in London, of heart failure, in the middle of the night, sitting on the toilet in the bathroom of their mews cottage. She was forty-six years old and weighed less than five stone.

If a history of Judy Garland traced along the lines of those things which produced and maintained her addiction reads like a bizarre nightmare, then it is exactly because it *was* a bizarre nightmare. And this account is by no means the whole gory story. Away from the show business hype, it is a story of the most abject neglect of a distressed and exploited human being whom no one was finally willing to help. She was for that whole time one of the most adored public figures of the century. The inhumanity of such a story is almost unfathomable, and almost unthinkable outside a society which is both capitalist and patriarchal.

Although her physical voice, that which could be commercially exploited, was heard everywhere, no one heard the voice that often begged for help. Gerold Frank's biography of Judy is generally the most respected, and is a useful manual of blow-by-blow descriptions of events in her life. And yet in Mr Frank's italics there emerges the thread of an opinion that threatens every woman. Judy Garland said time and time again that she did not want to stay in show business; she repeatedly said that as soon as Ethel was set up she wanted to get out. Yet Mr Frank constantly tries to persuade that although this might have been what she said, it was not what she actually wanted. What she wanted, he claims, and what she always turned to, were the fame and the bright lights. But no one ever gave her an alternative, nor made one possible. And what Gerold Frank does by this repeated reference to Fate is restate the dictum that has for centuries governed attitudes to rape: no matter what the girl says, we all know what she really wanted. There was never a time in Judy's life when she was able to insist that No meant No. The failure to be heard drove her to addiction that was never treated at the root. For all the reasons that constitute discrimination against women, that addiction was not treated as heroic or romantic but as disgusting, degrading and, finally, weak, selfish and self-destructive.

In this way Judy is the archetype of the 'torn star'. Few listened to her, and it was in the interests of both employer and audience not to listen too carefully; for had she been taken seriously, millions of dollars would have been lost, and the western world would have lacked one of its idols. It was the same with Marilyn Monroe. There were few who were prepared to listen to what she thought she could really do with her life and her talent. Time and again Judy Garland described her own unhappiness, but no solution was ever forthcoming because no one was prepared to allow her to remove herself from the business that was killing her. To have done that might have meant just another 'ordinary woman' living out her life in obscurity. One argument suggests that without her misery, without her manic pursuit of career, there would not have been *those* performances, which is a sure sign of cultural bankruptcy. Garland was indeed an extraordinary performer, and she left a recorded legacy of her great talent. But, like most performers, she worked best when she was happy and healthy and free from anxiety; and it's most likely that she would have left that legacy without the horrors of her day-to-day existence. That she took it on with such courage is even further reason for regret.

To condemn Judy Garland as simply 'too weak' is to abdicate the battlefield of sexual politics to genetic determinism. To do that is to give up hope of a revolution in sexual politics and with it the belief that such a revolution can improve the quality of women's lives. The addiction of Judy Garland and the other women in *A Star is Torn* cannot be seen simply as private and personal failing. Somewhere along the line the effect of public indifference and society's greed has to be acknowledged.

**Round and round and round I go
Ridin' high and feelin' low
Round and round just like a top
I'm a-gettin' dizzy but I can't stop . . .**

'Honky Tonk Merry Go Round', Frank and Gardner

Patsy Cline died in 1963 at the age of thirty-one; in the most obvious sense she belongs in a collection of twentieth-century performers who died young. The other reasons for her inclusion have never been immediately clear: if Judy Garland was the archetype of the torn star, then grinning, yodelling, good-time Patsy, cut off in her healthy prime, bore no resemblance. But beneath the rhinestone glitter of Country and Western nostalgia, Patsy's story is as complex and as recognisable as any in this book.

Born on 8 September 1932 in Gore, a dot on the map fifty miles from Winchester, Virginia, on the eastern flank of Country's heartland, Virginia Patterson Hensley was her seventeen-year-old mother's first child. Precocious and wilful, Patsy took her matinee-movie worship of Shirley Temple home, where she tapped and twirled endlessly until her bemused mother Hilda finally bowed to pressure and entered her for a local talent quest. Patsy tap-danced her way to victory, self-taught at the age of four. Patsy's father, Sam Hensley, had a daughter by a previous marriage, and she, Tempie Glenn, was a pianist. Patsy begged to be allowed to visit her, or at least her piano, which she began to play at every opportunity. The Hensleys were not well off, and there was no question of lessons or an instrument – that had to be clearly understood. But by the time Patsy was seven, Hilda had somehow scraped together the money for both. The lessons didn't last long: Patsy's ear and ability were too quick and true for her teacher to enforce the discipline necessary to impart 'proper' musical training. It was a waste of time and money, she said; Patsy didn't need to read music, and she never did.

In reminiscing about her daughter, Mrs Hensley could never see her own contribution to Patsy's abilities. Finding the wherewithal for the precious piano was merely a matter of parental fact; moreover, she recalled, the Hensley household was not a musical one: the only singing Patsy had ever done was with the local Baptist church choir – duetting with her mother. Hilda's modest misreading of the facts illustrates the typical undervaluing by a mother of both her work and her cultural influence. The truth was that she was raising a daughter who was attuned and eager for music. By the time she was ten, Patsy was firmly hooked into Country music, glued to the radio to catch her favourite stars and, most important of all, the broadcast show on which she told everyone she too would sing – 'The Grand Ole Opry'. Even then Patsy's broad, bold personality gave her pronouncements such a ring of truth that no one seemed to doubt her.

In the early 1940s the family moved into Winchester to make it easier for Patsy and her younger brother and sister, Sam Jnr and Sylvia Mae, to attend school. Patsy in particular was making good progress at the local grammar. One morning, however, she set out on a typically forthright enterprise: she was fourteen and, in her view, ready to sing in public. Every Saturday, WINC in downtown Winchester broadcast a live Country show which Patsy followed avidly. She presented herself to its star DJ and bandleader, Joltin' Jim McCoy, with the request that she be allowed to sing with his band, that morning, on the radio broadcast.

Her song for McCoy led to a regular Saturday morning spot with his Melody Playboys and the opportunity to learn first hand from real Country musicians. In her spare time after school, Patsy did little else but practise and learn, a self-imposed discipline in which she was supported unfailingly by her mother until, one year later, Sam Hensley left his wife and their three children. Hilda was thirty-one, Patsy barely fifteen, and for most of her life her parents' marriage had been plagued by Sam's drinking and unreliability. Now they were penniless. Patsy dropped out of school and got a job as a clerk and soda-fountain attendant in a family drugstore run by a sympathetic couple whose understanding of their young employee's aspirations led to time off so that she could get to the singing jobs which had begun to come her way. Patsy's wages and the few dollars from these casual dates kept the family going. It wasn't easy for mother or daughter but in later years both recalled the time as the best ever. In one interview Patsy said:

> If I made a list of people I admire, Mom would probably fill up half of it. She could do anything and everything. And she'd do it for me. She was one person I could depend on. She never once let me down. I would never have got anywhere if it hadn't been for Mother's faith and support.

(*Patsy Cline*, Ellis Nassour)

Mrs Hensley felt the same about her daughter; like Lulu and Helen Morgan, like Sadie and Billie Holiday, the relationship was the happiest and most constant either was ever to experience.

One facet of Patsy's character displayed ebullience and deep personal conviction; the other showed a down-to-earth realism that appreciated how long and hard the way ahead would be. If she had any notion of overnight stardom it didn't reveal itself; Patsy's main aim in life was to sing, just that. Until her arrival as a major star, Country music was essentially a male preserve where the 'girl singers' were not much more than light relief and decoration both on and off stage. While family and church music might stand or fall by the strength of its women, epitomised by Mother Maybelle Carter, head of the famous Carter family singers, the only guiding light ahead of Patsy in the commercial field was Miss Kitty Wells, Queen of Country Music. And from the beginning it was clear that Patsy was not modelling herself on that gracious lady.

Patsy's voice was quickly recognised as a major force. She had a range and depth that soared easily beyond the tight bounds of the Country idiom in a way that was to become known as the 'crossover', the phenomenon that occurred when a singer bridged the gap between Country and Pop and made a hit in both areas. It was an achievement that Patsy herself neither considered nor aimed for. Her voice was powerful and true, the twang and yodel simply ornamentations that testified to her heartfelt musical roots. But she was perfectly serious when she said she wanted to sing Country and mulishly resisted what she suspected were attempts to draw her style closer to something more acceptable to a broader audience. Her single-minded attitudes cost her a lot all through her career, not least at the beginning when her rise would almost surely have been faster and less arduous if she had been prepared to jettison musical partners who, without Patsy's presence, were nothing but amiable no-hopers. It would also have happened quicker if she had taken advice and compromised over the material she sang and recorded.

In her personal life, which she lived (in company with the rest of the Country Music clan) fairly publicly, she inspired both adoration and opprobrium. There were fiercely loyal friends and fans, and equal numbers of raised eyebrows and pursed lips. If Patsy wanted something she generally took the shortest route. Whether it was a singing date, a friend, or a man, all were treated in the same forthright way: Patsy was a down-home country gal, and a strong bold woman.

The long haul to the top began on the morning she stepped up to the microphone at WINC in 1946, after which she was always working or chasing after work. Calculable public recognition eluded her for another nine years, and during that time she paid her dues in the hardest currency – on the road. For the majority of bands and singers on the circuit at that time, making a living from Country music was secondary to the spiritual need just to be in there doing it. When Patsy was still a teenager her mother drove her to dates, either staying for the show or returning later to pick her up. Hilda's place as chauffeur was eventually taken by a succession of faithful and protective boyfriends whose interest in Patsy was more or less what she allowed it to be – which could be a lot or very little, depending on how she felt at the time. What they all had to

131

learn, including her husbands, was that deep down, no matter how much she loved and wanted them, singing came first. That aspect of her dedication was to bring her any number of black eyes and heartaches, but it was always so, inexplicable though it may have been to those around her.

As she grew up it did not occur to Patsy to question a system that required her to travel almost constantly from venue to venue in order to sing her heart out then as rapidly as possible move on to the next stop. No one else questioned it; it was a fact, a part of the business. For some, particularly the young and unattached, it was one of the most exciting parts. There was a sense of freedom, of unreality and irresponsibility, and, for the men especially, there were multiple sexual opportunities with a built-in tradition of no-strings-attached. These concepts, both real and imaginary, were almost impossible for a young woman to grasp at that time without being stung in one way or another. For Patsy and her growing band of female friends and colleagues, one of the perennial topics of conversation when two or more got together in a dressing room or in the back of a beat-up Cadillac at one in the morning was how *hard* the business was for women. Given the mores and social requirements of their time and place, it was an irredeemable situation; if they wanted children and a relationship with a nice man (and none questioned the norm that they should want such things), then they would almost certainly have to curtail their careers. If they didn't, they stood to lose not only their 'reputation', but also their man to jealousy – 'you're on the road with him so he must be sleeping with you' – or to the tit-for-tat affairs which inevitably came to pass. There was very little sense of the faithful husband staying home to mind the kids whilst Momma brought home the bacon, then or now. Twenty years later, David Dalton of *Rolling Stone* magazine recorded just such a conversation between Janis Joplin and Bonnie Bramlett:

Janis: That's the good thing about women, man. Because they sing they fuckin' insides, man. Women to be in the music business give up more than you'd ever know. She's got kids she gave up, any woman gives up home life, an old man, probably, you give up a home and friends, you give up an old man and friends, you give up every constant in the world except music. That's the only thing in the world you got, man. So for a woman to sing, she really needs to or wants to. A man can do it as a gig, because he knows he can get laid tonight.

Bonnie: A lot of musicians are married and worship the footsteps their wives walk in, but they go on the road, and they ball, and they have a ball, but when they are home no-one is going to break their marriage up, there ain't nobody gonna hurt their children. But what man would have you and let you do what you must do?

Sincerely Yours
Patsy Cline
"Decca"
57.

Janis: That's the trouble, you either got to be as big a star as the chick or you got to be a flunky, and no woman, at least me, I don't want an ass-kisser, I want a cat that's bigger and stronger and ballsier than me. When I'm pulling my shit as a singer it's hard to find him, because the only cats that hang around dressing rooms are flunkies. They're all right for a night, but when you want to talk about a man, ain't no man in the world needs to hang around a dressing room. The men are out in some log cabin growing grass and chopping trees, and I never get to see them. But that gives you more soul, right . . . ?

(*Janis*, David Dalton)

Patsy became Mrs Gerald Cline in 1952, when she was twenty and he was twenty-seven. There was no question at that time that she would remain Patsy Hensley. But when her success began to draw fans to the stage and to their favourite floorside after-show table, it wasn't long before being Mr Patsy Cline drove Gerald to sulks, drink and affairs – which put the Clines about equal, because Patsy was no angel either. Indeed she was one of the few women in her Country circle who found it neither impossible nor reprehensible to acquire casual and relatively guilt-free sex with the flunkies, as Janis called them, while on tour – or, in fact, just about anywhere.

Whether Patsy would have 'fooled around' so much if Gerald Cline, and then her second husband Charlie Dick, had been able to tolerate her independence is another matter. Their jobs kept them tied to Winchester and home, whilst it was impossible for Patsy to stay in one place if she was ever going to make it to the top. Sometimes they would go on the road with her, but most often, particularly when the tours spread further afield, they did not. Thus, when the novelty of endless supplies of free drinks, back-slapping Country camaraderie and the company of living heroes like Ernest Tubb and Johnny Cash – a heady mixture for a couple of local boys – wore off, first Gerald, then Charlie, decided that Patsy's trekking steadily from bar room to dance hall, from tavern to honkytonk and back again, four maybe five nights a week, and then for weeks at a time across America, was selfish and probably unwomanly.

Both campaigned tirelessly to have her stay at home and be a proper housewife; for Charlie there was eventually the added weapon of their two small children, who could always be relied upon to be 'missing their mommy' and 'wishing she was here at home' whenever Patsy called, which she did without fail from wherever she happened to be. Over the years it was an added pressure that she resisted utterly, although she was the one who invariably ended up weeping. But early in her career she had given one of the Melody Boys a piece of advice which indicates with crystal clarity that Patsy understood where she was going, and why. Roy

Dayton had been pining for his girlfriend and pondering on music versus marriage. Patsy's prescription was typically direct: 'Hoss, you do what's gonna make you happy. If you really love her, marry her. With me, you see, it's different. I don't love nothin' more than Music' (*Patsy Cline*, Ellis Nassour).

Patsy stuck with her music, carried always by her own deep conviction and the tantalising tasters of recognition which came her way without giving her the final boost to stardom. Her sympathetic and dedicated biographer, Ellis Nassour, in passing attributes her long struggle to a failure of pragmatism, but a woman might view it differently. A good instance was her departure from a spot on 'Town and Country Jamboree', a broadcast live show on which Patsy was a popular regular. When she was fired, one reason given by the exasperated producers was that she showed up late for rehearsal after being out on the razzle with Charlie. That bit of unprofessionalism was just the latest in a series of aggravations which initially stemmed from her consistent refusal to take part in the square dances which formed an integral part of the Jamboree. Audience and performers alike took part in this rousing knees-up, and a girl would have to dance with whoever she found herself in front of. Apart from personal antipathy to such activity anyway, Patsy had two reasons for not wanting to take part: first, she didn't care to get her fancy white boots stepped on and messed; and second, she didn't like to 'prostitute' herself. She was hired to sing, that was it.

This reflective sense of self did not go down well with men who were accustomed to a Patsy who could outcuss, outdrink, outsing and outdo the best of them. A gal who would go after a man and then ask him afterwards if that wasn't the best fuck he'd ever had, had no business laying ground rules on behaviour. In Patsy's nature there was rarely an impulse to acquiesce or do what was expected of her. Indeed, her greatest difficulties stemmed from the classic conflict for an ambitious woman between career and marriage. The pressure to attain the latter at the expense of the former was ferocious and all-pervasive, with the final seal set by official government policy in the phase of post-war family reconstruction. As a woman of her time Patsy didn't stand a chance, and much as she railed against her pregnancies, hitting the bottle during the periods of enforced curtailment of her work and subsequent huge weight gains, she tried as hard to be a good mother as she did to be the greatest Country singer. She was an habitual nurturer, passing on to young singers, and then to her children and girlfriends, the same care, affection and ability to give herself as she had received from Hilda, who remained a constant rock at the base of Patsy's hectic life.

The mid-fifties saw a spate of brassy voices and up-tempo hits on the pop charts. Songs like 'Music, Music, Music', 'Come On A My House', and 'Shrimp Boats' kept the joint rockin', and even the slower songs like 'Wheel of Fortune' could be belted out by a woman singer in much the same way as Presley did in 'Heartbreak Hotel'. By 1957 Patsy had recorded such a song in 'Walkin' After Midnight', but it had not been released, perhaps because of her own lack of enthusiasm for it, even though it was going down a treat in her live performances. She was invited to perform on 'Arthur Godfrey's Talent Scout Program', a prime-time TV favourite; and in an act of typical mischief, Patsy broke the rules and had her mother, introduced innocently as Mrs Hilda Hensley of Virginia, sponsor her. She sang 'Walkin' After Midnight' and 'broke the applause meters'. The song was released and stayed nineteen weeks in the Country charts, sixteen weeks in the pop charts.

Although Patsy's personal appearance fees suddenly sky-rocketed, she was still in a dire contractual snag. She had signed an exclusive six-year contract with Four Star Records, who not only had her services as recording artist but also approval over the songs she recorded. As Four Star also handled music publishing, it was always in their interest to have her record songs which they owned. It was one of the reasons she had gone so long without a really good song. Since her signing, Four Star had done a deal with the much larger Decca, which proved highly lucrative for Four Star, but had been carried out with no renegotiation of Patsy's contract. She received in all some $900 for one of the biggest hits of the decade, and it meant that Patsy was still bound to the road not just to promote the record, but in order to make a living.

Thus another of the great show-business myths dissolved before her eyes. She had the hit she'd wanted, but she was still on the road, and although she negotiated better terms when the six years were up, the rest of her short life was spent in touring. All the women in this book spent much of their lives living out of suitcases, but touring wasn't just a physical condition. In an unpredictable and demanding non-routine that played havoc with sleep and diet, being on the road was a state of mind. For the very successful these discomforts could be somewhat minimised: Elvis Presley had customised jet planes, Bessie a live-in train for the summer tours down south. But for most performers, being on the road meant an existence very different from the regular routine of sleep, eat, work and play. The implications for women on the road, moreover, were – and still are – even more severe. Any woman who was still trying to keep up the notion of good wife, mother, homemaker even, was always at odds with the professional necessity of being away from home most of the time. None of these women really resolved that conflict, and for Patsy Cline in particular it proved fatal.

The prospect of follow-up hits, delayed by two Four Star duds, but confirmed in 'Crazy' and 'I Fall to Pieces', encouraged her to use the advance for a suitably modern ranch house just outside Nashville; it was equipped with the finest in fifties drinks bars and a locally famed gold-fleck bathroom. Here Patsy, Charlie and the two kids could pretend they were a regular family, except that Mommy was hardly ever there. This heightened sense of well-being soon ran them into debt and proved more than usually risky when Patsy, returning from a shopping expedition to buy braid for Hilda to sew on one of her costumes, was involved in a head-on collision in the car her brother was driving. She was badly cut, especially her face, and had injuries to ribs and limbs that kept her out of action and in costly medical care sufficiently long to jeopardise their financial situation.

Like Piaf after her car accidents, and Garland after her many and varied hospitalisations, Patsy was busting to get back to work, not just for financial reasons but because singing was the most important thing in an uncertain life. She was on crutches much earlier than her doctors advised, and almost immediately went back into the studio, where she had to lie down between takes because of the pain her broken ribs caused as she sang. Much sooner than anyone expected, life had returned to what was normal for Patsy and her immediate family: recording, touring, dashing home from anywhere at every opportunity to be with the kids; fighting with Charlie when he hit the bottle, having him thrown into jail one day, getting him out on bail the next. For Patsy, as with so many of these women, in the midst of a lifestyle unsatisfactory on many counts, the place she could feel most at ease and most confident was on-stage in front of an audience, doing what she knew she did better than anyone else.

At thirty years old, Patsy was in greater demand than ever before, and the pace of the Honky Tonk Merry-Go-Round was unrelenting. Early in 1963 she had been touring heavily, and was getting over a bout of flu, whilst at home her young son had bronchitis. A troupe of Country stars had travelled from various points in their own tours to do a benefit for a Kansas City DJ's family following his death in a car crash. After the benefit, Patsy was agitating to get home. She had been away for some time, and now had only a few days before she had to be off on a long tour. When she rang Charlie she didn't get what would probably have been a wife and mother's response: 'Everything's okay, take your time; the weather's bad and you don't feel up to it', but rather a plea to come back to her sick little boy who missed her badly. Instead of coming back by car, which would have taken longer, she opted to fly in a small plane piloted by her manager, who was an experienced flyer but not instrument rated.

It was partly foolishness, partly the fault of a freak storm. What is sure is that had there not been the pressure of desperately wanting to get home after endless exhausting work and travel or of the others in the plane desperately needing to get on to the next gig, and had there not been the additional guilt for Patsy of not being home to look after her sick child, it is unlikely they would have decided to fly in such inclement weather. Pilot Randy Hughes checked conditions all the way and before the last hop phoned home, from where they were told that the storms had cleared and the stars were out. Then, only ninety miles from home, they took off, and, not realising that the stars had probably been shining in the lull at the eye of the storm, they never made it. It was obvious from the scattered wreckage that Patsy, Hughes, and fellow Country stars Hawkshaw Hawkins and Cowboy Copas had all died instantaneously.

'Sweet Dreams', recorded only weeks before, was released, and became Patsy's final million seller. She was sorely missed by the Country music community, who recognised her great influence by posthumously electing her first woman in the Country Music Hall of Fame. Privately, among family and friends, it seemed that no one would ever replace her overwhelming presence in their lives. Contradictory remembrances of Patsy stemmed from two widely opposed views of her: the sensitive loving friend, and the raucous wild girl. Both were equally true, with Patsy using the tough, brassy exterior as many women use fat, to minimise the threat of occupying space in a male world and to maintain her authority within it. Country singer-songwriter Teddy Milburn once wrote a song which she instantly learned by heart, only to have it turned down repeatedly when it came to recording. It caught her own imagination and was obviously a clear image of herself as a performer in the style of Annie Oakley and Calamity Jane:

> I wore my guns so proudly
> I'd kill for just a thrill
> No man could ever back me down
> Not me, Dakota Lil

and the last verse:

> I wore my guns so proudly
> No more I ever will
> Though I must die, no one will ever forget
> The name Dakota Lil

('Dakota Lil', Milburn)

When Dakota Lil got up on stage, as she best liked to do, ostentatious and powerful in white, high-heeled, fancy stitched boots, white Stetson, and a fringed and braided cowgirl outfit made always by Hilda, she was twenty years ahead of her time in Country, and prefigured the bold, free, solo presence of Loretta Lynn, Tammy Wynette and Dolly Parton. But if Patsy had continued to lead the way (she would have celebrated her fiftieth birthday, and perhaps the peak of such a voice, in 1982), it is tempting to speculate whether the strength of the women solo stars would still have been rendered more socially palatable by being clad in gingham frocks, frills, lace and long 'feminine' coiffures, or whether Patsy's no bullshit, rope 'em and tie 'em style might instead have prevailed. But just as Annie Oakley and Calamity Jane (and their real-life creators, Betty Hutton and Doris Day) were finally robbed of their independence and buckskins in the final reel in order that they be more fittingly clad in white wedding gowns, so might Dakota Lil have succumbed. Whether Dolly Parton would have felt quite such a need to disguise her own considerable autonomy with 'little girl' camouflage and to make such exaggerated efforts to be feminine if she had had before her a role model of equally flamboyant self-determination will always remain a matter of conjecture and regret.

For almost five years Patsy had hit the heights of her profession, and with three monster hits in the pop charts seemed destined to keep pace in the broader market with pop stars like Kay Starr, Theresa Brewer and even her young pal, Brenda Lee. Now her life and career had ended abruptly amid a dozen speculations about how she came to be on that plane, in that storm. It was the kind of 'if only she . . .', and 'it was pure

PATSY CLINE—A TRIBUTE

THEY voted her, in America, the top female Country 'n' Western star. And, with the building of a substantial following for this music-form in Britain, she looked like becoming a regular chart resident here, too. But now Patsy Cline is dead.

Killed in a plane crash in the States, on her way back to Nashville, Tennessee, her spiritual home, from a charity show in Kansas City. With her, and also dead, were singers **Cowboy Copas** and **Hawkshaw Hawkins**, and her manager **Randy Hughes**, who piloted the light craft.

Patsy had had only one substantial hit here, with **"Heartaches"**. But she's built her following, slowly but surely, with others

DETERMINED

But, at 31, Patsy was, according to reports from the States, determined to make a real stab at fame in Britain. She was planning "more sophisticated" numbers for release here. A concession, sure —but she felt that if she got in on more commercial numbers her chance to sell her own loved C and W music would be all the stronger.

There was talk, too, of her visiting the Continent later this year—and her big ambition was to call in on London, meet some of her followers, maybe do some radio and television work. And get a closer look at the disc scene she so much wanted to conquer.

Patsy Cline had great talent. She'd even been called the "female Ray Charles". But she had something else— something vitally important in the world of popular music. She had courage.

In the summer of 1961, Patsy was involved with her brother in a serious

head-on car crash. Two people were killed outright. Patsy was seriously injured and she was warned, firmly, in hospital, that she could forget all about singing.

"I'll show 'em", she said. And despite appalling injuries, including damage to her brain, a dislocated and fractured hip and disfiguring facial injuries, she did just that. The staff of the main hospital in Nashville could not remember a recovery like it . . . right against all the odds.

Her record at that time was "I Fall To Pieces", which is a sadly ironic title. It was a huge hit in the States and nibbled at the lower chart placings here. But "Heartaches" was the big one, with (in the States) numbers like "She's Got You" (which **Alma Cogan** "covered" here), "Crazy" and "When I Get Through To You", all doing well in the States.

Patsy's latest release was "Leavin' On Your Mind", a strangely-titled piece which has built substantial sales without actually making the charts. And her album on Brunswick was "Sentimentally Yours".

The album was a sign of her efforts to find a world commercial success. She was pop-ish on several of the tracks, but she did include "Your Cheatin' Heart", "Heartaches" and "Lonely Street".

Now that fightback and that determination has gone. Finally ended in a plane crash which brings back to memory that dreadful affair of four years ago when **Buddy Holly**, **Big Bopper** and **Ritchie Valens** all perished in a similar type of aircraft in a similar type of crash.

Virginia Patterson Hensley, her real name, was surely on the threshold of enormously increased prestige here in Britain. She was on the verge of the big breakthrough.

I wonder if her posthumous career will approach that of Buddy Holly. I do know there is a great stack of hitherto unreleased Patsy Cline material in the vaults of the studios of Nashville, Tennessee.

And I also know that she will be sorely missed by millions of fans throughout the world.

PETER JONES

chance . . .' reasoning that might have been applied to Patsy's frantic on the road existence almost every day of her life. And it was a condition that most entertainers tacitly accept.

Going on the road has always been a part of show business, from travelling circuses and troupes of wandering minstrels, to the multi-truck convoys and jet-in-jet-out one-night stands of modern international pop tours. Fatalities are high. Being on the road killed Bessie Smith and Patsy Cline, severely injured Edith Piaf and Jane Froman and has claimed dozens of other lives and generated even more close calls. And it isn't as simple as reckoning that those deaths and injuries are just the standard percentage within the entertainment profession that are destined to fulfil the statistical probabilities of road and air fatalities. Many of these accidents, like Patsy's, and even more in the case of the road crews who work behind the scenes on tour, occur because of tight scheduling (with an eye to minimising costs), and the necessity to move to the next job still exhausted from the last.

In a few notable cases, however, the circumstances really have been extraordinary. During the Second World War, for instance, Carole Lombard was killed in a plane crash while on a government bonds selling tour: it was by no means part of her regular routine. And the flight that so drastically affected Jane Froman's life and career was also something of a rarity. Jane's professional career as a singer had been mainly as a band vocalist, and it was in that role as a classic interpreter of all-American standards that she joined a wartime USO tour of American troops in Europe. The details of the accident furnished Hollywood with the very substance of Fate when it came to tell her courageous story. She had swapped seats with another woman just before take-off; when the plane crashed, the other woman was killed. Jane was alive, but badly injured. She was rescued by the pilot of the plane and later married him, which was approximately where the biopic ended, fortunately not spoiling the screenplay with the subsequent divorce.

It was undoubtedly a tale of great fortitude and endurance. Jane was expected to lose both legs through injury, and over the next ten years had to endure multiple operations, setbacks and understandable lapses into despair and the bottle before she finally felt able to stage her remarkable comeback in 1952. That was the spur for Hollywood to retell the story, with Susan Hayward as Froman miming an original soundtrack recorded by Jane herself. They became friends during filming, and it was a sad irony that Froman outlived Hayward, the woman with the best shoulders in Hollywood, who died of a brain tumour at the age of fifty-three. The movie *With A Song In My Heart* is the archetypal tale of survival; the story of a woman who battled against terrible odds to pursue a life and career she loved. Despite repeated knocks she managed to hold out until her efforts were recognised, and she went on to live out a full, rich and respected life, comforted by the knowledge of her triumph. While not

Jane Froman

wanting to detract from Jane Froman's undeniable courage in this real-life saga, it's important to recognise that all the women in this book overcame immense odds and constant setbacks in trying to achieve a similar fulfilment and dignity in their lives. The principal difference between Froman and the others is that she lived to a ripe old age, and they did not. That Jane Froman was able to *sustain* her comeback might be attributable to several factors which made her life significantly different from theirs.

Jane's father died when she was young, and she was raised by her mother, who remained a teacher of music until retirement. Her rearing in America's midwest was based on a stability of environment and consistency of education which led to her majoring in journalism at college. By the time Jane Froman started to sing for her supper, she was an accomplished and assured adult woman, bolstered by a hardworking academic mother and the advantages of her steady, if not large, income. And Jane's modest ambitions to be a good true singer of wholesome American songs did not conflict with her mother's vision. Mrs Froman was a self-contained woman with a career and life of her own; she was proud of what she had accomplished and was not relying on Jane for reflected glory or security. And Jane, unlike Janis Joplin, unlike Nina Simone, had ambitions after the duty of her college education which did not disturb her mother's expectations. Most of these singers tried on the one hand to please mothers whom they saw as disappointed by life, and on the other, deeply resented the expectations placed on them. Neither was true of Jane Froman. When she met her first great challenge she had years of positive, uninterrupted nurturing to fall back on, as well as the advantages of a degree of objective rationale, a dubious quality for purveyors of emotion, except, as in Jane's case, in states of emergency.

Secondly, when the accident occurred, it happened in circumstances that surrounded the injured Froman with legions, literally, of fellow-sufferers. She insisted on continuing the tour as best she could, and the USO saw the advantage in this. As Froman, on crutches and in pain, sang patriotic songs to thousands of soldiers similarly on crutches and in pain, the benefits were mutual. Not only was she a fellow American, but she was also a fellow sufferer, and it may well have been the tour and such evidence of suffering that made her more able to bear her own. Froman saw American manhood in a rare state – vulnerable, injured and frightened.

During the First World War Marie Lloyd incorporated patriotic call-up songs into her Music Hall repertoire: the image is indelibly fixed in the film version of Joan Littlewood's *Oh What A Lovely War* when Maggie Smith boasts 'I'll make a man of any one of you', as women from all walks of life were organised into homefront labour to support the war effort. In the Second World War the process of co-option was even more evident. After years of misery and no work for themselves or their men, women

After the plane crash, Froman marries the pilot who saved her life

were suddenly propelled into every conceivable kind of labour, from previously acceptable nursing to unthinkable jobs in mechanics and industry. The effect was felt in entertainment too. The mood of the times and of productive women's work bred entertainers who gave the impression of being able to stand and fight with the best of them: Vera Lynn, Kate Smith, Marlene Dietrich, 'GI' Jo Stafford, Sophie Tucker, even Gracie Fields, who nevertheless suffered opprobrium because of an Italian husband and American residency, despite the millions she raised for the war effort in Canada. Without exception these women came from early lives of comparative stability: in times of adversity they had plenty of reserves, and professionally came into their own.

The war brought Carmen Miranda into her own too, but with quite different results, and for equally different reasons. With the European market suddenly cut off, Hollywood cast about urgently for new outlets. South America was the obvious alternative, and the studios quickly

Judy Holliday,
the dumb blonde
who wasn't

imported Latin American stars to add the necessary ingredient for South of the Border sales. By the end of the war, through film exposure that was both racist and insulting, given her professional achievements and status in her own country, Carmen was one of the highest-paid club performers in the US, which was just as well: when VJ Day dawned, Hollywood speedily discarded the Latin quotient, including Carmen Miranda. Whilst some of the men continued to scrape along with bit parts as gangsters, swarthy bandits and other stereotypes, there was no place for tempestuous senoritas and darkly passionate senors. Carmen was left with the grind of club circuits. She died at forty-three of a heart attack, and of unrelenting overwork.

If the vicissitudes of politics worked indirectly on the career of Carmen Miranda, their effects were more straightforward in the case of those, like Judy Holliday, who fell foul of Hollywood's obsessively patriotic stance. Like most other women in this book, Judy's background included a father who deserted his family (for another woman), and an upbringing dominated by her mother and grandmother. Born Judith Tuvim into a strongly militant East Coast Jewish family, Judy was only too aware of her mother's distress at having been deserted in middle years, and she concentrated her own passions on education until her first big romance with an older, academic Jewish woman, with whom she remained friends for the rest of her life. The in-built streak of non-conformism didn't last long in her sexual life, but it certainly persisted in her career. There were a lot of Jewish men running the show in Hollywood, but not many openly

*A fruit-free
Carmen Miranda*

Jewish women were in front of the cameras, and Judy railed against that discrimination as hard as she did against her type-casting as the eternal dumb blonde. Given her fairly consistent battle mentality, it's not surprising that she too died at the age of forty-three from what is increasingly considered to be a stress-related disease – cancer.

Future research may well show that it is not as easy to put women like Judy and Carmen into the straightforward 'death by natural causes' bracket. When it comes down to the unadorned facts of death certificates, Judy Garland died of a heart attack too, and that is clearly not the whole story. In Dinah Washington's case the cause of death by heart attack was more directly attributable to an accidental overdose of diet pills and alcohol, but the indirect cause may well have been just as potent over any number of years.

Born Ruth Lee Jones in August 1924, in a clapboard shack in the deep southern town of Tuscaloosa, Alabama, her family moved to Chicago's South Side when Ruth was three. Chicago was one of the towns that had seen mass immigration from the South during the First World War, and especially an influx of New Orleans musicians. The *Chicago Defender* reported at the time that 'the fire department is thinking of lining 35th Street with asbestos to keep those bands from scorching passers-by with their red-hot jazz music.' During the twenties and thirties Chicago saw the emergence of countless bands and venues, but for Ruth Jones they remained out of bounds throughout her first decade in the Windy City.

Like Helen Morgan, Judy Garland, Judy Holliday, Frances Farmer, Doris Day and Patsy Cline, Dinah's father wasn't around much. Alcohol claimed a great deal of his time and energy. But like the others, she too had a loving mother whose every effort went into keeping her child as best she could. In her case, much as in Billie's mother Sadie Fagan's, this forced her to leave the little girl alone at home whilst she was out working as a domestic, something that left a lasting impression on the child. What time they could spend together was devoted to the activities of St Luke's Baptist Church. Dinah was one of the many black women singers who got her start in church. For all of them such an environment meant not only spiritual relief, but also free lessons in rhythm and harmony, and a simple and direct road to maternal placation. By the time she was eleven, Ruth was playing piano for the church, and she and her mother 'toured' to other churches to sing gospel. Mrs Jones clearly disapproved of jazz – the devil's music – but in a town as hot as Chicago, nothing, not even mother, was going to keep the energetic and fun-loving Ruth away from it for long. As Ruth's first singing teacher, Sallie Martin, once said: 'Dinah could certainly sing! But then she would catch the eye of some *man*, and be off outta that church before the minister finished the doxology!'

Having won an amateur contest at the Royal Theater at the age of fifteen, and secured her first blues gig at the Flame Show Bar, Ruth joined the Sallie Martin Singers in 1940. They were the first all-woman

The Queen of the Blues with Larry Wrice at New York's Cafe Society Downtown

touring gospel group, and included Clara Ward and her mother, Gertrude. For more than a year Ruth toured the south and midwest with them, offering her faith and availing herself of an invaluable apprenticeship in music and the performing arts in general. By 1941, at sixteen, she felt she was ready for the big bad world outside gospel. She landed odd dates at the Rhumboogie Club, the Downbeat Room and the famous Three Deuces; but it wasn't until Joe Glaser (Billie Holiday's agent) was encouraged to listen to her in one of the rooms he booked, the Ladies Room of the Garrick Lounge, that she found herself in regular work. Glaser got her an audition with a brilliant young percussionist who, incidentally, was the nephew of Bessie Smith's man, Richard Morgan. Lionel Hampton hated Ruth's name, which he had her change to Dinah Washington, but he loved her voice, and she stayed with his band for the next three years.

Dinah's idols were Bessie and Billie. Like Bessie, she could growl the blues or sing them full-throated and true; like Billie, she played dangerously with phrasing, purposely spitting out the end of a word, chopping it off with a consonantal attack that hung over the empty gap, and creating tension for the start of the next line which, by contrast, might be lazy or soft. With a sense of pride, adoration of the Empress and the Lady, and inimitably comic terms of self-reference, Dinah bestowed upon herself a title: when she answered the phone with 'This is Dinah Washington, Queen of the Blues' there weren't many who were about to dispute the claim.

She was as rumbustious a character as Bessie or Patsy, and constantly sought and failed to find *the* man, the one who would be big enough, fun enough and sure enough to handle it. She felt compelled to legalise her situation at every opportunity, or at least to acquire the piece of paper which officially gave her the security she craved. Dinah held to the belief that if she loved a man enough to go to bed with him, then she loved him enough to marry him too. She doggedly pursued that belief through marriages to John Young, George Jenkins, Robert Grayson, Walter Buchanan, Jimmy Cobb, Eddie Corblee, Rusty Maillard, Raphael Campos and, finally, the one who did seem to fit the bill – football star Dick 'Night Train' Lane. That Dinah found something like her ideal in a football hero, and Piaf found hers in a boxing champion, is worth consideration. These men had their own professions and, more importantly, both the footballer and the boxer were specifically famed for their masculine strength. No matter how much praise their wives received, these men had unassailable public testimony of their prowess, and it was unlikely that that would be diminished by their wives' success, or that they would ever suffer the Mr Washington or Mr Piaf complex. Nor were Dinah and Edith sex symbols in the way that so alienated baseball star Joe DiMaggio from Marilyn Monroe. Audiences found them sexually attractive and fascinating, but the attraction lay in a combination of sensuality in their voices and in the interpretation of particular songs. Whereas Joe DiMaggio felt he had to compete with ten thousand GIs for his gorgeous wife's attention, the long line of lovers and husbands pursued by Dinah and Edith were merely competing with the women themselves. Most dropped out of the competition because they couldn't stand the pace. Dick Lane and Marcel Cerdan were companions who could keep up, and were proud to do just that.

But like Piaf, Dinah's needs were not satisfied only by sexual pursuit and conquest. Collecting husbands was not the only way she put buffers between herself and early deprivation. Her extravagant stage outfits became a trademark; and in private she affected quantity as well as quality. It was said that there was always a rack of fur coats, all with the labels ripped out, hanging in Dinah's wardrobe; she sported outrageous blonde wigs, half a dozen tiaras, and her particular ruling passion was shoes – she had at least two hundred pairs.

Unlike most of the women in this book, both Piaf and Washington lived to positive rather than negative excess, more like the male stars, and this ran them into similar problems. A much-quoted remark was that 'Dinah had a pill for everything.' Like Judy Garland, her use of pills to sleep, wake and, in particular, to lose weight, began early and remained a continuous fact in her life. Unlike Judy, however, documentation of her life is scarce, so there is no way of knowing whether she took the pills because she had been schooled to believe she was overweight, or whether it was Everywoman's legacy of dissatisfaction with her body. The constant streamlining process required to bring that body into line with an image of desirability had a particular importance for those whose bodies went on display as they exercised their special talents. Certainly Dinah could be heard complaining about the injustice of hair that was 'as short as dust on a jug', or lamenting her expanding waistline: even surer is the fact that after an accidental overdose of diet pills and alcohol her heart gave out. The strain of twenty years of ferocious dieting finally caught up with her body's tolerance of wild fluctuations in weight. When she died, at the age of thirty-nine, Dinah weighed, like Judy Garland and Edith Piaf, a skeletal five stone.

Along with dieting, dressing up and great, great singing, there was a policy of living it up and raising various kinds of hell. Among her contemporaries, everyone is reckoned to have a wild story about Dinah. Those who knew her from her enormous packed-house successes at the Apollo in the fifties remembered how she always needed large advances on her large salary. By the end of a week her pay packet would be filled with nothing but debit slips. And the papers had a ball documenting Dinah's escapades. There was an incident with a dressmaker who swore that the Great Miss D pulled a gun on her in a dispute over a bill for either $700 or $7000, depending on the newspaper. The woman later admitted that she didn't exactly *see* the weapon – that yes, it could have been a comb or a pen that Dinah was pointing at her – but the incident simply served to swell Dinah's wild reputation.

Another report from 1958 records her 5 a.m. arrest with friends at the Comedy Club in downtown Baltimore. Dinah was appearing at the nightclub at the time, but that didn't affect the charge of after-hours drinking. Outside of a miniscule stratum of sophistication, centred exclusively in one or two cities, greater America was extremely ambivalent when it came to drink and the social life around alcohol. The uncontrolled growth of cities in the first two decades of the century had produced a period of lawlessness and corruption which permeated urban American society to a degree unknown since the wildest days of the West, the unsavoury reality of which had anyway been sufficiently sanitised by folk tale and Hollywood as to have vanished. Prohibition was introduced to help curb these problems but ended up exacerbating them in many ways, and producing other kinds of violence. The double stigma of both old and new lawlessness thus attached to public drinking did not disappear with the repeal of the Prohibition laws, and for many years – and in some parts to this day – the social acceptance of alcohol was confined to high days and holidays, to specific drinking establishments and to certain types, including men in general, and women of dubious reputation. To add to the difficulties of such party-loving gals as Dinah and Patsy was the fact of their gender.

Dinah in 1959, her blonde wig phase

For white country boys the decade of the fifties was a time for psychic relief and reconstruction of their male identity. They had finished the Second World War as heroes, whether or not they had actually departed the shores of the United States. Korea and the build-up towards the Cold War and anti-communism gave new impetus to the conventions of masculinity, and society smiled benevolently upon the hard working male letting his hair down and raising the roof as his reward. Quite the opposite was expected of women, and it was a difficult time to be a good ole gal.

Despite the new black consciousness that world war had spurred on, black women were in a similar position in relation to their men: a perspective not truly taken up or acknowledged by them until long after the inherent sexism of the later Black Power movement had exposed the doublespeak that had been going on all the time. In the 1950s black women were again seen as they had been by black feminists in the latter part of the nineteenth century – as the hope of the race. To that end, the burdens of upright and moral behaviour, which would be rooted in family life, were heavy; in that light, the Queen of the Blues was not a good thing, no matter how great her cultural contribution.

But Dinah was unstoppable, and her influence undeniable. By the mid-fifties she had boosted a widespread rediscovery of Bessie Smith (Columbia, now better known as CBS, did their first massive re-release of Bessie's songs in 1956), and her own musical legacy would be heard wailing into the eighties, not only on her own recordings, but also in the styles of singers like Nancy Wilson and Esther Phillips, who did a successful remake of Dinah's greatest hit. 'What A Diff'rence A Day Makes' signified Dinah's desire to do her kind of crossover, from rhythm 'n' blues to pop. Unlike Patsy, to whom the crossover from Country to pop represented a certain infidelity, Dinah wasn't going to be limited by anyone's tight conceptual framework: if gospel had been too restrictive in her teens, blues was too constricting at the height of her career, even when her devotees insisted that she was the greatest since the Empress. No matter that there were recordings revealing a classic jazz interpreter (re-issued by Verve as 'The Jazz Sides'); Dinah was determined to extend her audience in a way that Billie had never been inclined or able to do. Dinah softened her tone a little, ironed out her phrasing just enough not to alienate either side, added lush strings to the funk, and came up with two of the biggest hits of the decade. The other was 'Unforgettable' and that's just what Dinah Washington intended to be.

If nine husbands, two sons and a breakneck pace of work weren't enough to keep Dinah busy, she also opened a restaurant in Detroit, started a civic welfare group called the Ballantine Belles, and formed her own booking agency – Queen Attractions – which handled work for Sammy Davis Jnr, Muhammed Ali and Aretha Franklin, as well as the full list of commitments for the Queen herself. Nor was she by any means aloof from the vital movement of Black America which was taking place all around her. In 1960 a radio station in Louisiana sourly noted that it would be 'quite willing' to go along with Dinah Washington's demand for a boycott on the sale of her records to Southern segregationist states; it would be happy to box up her records and send them back to her. In 1963 Mahalia Jackson announced her intention of raising thousands of dollars for 'Dr Martin Luther King Jnr, negro Internationalist leader', as the *New York Times* described him. Mahalia was in the process of organising a benefit concert which she hoped would include Dinah Washington. It seemed, at last, that it was time: the singing of a song like Billie's 'Strange Fruit' would no longer be a solitary act of bravery. That was the year Dinah died. As she was still young and very popular it's likely that her involvement in that movement would have gone on to redress the balance of her reputation as a self-absorbed pleasure seeker. Just as Patsy Cline had prefigured the crossover and immense range of appeal of a Country star like Dolly Parton, so Dinah Washington had achieved her pop successes and widened her audience from the inner circle of rhythm 'n' blues devotees. That kind of popularity could have been very valuable. On the other hand, the forces of opposition could just as easily have seized on her success for their own cultural hypocrisies. It is significant that in 1984, the year that Jesse Jackson brought the possibility of a black president into the consciousness of the United States for the first time, the incumbent white president made sure he was seen shaking hands with Michael Jackson, the most broadly popular black American in history.

As it happened, Dinah passed into the history of blues and jazz as a descendant of Bessie and Billie, and as the musical rather than political ancestor of an artist like Nina Simone, who, at the time of Dinah's death, was really beginning to spread her wings for a flight from classical music into music which was not only beautiful and original but also informed by resolute political awareness. In most minds, Dinah is remembered as a character who lived too wildly for her own good. Despite the positive energy with which she grappled with life – amply evident in her singing – she is still labelled 'self-destructive'.

It is this description that is perhaps the most unjust of all those applied to the women who make up *A Star is Torn*. Seen through a veil of social expectation and demand, the description seems to have been used for any woman who did not fulfil that expectation or demand. The tacit judgement is that if they refused to stick to the rules then they were really asking for it all along: it was sad that they died so young, so talented, but it really was their own fault; they destroyed themselves.

Janis Joplin saw very clearly how F. Scott Fitzgerald's hell-bent existence was regarded as romantic and tragic, while Zelda was considered just crazy. The same could be said of all these women. When Judy Garland broke the rules it was not rebellion but self-destruction; when

Patsy wouldn't do what she was told it was career madness. When any of them drank, screwed or partied with the same freedom or pleasure as men in the same business, it was not to be admired or glorified but seen as a reinforcement of their reputations as vamps or sluts who would come to grief by their sins and their destructive way of life. But they were not setting out to destroy themselves or anyone else. They may well have sought to block out certain areas of their experience, but against all the odds their gender laid against them, what they were all hell-bent on was survival, and more. They saw what life had to offer, and each in her own way went right out to grab it. They could not be physically stopped from pursuing these various fulfilments, but when they went under what society could say was 'I told you so.' It is precisely that resentment of their battles that pervades the label 'self-destructive'. And for none was it more of a dangerous misnomer than for Marilyn Monroe.

Times Telephone Numbers:
MAdison 5-4411—Classified Advertising
MAdison 5-2345—For all other calls.
Circulation—Largest in the West:
772,435 Daily; 1,120,183 Sunday.

Los Angeles Times

EQUAL RIGHTS
LIBERTY UNDER THE LAW — TRUE INDUSTRIAL FREEDOM

Copyright © 1962 The Times-Mirror Company

MARILYN MONROE FOUND DEAD

Sleeping Pill Overdose Blamed

Red Super Bomb Kicks Off Series

High Altitude Test Reported as Being in 40-Megaton Range

UPPSALA, Sweden ⒫—The Soviet Union exploded a big nuclear bomb high in the atmosphere Sunday.

Swedish scientists estimated it to be in the 40-megaton range, second only to the Soviet 50-megaton bomb set off last Oct. 30. A Norwegian scientist said his instruments showed only that it was smaller than that one and U.S. officials would say only that it was "in the megaton range."

The Japanese Meteorological Agency estimated the blast to be in the 20-megaton range.

Whatever the size, the blast carried out Premier Khrushchev's threat to resume testing in retaliation for U.S. Pacific tests.

At High Altitude

Uppsala University's Seismological Institute, which classed the blast as in the range of 40 million tons of TNT, said it occurred at a higher altitude than the Soviet series of 1961, which was climaxed by the superbomb.

Recordings at the institute indicated the test was carried out at the Soviet atomic testing ground on the island of Novaya Zemlya, in Siberia 1,350 miles east of Uppsala.

In Washington, the State Department deplored Soviet resumption of atmospheric testing as a "somber episode." In Japan, only nation to feel the wrath of an atomic bomb in wartime, a government spokesman said the

new Soviet testing "is regrettable for world peace."

The big blast appeared to have kicked off a new round of Soviet military maneuvers in the far north designed among other things to test new nuclear weapons.

The Soviet Foreign Ministry refused to comment on the report of a new test, and tight security blanketed the military maneuvers in the Arctic Circle. The Soviet government announced two weeks ago, however, that land, sea and air maneuvers would begin Sunday.

'Various Weapons'

That Soviet announcement said the Soviet northern fleet, together with rocket troops and air force units, would participate.

The announcement followed a Soviet government's statement that it had ordered a new series of nuclear weapons tests.

The Soviet Defense Ministry said the troops would "conduct maneuvers with the actual use of various types of modern weapons."

Western military experts said the new tactical weapons would probably be tried out under battlefield conditions during the 11-week period, as well as a series of experimental nuclear blasts.

They said the Soviet *Please Turn to Pg. 13, Col. 1*

Junta Pledges to Seat Victor in Peru Election

BY BEN F. MEYER

WASHINGTON ⒫— The President of Peru's military government junta, Gen. Ricardo Perez Godoy, promised Sunday that Peru's 1963 presidential elections will be absolutely impartial and that the winner will get the office.

That point was mentioned by President Kennedy at his news conference last Wednesday as one on which "clear assurances" are desired before the United States recognizes the Peruvian regime

which took power rather than accept the results of this year's voting.

The viewpoints of Perez Godoy were expressed in cabled replies to questions submitted by this correspondent in Washington.

In addition to his comments on election plans, Perez Godoy pledged a clean government in Peru, operating on a balanced budget, announced Peru's readiness to join other hemisphere nations in collective action *Please Turn to Pg. 18, Col. 1*

Nixon Team at Helm of State GOP

BY RICHARD BERGHOLZ
Times Political Writer

SACRAMENTO — Moving quickly and easily, the Republican state organization changed leadership Sunday with Richard Nixon in tight control.

The 864-member State Central Committee, without an apparent ripple of dissent, selected new leaders for two-year terms and adopted a series of policy resolutions, closely attuned to the views of the former Vice President, now the Republican nominee for governor.

Conservative elements of the party which had opposed Nixon's candidacy in the June primary election never raised their hands in a serious challenge to Nixon's obvious control of the proceedings.

Weinberger Chairman

Elected new chairman was 44-year-old Caspar (Cap) Weinberger, San Francisco attorney and former state assemblyman. He succeeded John Krehbiel of Pasadena.

Named vice chairman was another 44-year-old, Dr. Gaylord Parkinson, an El Cajon obstetrician. He succeeded Weinberger in the No. 2 post and in the usual progression would be in line for the state chairmanship in the 1964 Presidential year.

Other new state committee officers include: state Sen. John McCarthy of San Rafael, secretary; Mrs. Athalie Clarke, of San Marino, assistant secretary; Robert Rowan, of San Marino, treasurer; Assemblyman Don Mulford of Berkeley, assistant treasurer, and Mrs. Lee Sherman of San Francisco, Dorothy Misenhimer of Hanford and Mrs. Gladys O'Donnell of Long Beach, women's vice chairmen.

"This meeting was evidence that there is no breach in the party," Weinberger said. "It was a very harmonious and youthful meeting which, if continued, will produce

LIFE IS ENDED—Marilyn Monroe, the most famous blond of the screen, in a recent photo. She was found Sunday, dead of apparent overdose of sleeping pills. *AP Wirephoto*

SAD CHILD, UNHAPPY STAR

Help She Needed to Find Self Eluded Marilyn All Her Life

BY CHARLES E. DAVIS JR.

When they found Marilyn Monroe, one of her hands grasped a telephone.

She had been calling for help.

"Three husbands didn't help.

She had carried her problems to psychiatrists.

escaped it, despite the tremendous wages paid her by the film studios.

"I am trying to find myself as a person," she told an interviewer not long ago. "Sometimes that's not easy to do. Millions of people live their entire lives without finding themselves. Maybe they feel it isn't necessary.

"But it is something I must do. The best way for me to find myself as a person is to prove to myself that I am an actress. And that is what I hope to do.

"For the 36 years she lived, she was trying to prove she *Please Turn to Pg. 53, Col. 1*

THE WEATHER

U.S. Weather Bureau forecast: Mostly sunny today and Tuesday but low clouds nights and mornings. High today, 84. High Sunday, 82; low, 60.

Unclad Body of Star Discovered on Bed; Empty Bottle Near

BY HOWARD HERTEL AND DON NEFF

Marilyn Monroe, a troubled beauty who failed to find happiness as Hollywood's brightest star, was discovered dead in her Brentwood home of an apparent overdose of sleeping pills Sunday.

The blond, 36-year-old actress was nude, lying face down on her bed and clutching a telephone receiver in her hand when a psychiatrist broke into her room at 3:30 a.m.

She had been dead an estimated six to eight hours.

About 5:15 p.m. Saturday she had called the psychiatrist, Dr. Ralph Greenson, and was told to go for a ride when she complained she could not sleep, police reported.

Her body was taken to the County Morgue, where Coroner Theodore J. Curphey said after an autopsy

More news and pictures of Marilyn Monroe on pages A, B, 2, 22, and 23, Part 1.

that he could give a "presumptive opinion" that death was due to an overdose of some drug.

He said a special "suicide team" would be asked to investigate Miss Monroe's last days to determine if she took her own life.

Further medical tests as to the nature of the suspected killer drug will be completed in 48 hours, he said.

An empty bottle found among several medicines beside her bed had contained 50 Nembutal capsules. The prescription was issued only two or three days ago and the capsules were to be taken in doses of one a night, said Dr. Hyman Engelberg.

Believed in Depressed Mood

It was learned that medical authorities believed Miss Monroe had been in a depressed mood recently. She was unkempt and in need of a manicure and pedicure, indicating listlessness and a lack of interest in maintaining her usually glamorous appearance, the authorities added.

The coroner's office listed her death on its records as possible suicide while the police report said death was possibly accidental.

No suicide note was found.

Dr. Robert Litman, a psychiatrist serving on the sui- *Please Turn to Pg. A, Col. 4*

NEWS SUMMARY

Today's summary of world, national, local and state news appears on Page 2, Part 1.

Marilyn — Hollywood's most famous blonde since Jean Harlow — was born into insecurity and "never

A – B – C – D
Who's gonna file me under LOVE?

'I'm Gonna File My Claim', Newman and Darby

Marilyn Monroe's face and body – her *image* – are synonymous today with a particular kind of vulnerable and exciting female sexuality: the cotton candy blonde hair, richly pouting lips and sensuous body are instantly recognisable. More than twenty years after her death Marilyn is *known* almost anywhere in the world. Yet few know anything at all about the woman behind the image; and for her, perhaps more than for any other movie icon, that is how it has always been. For several years an image was all the public had of her. She had made no movie appearances and the only way in which she could be perceived by the mass entertainment audience was by way of a series of pin-ups and modelling assignments which put her first of all into magazines as a 'young model', and then onto their covers as a 'young starlet'.

Meanwhile Marilyn had been putting together some kind of personal identity from the unkind wreckage of her early life. The result was someone almost as interesting as the person herself: an amalgam of truths, fairy stories, myths, misunderstandings, lies, misremembrances and other morsels. In short – an image. At the beginning of her career fans knew nothing of Marilyn's personality and had little interest in any aspect of her other than whatever suggested itself through the cheese-cake pictures that made up her only public work to that point. In that way, lack of curiosity was helpful in her early years, as she hadn't actually *done* anything but survive; in the end it rebounded, because when she did have something to say and something to offer, which in her terms meant the use of brain as well as body, still nobody was interested.

At the height of her fame as a living movie star in the late fifties and early sixties, fan mail arrived at the rate of twenty-five thousand letters a week. Now her image is as potent as ever. She is the subject of dozens of picture books and biographies ranging from careful works of loving and reasonable research to the seemingly inevitable I-once-met-her-in-an-elevator-and-she-said-I-was-her best-friend exploitation that comes with untimely death. So who or what is Marilyn Monroe?

Marilyn's thirty-six years comprise one of the most documented yet ill-served lives in modern times: popular memory has an uncanny way of distorting. It recalls and highlights, deletes and rewrites as firmly as any editor. It began in Marilyn's lifetime, frequently at her own instigation, and went far back into her childhood. At the time it was seen as evidence of her innate chicanery, but in retrospect it is equally possible to see the mechanics of self-protection at work.

In 1926 Rudolph Valentino died and 'talkies' were born with Warner Brothers' historic Vitaphone system and *Don Juan*. On 1 June of that year, some two years after the departure of her second husband, Martin Mortenson, Mrs Gladys Pearl Baker gave birth to a daughter at Los Angeles General Hospital. She was twenty-four; two previous children were in the care of her first husband's family and her third child's father was given as 'Edward Mortenson'. Marilyn used the name for official purposes all her life, although she knew Mortenson was not her father. Gladys Baker was a film cutter at Consolidated Film Industries. Along with thousands of other movie ancillaries, she shared the Hollywood dream: her baby was named Norma Jean (on occasion Norma Jeane) – for Norma Talmadge and Jean Harlow. A single mother with no means of support other than her own earning capacity was in desperate straits in mid-twenties America. There was no form of welfare safety net and no possibility of aid other than self-help. Mrs Baker was soon back at work, a move that was to be interpreted by an uncomprehending Norma Jean as abandonment. Marilyn herself claimed to be an orphan in early studio publicity, not only because she *felt* like one, but also to hide a mother who by then was living within the shameful environs of a state mental institution. And she was also terrified of 'catching' the family weakness herself. Much has been made of the insanity that ran through her family and of her abandonment, but Gladys did not abandon the infant Norma Jean and had no intention of ever giving her up. Her goal in life was to make a proper home for her daughter, and this she finally did; but not until the child was seven years old.

Nevertheless, it isn't difficult to see why Marilyn might look back upon her childhood and believe that she had been a deserted orphan. By the time she was weaned Norma Jean was placed with Ida and Wayne Bolender in the almost rural suburb of Hawthorne. The Bolenders weren't strangers; their modest but comfortable home was across the street from Gladys's mother and they were a respectable, God-fearing couple. For their part, as America's economic crisis deepened, they also needed the money Gladys provided for her daughter's keep. Norma Jean lived quite happily with the Bolenders. She was well fed and cared for, was sent to school, had piano lessons and was visited most weekends, for a few hours at least, by a pretty woman who brought her presents and was called her mother.

The summer of 1933 was a good one for both mother and daughter.

*Norma Jean and
the Bolenders'
young son*

Gladys was close to her dream of buying a house and she felt confident
enough to talk to Norma Jean of her plans when they went to the beach
together during her Saturday visits. In the autumn Norma Jean said
goodbye to the Bolenders and she and her mother moved into their new
home. Gladys, however, could not afford the repayments on the house
on her own and she had arranged for lodgers to move in too, keeping two
rooms for herself and Norma Jean. The tenants were English and also in
the movie business; she as a registered 'dress' extra and he as George
Arliss's stand-in. Their grown-up daughter lived with them too, and
eventually became Madeleine Carroll's stand-in. They smoked, drank,
played poker and did not go to church. They weren't 'bad' people, but
they were a world removed from Hawthorne.

Gladys's happiness at the end of her seven-year struggle didn't last
long. She had been so eager, to the point of desperation, to set up home

with Norma Jean that the circumstances under which she finally achieved it were highly unsuitable. Since before her daughter's birth she had lived frugally, and mostly alone, spurred on by hopes for the perfect little home where she would be able to bring up Norma Jean, probably with a new husband and certainly happily ever after. Reality was disappointingly different. Her own house was not her home and her baby daughter was by now an intelligent, boisterous girl who had to be contained within their two rooms and always reminded of her best behaviour. On top of that, Gladys had to work as hard as ever for what quickly seemed like a dubious reward, and her freedom, just about the only advantage of her former way of life, was curtailed to the point of extinction. Although an attractive and sought-after woman, Gladys's bouts of depression and introspective withdrawal had generally caused men friends to fade away after a few months. Now, with every corner of her life filled with small daughter or tenants, a new permanent relationship became a distant prospect.

By the beginning of 1934 Gladys's depression had become profound. She had failed to provide a home for Norma Jean, failed to find herself a husband and, slowly but surely, she felt she was 'going mad' just like her mother, brother and father before her. The future could never have looked more bleak. One morning when Norma Jean was at school, Gladys finally buckled under the weight of her own hopes and expectations. Her depression turned to hysteria, an ambulance was called and after a struggle she was taken under heavy restraint, then sedation, to hospital. After observation she was diagnosed as suffering from paranoid schizophrenia – just like her parents. She was transferred to Norwalk asylum where her mother had died seven years before. When Norma Jean got home from school she discovered that her mother had 'gone to hospital for a while' and that the tenants would take some kind of care of her. Gladys had one good friend in Grace McKee, a fellow employee at Consolidated who was to commit suicide by barbiturate overdose in 1953. For a few weeks the company continued to pay Gladys's salary to Grace who doled it out to the English couple for Norma Jean's keep. When they were no longer able to maintain payments on the house, it was repossessed by the bank, and for a short time Norma Jean lived with them in a small apartment. Eventually they returned to England and Norma Jean was put into County care with Grace McKee named as guardian. Although Grace visited the child regularly and took a genuine, rather than merely official, responsibility for her, it seems that her pending marriage to 'Doc' Goddard and the care of his three children by a previous marriage prevented her from taking Norma Jean into her home right away. From the asylum Gladys insisted that her daughter was not to be put up for adoption, even when there were two confirmed offers: she hung on to her conviction that she would eventually make a proper home for her daughter, but with the best intentions, Gladys was condemning Norma Jean to a childhood of continual upheaval. One way or another it fell to

Norma Jean to look after herself.

From that point until her marriage at sixteen to Jim Dougherty, Norma Jean no longer belonged to anyone, and it was the experience of those years after her short-lived home with her mother that gave rise to her bitter memories of Gladys. At the time she had been told only that her mother had had a nervous breakdown, and that didn't seem sufficient to warrant what she saw as total rejection. At the age of nine, Norma Jean was committed to the care of the Los Angeles Orphans' Home Society. She could read the sign and knew what 'orphan' meant. She had to be dragged into the building, and her cries of 'I'm *not* an orphan' were quieted only when the other children came to stare. Despite the later assurances of the staff that the home was much like any other and that they tried their best for the kids, Norma Jean remembered it with a deep and fearful loathing.

It wasn't until early 1938 that Grace, now Mrs Doc Goddard, felt settled enough with her new home and family to ask Norma Jean to stay with them on a permanent basis. The ebullient little girl who had been known to stand up on the seat in a diner and sing 'Jesus Loves Me This I Know' right through for the Bolenders and other customers was a long way from the quiet, introspective creature who, for a few months at least, was nicknamed 'Mouse' by the Goddards. She shared a bedroom with Doc's daughter Beebe, who was the same age as Norma Jean and who had suffered similar disruption during the course of her parents' divorce. It took Norma Jean a long time to regain any kind of confidence, but as with her years with the Bolenders, being taken in by the Goddards gave her a second period of stability, and she finally responded with the resilience which marked her whole life.

Biographers and commentators continually portray the adult Marilyn as seeking a father figure to replace the one she never had. Clark Gable and Arthur Miller, co-star and husband, are cited as the fantasy on the one hand and realisation on the other. However, all the information, written but never emphasised, points to the fact that she most fiercely and successfully sought to construct mother-daughter and familial relationships with other women and their families. Grace Goddard's elderly aunt, Ana Lower, was the first of these and her influence on the young Norma Jean was profound. Another enduring aspect of the Marilyn image is the way in which she could discard people when their usefulness to her was at an end. Such an impulse could again be differently interpreted as a refined method of self-preservation when life's one sure lesson so far has been trust and love nobody, they will all leave, reject, die or simply not be there in the end. Marilyn's way of not sinking in her turbulent life was to let go the moment she suspected betrayal, but not before she had the next handhold in her grasp. It ensured that she remained afloat while at the same time reduced the chances of being abandoned, even in a small way, yet again. Ana Lower would never reject nor willingly leave her; only her death in 1948 ended the longest and mutually least exploitative relationship in Norma Jean's young life.

Norma Jean had moved in with Ana after Doc Goddard had made a grab for her after several drinks too many. By that time she was fourteen, had reached her adult height of five feet six, and was already 'well developed'. A year later Grace sought to place her outside the family once again: Doc had been promoted and the family had to move to West Virginia. The County support money for Norma Jean would cease if she left California, and the Goddards could not afford to keep her without it. Marriage to the boy next door was the solution. Jim Dougherty was a pleasant, eligible young man with a job and a car of his own; he needed no help finding girlfriends or indeed a wife. Accounts vary as to whether Norma Jean was in love with him, whether they were in love with each other, or whether they married, then found something to be 'in love' with in each other. Norma Jean was still fifteen and Jim eighteen when the plan was first tabled by Grace. In the event she was given away by Ana at a ceremony in their apartment living room a few weeks after her sixteenth birthday in 1942. The Goddards had already moved to West Virginia and sent a telegram of congratulations, but the Bolenders were there and it was a happy occasion. The newly wed Doughertys were relatively untouched by the Second World War until Jim, embarrassed by his safe billet on Catalina Island, finally shipped out on a freighter bound for Australia and the Far East. He took care to ensure that Norma Jean was safely ensconced with his parents, then he was gone.

For a while she continued her daily routine of conscientious housework and occasional trips to the beach – much curtailed by fuel rationing – but finally she managed to get a job with her mother-in-law at the Radio Plane factory. Her first assignment was on the parachute packing line. She quickly became proficient, and bored, and transferred to the spraying plant where fuselage fabric was prepared for aircraft. In later years a journalist turned the transfer request into a sacking after her sloppy work had caused the death of an airman when his parachute failed to open! In fact the only hostility Norma Jean encountered was similar to that faced by her own mother in the film cutting room years before and was caused by her own zealous attitude to work: when she was awarded a certificate for excellence by the management the other women responded with a collective cold shoulder.

Norma Jean had no reason, other than the usual dreaming over movie magazines, to believe that she had any future outside the commonplace, but she was also increasingly aware of herself and always made the best of what she had. When an army photographer visited the factory and wanted a model in his shots he headed unerringly for Norma Jean. Private David Conover spent three days photographing her in various modes of work all over the plant. Another photographer saw the pictures and was so taken with the young woman that he sought her out for a weekend's colour shooting. These pictures were put in front of Emmeline Snively, whose Blue Book Agency was the one with which any aspiring model sought to sign. Miss Snively sent Norma Jean a brochure for her three-month modelling course and she grabbed at the opportunity. She reported sick at the factory and went off at Miss Snively's instruction to an industrial show where, as a stand hostess, the ten dollars a day enabled her to work, attend the course each evening and pay her way. After the first photo session others followed – spasmodically, but often enough to buoy her optimism and new-found belief in herself. She also began to learn about the camera.

By 1946 young Norma Jean Dougherty's exuberant face and figure had appeared on forces magazine covers and in various other guises nation-wide: in her own mind she was definitely getting somewhere. After a

Early cheesecake

childhood of little or no positive self-image this new person was something she could work at. She was living with the ageing but supportive Ana again, learning as avidly as financial restrictions permitted and was changing rapidly. One important development, in which she was backed by Ana, was divorce from Jim. Another world of possibilities had been opened up for her by Emmeline Snively and the photographers who were by now saying to her, in some form or other, honey, you should be in pictures. Miss Snively introduced her protegée to Helen Ainsworth's National Concert Artists Corporation and, after an interview at which the most enduring memory of Norma Jean was her lack of confidence and extreme nervousness, they took her onto their books. Throughout her life and career Norma Jean displayed an astonishing capacity to take courage from the most insignificant gesture of belief in her potential ability. The signing by the agency was a good example: on the strength of it she pressed her best print cotton frock, combed out her long (and by now definitely golden) hair and took herself off to the offices of Ben Lyon, the head of casting at Twentieth Century Fox.

If Norma Jean thought she finally had one foot on the ladder when Fox screen-tested her, it was only to find that the ladder was propped against a brick wall. Head of production Darryl F. Zanuck was sufficiently taken by her appearance to have her placed on the usual six-month option contract, but in truth the policy of the studios was similar to that employed by trawler fishermen: scoop up everything that wriggles. She was put on the studio payroll in August 1947 at $75 a week, less than she'd been making as a model. At the end of her first six months she had acquired only a new name. Ben Lyon didn't think that Norma Jean Dougherty had much billboard appeal. He favoured 'Marilyn' after the stage musical star Marilyn Miller. Norma Jean, eager to please, didn't object but suggested her grandmother's name to complete it.

For almost a year she attended voice classes, movement classes and drama classes. With other hopefuls she was photographed at parties, restaurants, premieres, conventions, exhibitions and trade shows, but nowhere near a sound stage. Whatever Ben Lyon and Zanuck had seen in Marilyn (a quality grandly described later as 'flesh appeal') it was probably nothing more than the appeal of a cute broad with a great figure who might come in useful *but* whose main qualification had been a chance attack of boldness which had led her into Lyon's office in the first place. Fox had no need of what they could comprehend only as 'another blonde': they already had Betty Grable and a second-string version in June Haver. But Marilyn was eventually assigned a three-scene debut in a Haver comedy, winningly entitled *Scudda Hoo Scudda Hay*. By the time it was released in the spring of 1948, her contribution had been all but lost to the cutting-room floor.

In the next few years Fox used her as a prop or window dressing in any number of forgettable productions, but despite these minimal efforts, the young starlet commanded press and public attention out of all proportion to her screen achievements. She also netted good reviews for her parts in the 1949 classic *Asphalt Jungle* and in *All About Eve*, made the following year. In 1952, between publicity appearances, poses and other risible roles, she was loaned to RKO for the screen adaptation of Clifford Odets' *Clash By Night*. The result gave rise to the gurgles of praise and surprise which were to become standard critical response to a dramatic performance by Monroe. Finally, later that same year, Fox put her in *Don't Bother To Knock*. It was her first official starring role and by the end of the year it should have been obvious that she was not only an actress of some ability but also a star of extraordinary pulling power. In 1953 she and her friend Jane Russell were recorded placing their hand and footprints in the cement outside Grauman's Chinese theatre. They had just made *How To Marry A Millionaire* together with Lauren Bacall and Betty Grable. In that company Marilyn had begun to realise and revel in her growing status. The exalted position of her co-stars also resulted in extreme nervousness and the inevitable lateness which was to become a trademark of Monroe-in-trouble.

With the benefit of hindsight and the freedom of what is, in 1986, admissable evidence, it is now easier to see that Marilyn's erratic behaviour and chronic insecurity had causes that not only went far back into early childhood, but were also attributable to her experiences as a struggling actress in Hollywood. Along with her stints as a model and hostess, she also earned the rent or a square meal in the oldest way open to a woman in those bit-part years. It was no big deal – except in the tightlipped moral climate of the 'family' oriented post-war 1950s. What did make a difference, both to Marilyn's enduring perception of her own worth and the perception of the industry men who effectively controlled her career, was the nonchalant use of the casting couch.

In 1954, after a great deal of indecision and a press-dogged 'courtship' Marilyn was able to say to a journalist friend, with evident triumph and relief, 'I've sucked my last cock', when her engagement to all-American baseball hero, Joe DiMaggio was announced. Joe was quite unlike any of the men she had known hitherto. Quiet, old-fashioned, a 'man's man' and proud of the Italian virtues of his tough San Francisco-Sicilian background. He was also as famous as Marilyn and one day when she breathlessly asked him if he had *any* idea what it was like to have ten thousand fans stand up and roar for you, he was able to recall his career with the New York Yankees and say yes, seventy-five thousand Yankee fans had stood for him on a hundred occasions. Above all, Joe seemed to offer a solid kind of devotion and – most of the time – it was what Marilyn felt she needed.

Although a fishing trip to a remote mountain cabin marked the beginning of their marriage, it didn't long continue in this idyllic vein, and indeed it could not; Joe and Marilyn were two of the most famous

and sought after people in America – and in the Far East too. Joe's fans in Japan meant that he was soon scheduled to visit there. The State Department meanwhile had made enquiries about Marilyn's availability for a tour to boost the morale of US troops stationed in Korea. Joe quickly and reluctantly realised that he would have to get used to sharing his wife with millions of other joes. Whilst Marilyn had – and would – make efforts to sit quietly in the background when her husband was being Joltin' Joe DiMaggio, hero of the ballpark, taking a back seat to his wife wasn't a lesson Joe ever put much heart into learning. Marilyn's Korean war effort, singing and joking on makeshift, wintry, outdoor platforms, did for the boys what Betty Grable had done for the Second World War, and skimpily clad as ever, she returned to Joe and home with mild pneumonia.

Back in San Francisco Marilyn tried hard to play the wife and home-maker, but as Joe's idea of fun was beer and sports on TV whilst Marilyn went about her domestic duties, it quickly palled. From her point of view it was a difficult situation to come to grips with, she was twenty-eight and the most sought after woman in America. Much as she yearned for a home, family and security, she also craved success as an actress. The pull of the latter – with the full weight of Hollywood behind it – was soon irresistible. The marriage came to an end quickly with the making and release of *The Seven Year Itch*. The film, directed by Billy Wilder, con-firmed Marilyn's ability as a comic actress and also provided one of Hollywood's most enduring icons when she stood over a New York subway grating and her full white skirt swirled up around her ecstatically laughing face.

For Joe it symbolised everything he would not tolerate about his wife's relationship with both her body and her public. He walked angrily away from the location during the shooting of the scene. Their marriage had not lasted a year, but he remained a constant prop and presence in her life, and after her death.

By 1955 Marilyn's dissatisfaction with Hollywood was deep. Her grow-ing desire to improve herself, coupled with her frustration at the endless stream of dumb blonde roles she was offered by Twentieth Century Fox, was further compounded by increasing resentment at the financial terms of her contract. It had meant that whilst sharing top billing with Jane Russell for *Gentlemen Prefer Blondes* (in 1952), her salary had been $18,000 to Russell's $100,000. That the studio had now started calling her 'Miss Monroe', in recognition of her star status, also made her even more determined to show Hollywood that she had well and truly escaped the casting couch. With the encouragement and backing of New York friends, Milton and Amy Greene, she stunned the film capital by turning her back on the studios and taking an extremely avant garde step: the setting up of her own independent film company – Marilyn Monroe Productions – with offices in New York and Milton Greene as vice president.

Marilyn and Greene were able to secure her release from the crippling contract with Fox as well as some startling concessions: she would only be required to make one film a year for them and she would have approval over the choice of director as well as script consultation. With all that on paper she was free to spend a year on the East Coast and her desired learning process. It led her to the influential Actors' Studio where Lee and Paula Strasberg propounded the Stanislavsky Method to the thinking talent of the day. Marilyn tentatively joined the class, as anonymous as she could be in sweater, slacks and dark glasses with her hair scraped back in bunches. She was scoffed at by the press and regarded with suspicion and derision by other actors, but later that year the first fruits

Arthur and Marilyn

of her efforts (and Marilyn Monroe Productions' first project) became public in the role of Cherie, the 'shantoose' from the Ozarks, in Joshua Logan's *Bus Stop*.

Any question about her ability should have been answered once and for all with that role, but it didn't work out that way. Marilyn's image as a pin-up girl and piece of studio property was a long time dying with the Fox men. It was the same with her singing. Marilyn was a much better singer than she is given credit for, and her very first review in October 1948 had actually focused on that talent. An appearance in Columbia's *Ladies of the Chorus* in which she sang 'Every Baby Needs a Da-Da-Daddy' drew the following comment from the *Motion Picture Herald*: 'One of the brightest spots is Miss Monroe's singing. She's pretty, and with her pleasing voice and style, shows promise.' Marilyn was never going to be a great innovative singer, but many an actress was allowed to use her voice and develop her talent in a way that was forbidden Marilyn by her image makers. If she was going to be everyone's idea of a dumb blonde then she was going to sound like one too, and she was never encouraged to take it further. In the same way that her aspirations towards serious dramatic acting were generally ridiculed, so it has been deemed inconceivable that she might ever have been a good singer. Yet 'Heatwave', 'Diamonds Are A Girl's Best Friend', 'I'm Gonna File My Claim' and, particularly, 'A Fine Romance' all indicate that she might well have taken her vocal potential as far as Judy Holliday, the dumb blonde who fought back, and who not only launched one of the great standards 'The Party's Over', but with the encouragement of her lover Gerry Mulligan also went on to co-write and sing an album of songs with him. Just as Janis Joplin's uncompromisingly sexual performances always turned off the serious music critics, so Marilyn's equally dangerous image as seductress blinded most to her real potential.

Director Joshua Logan was one of those who did see and, more importantly, understand what Marilyn had to offer. He was not one of those who scoffed at her seeking after the inner truths of the Method – he had worked under Stanislavsky in Russia himself. Although the making of *Bus Stop* wasn't easy, and Marilyn's insecurity and deep unease often made work impossible, he never stopped singing her praises and in his not inconsiderable opinion, she was the greatest ever. *Bus Stop* was well received, and Marilyn felt at last that she was forcing the movie establishment to afford her a measure of the respect she craved. It also meant that she went into the next film with high hopes, and Joshua Logan had already given her next director the benefit of his own insight and experience of working with a fully creative Monroe.

Adapted from Terence Rattigan's play 'The Sleeping Prince', *The Prince and the Showgirl*, on paper, with Laurence Olivier as co-star and director, looked like a logical progression for her ambitions. In reality the experience was an unhappy one. She arrived in England with her husband of two weeks, playwright Arthur Miller. The British press went crazy, and neither Olivier nor his wife Vivien Leigh could be seen for popping flash bulbs and overflowing superlatives. Miller smiled enigmatically. He was already accustomed to life in Marilyn's goldfish bowl, and he was also sure enough of his own position to be content with the reflected glow of his wife's presence. But somewhere along the line Olivier's approach to the task of director brought the project to near disaster. Marilyn was already notorious for her lateness and insistence on perfection, in her own work at least. It was always exaggerated by insecurity; and an early exchange between director and star began the downward spiral. Olivier, in a jokey reference to her screen persona, walked on set one morning and instructed his star: 'OK Marilyn, be sexy.'

Aware of Olivier's huge reputation and the fact that his beautiful wife had already played the role to acclaim on the London stage, a tense Monroe failed to detect the intended humour. She crumbled into confusion, bewilderment, then panic. Insomnia and fright took over with a vengeance and she became ill. It was a classic Monroe reaction and no one appeared able to reassure her out of it. *The Prince and the Showgirl* over-ran its budget and schedule; on release it received its share of critical raspberries, yet Marilyn had never looked better and had been deftly directed by her co-star to shine in their double act. She was nominated for and received a handful of continental film awards and was recalled by co-star Dame Sybil Thorndyke with fondness; the same could not be said for star and director.

In 1957 Arthur Miller was required to testify before the House Committee on Un-American Activities. He refused to name names and was fined $500 with a thirty-day suspended sentence. Fox tried to keep Marilyn out of that particular spotlight but she went with her husband to Washington and further branded herself as some kind of unsavoury trouble in the eyes of Hollywood. In August she suffered a miscarriage and spent the rest of the year in seclusion at the farm they had bought in Connecticut.

Marilyn's desire for a child would eventually become obsessive and the loss of this one, a boy, was a severe blow. That she could ever have carried a child to term must be considered doubtful as it seems likely that she had already had possibly twelve abortions as well as continual menstrual and gynaecological problems. Nevertheless, her empathy with children meant that they gravitated to her unerringly and she established affectionate relationships with both DiMaggio's and Miller's children by previous marriages.

In 1958 Billy Wilder presented her with the script of *Some Like It Hot* and the role of Sugar Kane. Meanwhile Arthur Miller was not writing, despite spending hours closeted at his desk. He could not be persuaded from either the farm or his study in their New York apartment and Marilyn's boredom and guilt when she did disturb him were slowly souring into disillusionment and a dangerous realisation of just how *alone* she felt.

The first thing that happens to the 'star' is that she is, in her own lifetime, isolated as a unique personality. This is reinforced by the accepted images of The Star: the pin-up, the publicity still and the information which is made available to the public. They all serve to present the woman (and even that description is difficult because the impersonal, non-gender defined 'star' has come to seem so much more appropriate) in isolation, either quite literally in the posed pin-up, or as the epicentre of a contrived scene for a movie still. Even candid images are frequently taken from situations quite alien to the normal experience of the observer: in night clubs, arriving at or leaving an airport, getting into or out of a limousine – often with the subject caught unprepared and actually *looking* alienated. Very rarely is the woman represented by any everyday image easily recognisable by other women or by herself. She is always presented as either perfectly groomed and glamorous, or as the very opposite, dishevelled and unhappy to the edge of distraction. Her life, that which occupies her when she is not before the cameras, is never seen. The rare exception occurs when an image, like that fixed early on for Doris Day, required that she be portrayed in such a context: at home with her child. Yet even that seemingly guileless, homespun presentation was loaded. Warner Brothers felt they had to downplay Doris's raunchy beginnings as a band-singer with a wife-beating trombonist and eventual suicide as the father of her small son. Then her status as a divorced mother required adjustment to their own perceived role for her as the good girl-next-door. The studio version of reality bore little relation to life, either Doris's or any other woman's.

For generations of women who have come after that star-making process, those carefully created images have had an even more distancing

effect. They began a process by which the strengths and positive aspects of the stars have been gradually and effectively obliterated. Doris Day's dramatic capabilities were effectively killed off by the girl-next-door image; it's difficult to find an image of Marilyn Monroe *doing* anything, except posing. Women like these are now represented for the most part as drunks, junkies, weirdos, inadequates, bitches, fools and ingrates. The men who surrounded them, either as husbands, lovers, managers or a combination of all three, are presented, usually by themselves or other male writers, as the long-suffering victims of monsters, gobbled up and spat out by harridans, or as luckless fools who were nevertheless thoroughly trampled by their personal Medusa.

To isolate a person in this way is to render her powerless and to refuse any kind of perception of her as a woman, a member of society. From the accounts available, it would be easy to believe that they existed in a cocoon of self-love, self-interest, indeed just plain *self*. They are rarely pictured with each other, which is to say that officially released photographs always show them alone: and it is difficult to imagine them as friends, even though many were. It is easier (and common) to think of them as rivals, distrusting or disliking one another, because that is how the studios preferred it. It was also good for business if public interest could be aroused by an apparent feud between two women stars. Sisterly solidarity was not good box office: Betty Grable's kindness and compassion towards her clearly intended successor was not what the publicity department wanted to hear and not what it leaked out to the public. That neither Grable nor Lauren Bacall could be drawn into criticisms of Marilyn during *How To Marry A Millionaire* was a similar source of frustration. In the wider context of America in the late 1940s and 1950s, it was not in the interests of that society for its female role models to be seen placing their allegiance anywhere but with their men, whether he was Darryl F. Zanuck or a husband.

When Marilyn Monroe began in her way to refuse the American dream, she was punished, as was Frances Farmer before her; neither was unusual in that, merely obvious. These young women had everything that their society held dear: money, fame, beauty and the adulation of millions. When this proved insufficient, their rebellion was not only an insult to the industry and the audience who had bestowed such riches but was also, and more gravely, an overt threat to the underpinnings of the society: if this zenith, striven for and romanticised throughout the nation's history and of which Hollywood itself was an exemplary micro-cosm, then what price America itself?

Marilyn compounded her sin by being a stupid broad who hankered after intellectuals. She wanted to learn, and she sought out books and the people she felt had the key to what they contained. That many of these people found her to be anything but stupid was neither consolation nor even a source of pride to the Hollywood men who found her ambitions so threatening. A frontier society has little room for intellectuals and Hollywood Americans were too insecure to see such people as anything but trouble. To cut down to size the fear of the unknown, intellectuals were deemed tainted by homosexuality or communism or both (and often rumoured of Marilyn) and the suspicion that they in their turn despised the honest, God-fearing citizen left no room for generous consideration of Marilyn's aspirations.

Her frustrations with her career were enormous in spite of, and often because of, Marilyn Monroe Productions. No matter what she may have hoped or believed at its inception, the company could not give her true independence from the Hollywood machine. At the height of her greatest fame she had but one way to influence her working life: like any other factory hand, the only effective weapon at her disposal was the withdrawal of her labour. She did this by means of extraordinary lateness, illness and sometimes downright no-show. Just as in other industries, her employers got back at her by withholding salary, benefits and further work. Marilyn was aware of her importance to the studio and of the fact of her stardom, but her ego was undermined by an equally powerful insecurity, which meant that her fragile sense of self could easily be damaged by the insensitive or uncaring approach.

Her attitude towards men and sex also made her peculiarly vulnerable when coupled with her frail psyche. In one crucial way she was very much a woman of her time: she continually sought the One Great Love, the shining knight who would love, protect and fulfil her every need. But her every experience of the sexual act, aside from the other-world of marriage to Jim Dougherty, was of use and abuse. More than one lover reported her to be 'a lousy lay' and this assessment was frequently and anonymously bandied about. Even the mythical knight would have been hard put to fulfil her needs: it's doubtful she ever understood that she might legitimately have any. Orgasms were rare, satisfaction most likely to come from knowing she had, in some way at least, lived up to her image as the ultimate sexual being, the heavenly enchantress, the object of Everyman's desires. Unfortunately for Marilyn, the age of the caring (male) lover was still some years in the future. 'How was it for you?' was a rhetorical rather than realistic question; whilst the definition of a good time in bed was the male prerogative and probably not something that Marilyn would have dreamed of demanding for herself.

Paradoxically the world's greatest sex goddess had a lousy sex life and it served only to heighten her feelings of failure and rejection. And as a consequence, rejection was exceptionally hard to take. When she suspected it, her defences sprang into the action that others would call self-destruction. Indeed, the enduring memory of Marilyn today is of a woman who was bent on destruction, and succeeded. But as Susie Orbach points out in *Fat Is A Feminist Issue*, 'feminism has taught us that activities that appear to be self-destructive are invariably adaptations, attempts to

171

cope with the world . . .'

Marilyn's protective mechanisms, perfected since childhood against an uncaring and unreliable world, may well have been sufficient to carry her through life but for two things: her profession and drugs. The industry in which she was engaged had no room and no means of providing room for the ultra-sensitive, unguarded personality. The very essence of what made Marilyn's screen presence so appealing and so powerful was also the most dangerous aspect for her mental health and physical well-being. Giving her best performance meant stripping away protective layers which she had been busily constructing for most of her life. The combination of continual questioning and rebuilding of a persona of which she was fundamentally unsure, together with the physical and mental pressures of the film set, were frequently overwhelming. It was exacerbated by her increasingly indiscriminate use (parallel with Judy Garland's) of 'medication'.

Marilyn's insomnia was the crippling symptom of her insecurity. For years her bedroom, wherever she was living, was furnished with the heaviest blackout drapes at the window and dozens of pill bottles at the bedside along with new scripts and the inexhaustible flow of books that always accompanied her waking hours. As the years went by her tolerance of dangerous drugs became dangerously high, making accidental overdose and a semi-comatose state a frighteningly commonplace occurence. Coupled with the primary effects of massive doses of tranquillisers and sleeping pills, were the side effects – still relatively unappreciated at that time – of depression, general malaise and feelings of paranoia. But in the late 1950s it was not part of the culture or working way of life to question whether the 'problem' might lie elsewhere than at her own selfish star's feet. It has been said of the last years of her life that if she had been anyone but Marilyn Monroe she would have been certified and institutionalised, it could also be said that if she had been anyone but the world's most famous star to whom nothing was refused if she had the dollars to pay, she would not have required the attentions of an institution. As it is, despite the almost constant attention and care of a responsible psychiatrist and physician, she was always able to secure prescriptions for huge amounts of drugs, primarily and most dangerously, Nembutal.

After a hot summer on location at Coronado, California for *Some Like It Hot*, Marilyn miscarried again just before Christmas 1958. She had been in constant trouble on the set as she struggled to perfect one of the all-time great film comedy performances, achieved by multiple retakes during which she got better and better, but which co-star Tony Curtis believed had destroyed his own spontaneous style. He had grown to loathe her in consequence and later commented that kissing her had been like kissing Hitler. It was a fairly strong statement coming from a Jew and has not been tempered by time. Once again, however, the finished on-screen product of Marilyn's agonising was incandescent and timeless. Meanwhile the Miller-Monroe marriage was by then perceptibly crumbling and as was always her way, Marilyn reached for affirmation wherever she found it. Her underlying insecurity and need for proof of her powers of attraction meant that despite the prevailing social mores, sexual fidelity was never her strong suit. She had engaged in long running, if spasmodic affairs throughout her long 'courtship' with Joe DiMaggio and even after it was publicly announced that she was to marry *him*, she had already told a colleague that she planned to marry Arthur Miller one day. Then, whilst conducting a year-long secret affair with Miller before their marriage, she had also found time for any number of other more or less casual bed relationships.

In 1960 there was yet another brief and dangerously unsatisfactory respite from loneliness for Marilyn when Yves Montand was signed to co-star with her in another comedy. *Let's Make Love* was not a success: Montand was out of his depth in every way, and the affair between them created a minor scandal until he fled back to France and the safe haven of his wife, Simone Signoret. Marilyn's belief that Montand would eventually marry her was some time dying however, in a pattern of the impractical and unrealisable fantasy that would fatally re-assert itself two years later. Now, whatever his own wishes might have been, Arthur Miller was unable to breach the chill that had set in, even though he was by then engaged in writing a screenplay for his wife.

The 1960 production of *The Misfits* was a harrowing experience for all concerned. From mid-July it gathered together a glittering line-up of talent in what was seen as Miller's tribute to and acknowledgement of Marilyn's dramatic ability. The rest of the cast included Clark Gable, Eli Wallach and Montgomery Clift. The director was John Huston, for whom Marilyn had worked years earlier in *Asphalt Jungle*. On the face of it, all the signs pointed towards a major movie success. In reality (and in retrospect) *The Misfits* can be seen as a remarkably cruel piece of writing. It required Marilyn to go before the camera and virtually flay alive her inner self. The harsh desert location, near Reno, Nevada, was equally unforgiving and delay piled on delay as the star of the piece struggled to deliver of herself through a haze of barbiturates and terror.

In November, the shoot finally over, the Millers returned to New York – on different planes – and on 11 November the press announced their impending divorce. A few days later Clark Gable died of a massive heart attack. Audible whispers laid the blame at Marilyn's feet because of the much-prolonged desert shoot; Marilyn was inconsolable. The following spring however, Gable's widow Kay specifically invited Marilyn to the christening service for her baby son John Clark Gable – born months after his father's death. It was Joe DiMaggio who picked up the pieces once again at Christmas 1960; then in February when the hoped-for success with *The Misfits* evaporated into stinging reviews, Marilyn was admitted to a New York clinic to de-toxify. She found to her horror that there were bars on her window and she was locked in. The spectres of Gladys and of grandmother Della Monroe Grainger howled and Marilyn could not, would not, rest. She wrote a frantic letter to Lee and Paula Strasberg, begging them to get her out, but in the end it was the ever-faithful Joe who secured her transfer to a less frightening environment. In June, after further hospital treatment – to remove her gall bladder – and after spending enough time in DiMaggio's company to kindle the remarriage rumours, Marilyn returned to California looking as well as she had for a long time.

In 1963, while researching for his book *Goddess*, Anthony Summers spoke to Dr Lee Siegel. He had once been a Twentieth Century Fox studio doctor and had treated, among others, both Marilyn and Judy Garland. His memory of the stars' 'medication' habits is illuminating: 'In those days pills were seen as another tool to keep stars working. The doctors were caught in the middle. If one doctor would not prescribe, there was always another who would. When I first treated Marilyn, back in the early 1950s, everyone was using pills.'

Whether or not Marilyn was addicted to the contents of her pill bag, what she did crave was sleep and release from the ever-present loneliness and sense of failure brought about by her lack of a permanent partner. At thirty-six Marilyn had reached the age when in movie industry terms she was past it. Betty Grable lost out to Marilyn at around that age, and Alice Faye before her, and so on down the line. Photographer Eve Arnold said of her 'she had lost the contours of a young woman by then . . . but she refused to acknowledge her body was becoming mature'. It was a curious statement and perhaps says more about what was then – and now – perceived as a desirable and ideal female body. Nevertheless, Bert Stern's photographs for *Vogue* from about the same time tell another story, as does the shoot from the set of *Something's Got To Give*. Those pictures reveal a vibrantly beautiful woman, complete with crows' feet and laughter lines and still, two decades on, breathtakingly lovely. Beneath the surface however, the downward spiral of barbiturate-depression had not been halted; moreover she had unknowingly drifted perilously far out of her depth in a milieu that was possibly even more vicious in its attitude to women than show business.

From its earliest days much of Hollywood's funding had come from organised crime. The movie business offered not only the possibility of huge profits, but also the irresistible glitter of Stars. And where the mobsters went, politicians weren't very far behind, either in hot pursuit or hand in glove. John F. Kennedy came to the presidency of the United States on a joyous tide of romantic hopes for a new era of civil rights, social responsibility and a clearly stated intent to make America a country fit for such an heroic figure. At his side, in the post of Attorney General, was his younger brother Robert. Between them they intended to rid their country of what they saw to be its number one cancer: organised crime.

To the public they were glittering figures, as starry as anything ever produced by Hollywood, and inevitably the two worlds were drawn together.

Reality has never been Hollywood's strong point and its entire existence encouraged the pursuit of fantasy, grandiose or otherwise. So rarefied was the atmosphere in which its golden people moved that any desire or passing whim could be translated into fact and as quickly undone if it pleased the princes and princesses. It could also reveal itself as a cruel illusion, and Marilyn's life was spent swinging back and forth between the extremes of having and lacking. By the beginning of the 1960s it seems clear now that she thought, not unreasonably for the symbol of American sexuality, that she could have America's symbol of family manhood. What she neglected or refused to understand was that the President (and to a lesser extent, his brother) was as long accustomed to Hollywood-style sexual relationships as any studio mogul. Given the prevailing moral climate of the times, Kennedy's indiscriminate sexual habits show a breathtaking disregard for the possibilities of scandal, or merely the inborn arrogance of a silver-spooned self-made aristocrat.

Of all the men she could have chosen, the President embodied both the dream and the nightmare elements of her adult life: a godlike consort for a goddess at first glance. In reality Kennedy was a powerful, ruthless man who was not about to jeopardise his own great American Dream for any broad. The Attorney General followed his brother into bed with Marilyn but was not quite the bedroom cavalier that made John Kennedy notorious. Nevertheless, it didn't stop him meeting Marilyn, with little attempt at secrecy, even after receiving clear warnings from his department that he and his brother were prime targets for a smear and exposure campaign that was likely to be instigated by the crime leaders the Attorney General was pledged to destroy. At the time of Marilyn's death there were half-hearted rumours and the predictable scandal sheet allegations of murder, suicide and famous name involvement. Nothing came of any of these murmurs and it wasn't until Anthony Summers began a new and thorough research at the beginning of the 1980s – twenty years after her death – that the truths and the reasons for the silences became clear at last.

The tangled, seamy machinations that surrounded Marilyn's 'private life' still have an aura of incredibility, despite Watergate and all that is now known about the extent of 'dirty tricks' work that goes on in the vicinity of power and money. In 1961 it was still possible, and in Marilyn's case, probable that any suspicions she might have voiced about her phone being tapped, her house bugged, that she was followed, or that she received threatening anonymous phone calls, would be treated as paranoia and the actions of a woman who was determined to put herself at the centre of concerned attention no matter what. Her unhappiness as she began to understand that there was no future for her, other than as a plaything, with either Kennedy brother, was then compounded by real

fear that something was going to happen to her. The possibility that harm might be done by the Mafia could not have escaped her mind. Many of the night spots and watering holes that she frequented were owned by organised crime, and it is also highly likely that many of her long conversations with Bobby Kennedy would have been about his aspirations towards the mobs.

In her despair at being so easily discarded by her two shining white knights Marilyn began to talk freely both about the relationship she had shared with them and about the notebooks she had kept of what had passed between herself and her lovers. It was not a wise course of action to take, but Marilyn was too outraged and unhappy for wisdom. She also began making fresh plans for her future. Her major disintegration over the loss of her 'lover' – the President – had coincided with the beginning of shooting *Something's Got To Give*. Initially she had not liked the script but champagne and a persuasive evening with scriptwriter Nunnally Johnson, a man she trusted, had secured her agreement; but it was destined to go nowhere. 'Illness' kept Marilyn away from the set more often than not, and the film began to run away from its schedule. Then on 19 May she was not only absent but on the other side of the continent. She had flown to Washington to sing the world's most memorable version of 'Happy Birthday To You' for President John F. Kennedy's forty-fifth.

It was a political rather than social occasion: a glittering array of entertainers had been gathered together to provide the bait to bring in rich Democrats willing to pay hundreds of dollars a ticket for party funds. Marilyn was in exalted company: other names on the bill included Ella Fitzgerald, Peggy Lee and Maria Callas. Nevertheless, it was Marilyn, terrified, drunk, sewn into her shimmering silver sheath, who walked away with the show. The next day she flew back to Los Angeles and the day after that, Monday, she was on set to film the 'nude swimming sequence' immortalised by the stills photographers.

On her own birthday, 1 June, she appeared with Joe DiMaggio at a ball game, tossed the first ball and looked radiant, having been given a huge cake and on-set party at Fox. A week later she was fired and Lee Remick was signed to take over her role. Marilyn retired to her newly acquired hacienda in Brentwood amid a flurry of suits and counter-suits, to sit out her punishment.

It was a time of fear and transition in Hollywood, as television transformed the old studio hegemony beyond all recognition. The industry was changing, faltering, groping for new directions: scapegoats were required to appease the frights and huge losses that were being chalked up. Fox had just lost an unthinkable amount of money on the monster epic *Cleopatra* and, unlike Elizabeth Taylor, Marilyn had not publicly and dramatically nearly died in harness, and was therefore a much easier target for punishment. Like Judy, Marilyn's need for 'medication' grew to alarming proportions once again. Her insomnia was almost total and when she did sleep there was the other terror that she would not be able to the next night, or the night after that. She could not sleep without handfuls of capsules; she needed more to wake up, and even more to keep functioning. She was also able to obtain them with murderous ease and regularity in a situation where her well-being demanded just the opposite. On the day before she died she had acquired twenty-five Nembutal on prescription – without the knowledge of her psychiatrist, a man she saw sometimes seven days a week.

Marilyn died during the night of 4 August of a massive overdose of barbiturates. It was trumpeted as suicide, then as murder. The overdose that killed her would, on its own, have accounted for a large horse or half a dozen ordinary unaccustomed human beings. Her tolerance for the drugs had become impossibly high and it is most likely that a handful of extra pills, taken on top of a dose already fuzzily forgotten, finally proved too much for her system. It was the kind of accident which had happened to Marilyn before and may well have happened again if her calls for help had been heeded. Unfortunately it seems that the phone calls she made while slipping towards oblivion were to people who were only too familiar with her drug habits, or to whom she had become a pest – to be ignored in the belief that she would then go away. What happened during the night of 4 August is now a maze of lies, dead witnesses, silent witnesses and at the very centre, a cover-up and clean-up operation that had the Attorney General at its heart.

It seems Robert Kennedy, reckless as ever, may have answered Marilyn one last time; certainly his own fascination had been only dampened by the most severe warnings from others. And it is likely that he was not only in Los Angeles the night she died but that his presence, and the subsequent need to get him away before he was overwhelmed by potential scandal, is why Marilyn's death was never properly examined, why the evidence for suicide was so cursorily accepted, and why no subsequent investigation was ever successful: the relevant records, specimens of her own vital organs taken at the autopsy, and her personal notebooks, diaries and other papers, went missing within hours of her death and have never been found. It means that the possibility and allegation that she was murdered by the Mafia, to bring about the downfall by association of the Kennedys, could be neither proven nor discredited. Certainly there is enough room for conjecture in that direction and the truth may never be known.

From Marilyn's point of view there is something rather more positive to be said. Much has been made of the events leading up to her death in the vein of 'this was her last major public appearance', 'this was her last week of life', that the title *Something's Got To Give* was grimly prophetic and so on. But none of it could be said without hindsight, and hindsight was something Marilyn was certainly not employing at that time. She was indeed as depressed as she had ever been: in the circumstances of a double cold shoulder from America's golden boys, it's hardly surprising – but suicidal she was not. On the contrary, she was planning work for the future and had scheduled appointments for the following week to discuss new projects. She was more determined than ever to prove herself as the dramatic actress she knew she was and could be. Her Brentwood house was slowly being put together, and its half furnished, half finished state is not necessarily the environment of someone on the last downward slide, as the otherwise sympathetic Anthony Summers sees it, but perhaps the tentative and experimental nature of a project new to its owner. Despite her wealth and opportunities, the house was the first one to be bought by the one-time rootless orphan.

Like Judy, the deep-seated drug problem was at the root of her troubles and it was the one thing that no one around her had the will or ability to help her out of. It would be another two decades before Judy's daughter Liza could talk of how her own life and sanity had been saved at the Betty Ford Clinic. For Judy and Marilyn there was no proper help, and for Marilyn, despite the intense and loving support of her psychiatrist, it was release from her drug dependency that would have made the difference to her struggle for independence and adulthood. At the time she died Marilyn Monroe was still conducting that struggle and was in the process of setting herself up to be one of the great survivors.

Don't you expect any answers dear
'Cos I know they don't come with age . . .
Well I'm twenty-five years older now
So I know it just can't be right . . .
But it don't make no difference babe,
'Cos I know that I can always try,
There's a fire inside every person,
I'm gonna need it, I'm gonna hold it,
I'm gonna use it til the day I die.

'Kozmic Blues', Joplin and Mekler

When Marilyn Monroe died in August 1962, five of the women who comprise *A Star is Torn* were still living. Edith Piaf had just decided to marry Theo Sarapo; Dinah Washington had recently completed a two-week season at the fifteenth anniversary celebrations at Birdland, and Patsy Cline was one day away from the release of her third album 'Sentimentally Yours'. By the end of the following year they were all dead. During that summer of Marilyn's death, Judy Garland was in London filming *I Could Go On Singing*, and Janis Joplin was in Austin raising hell at the University of Texas. Seven years later Judy was dead too. It was 1969, the year Janis recorded the Garland standard 'Little Girl Blue', and *Rolling Stone* magazine asked: 'THE JUDY GARLAND OF ROCK'N'ROLL?' The following year she fulfilled their expectations and ended this line of women stars in the centenary of Marie Lloyd's birth.

Janis's twenty-seven years bore all the marks of the post-war generation that was said to have liberated itself via sex, drugs and rock'n'roll. Her adolescence was rebellious, her performance was overtly sexual in a raucous sweaty way and, along with millions of her peers, she experimented with numerous fashionable drugs before acquiring the heroin habit that eventually killed her.

Compared with the rest of the women in this book, Janis looked like, sounded like, talked like, someone from another era entirely. Yet with one battered silver shoe standing firmly in the present, Janis also trod the old familiar ground. Despite appearances, she was a classic in the line, and her life reiterated many of the conflicts of the women in this book. From her early teens onwards she deliberately created personae which dared to live on the wild side, but time and time again she drew back from these dangerous characters and just as deliberately tried to construct the conformist – the diligent, sober, middle-class girl who would eventually settle down to marriage and a family of her own. Whatever her various images of rebellion and independence may have done for a new generation of young women hungering for such a model, Janis succeeded in liberating herself from very little – not even the values of the society she so vehemently criticised.

Janis Lyn Joplin was born on 19 January 1943 and raised in the oil refinery town of Port Arthur, Texas. Her father, Seth, was a supervisor at the refinery. His demeanour was that of the quiet philosopher, absorbed in his work and his own reading, an easy-going, small-town stereotype of middle-class America in the sixties. Dorothy Joplin, on the other hand, has been described as 'industrious, disciplined, shrewd, stalwart, precise'. She worked as a businesswoman and college registrar. In a parental environment reminiscent of Marie Lloyd's, Janis was reared by a mother who was intent on imparting respectable values to her eldest girl, and at the same time nurtured strong ambitions for Janis's academic and artistic success, albeit in rather more acceptable fields than she chose. A schoolfriend of Janis's said Dorothy was like

> . . . a Victorian father . . . wanting to be close, but duty bound and obligated to 'prepare her child'. She just couldn't give that last inch, but Janis was the apple of her eye.

(*Buried Alive*, Myra Friedman)

Janis's response was typical of the generation which had grown up amid post-war affluence and materialism:

> A lot of my generation and younger, we look back at our parents and see how they gave up and compromised and wound up with very little.

(*Janis Joplin*, Deborah Landau)

It was the sterility of that compromise, coupled with an equally sterile environment, that led Janis to early rebellion. Her father described her at fourteen as a 'revolutionary'. Janis saw it more simply as just not fitting in:

> Texas is okay if you want to settle down and do your own thing quietly, but it's not for outrageous people and I always was outrageous. I got treated very badly in Texas. They don't treat beatniks too good there . . . people thought I was a beatnik and they didn't like them, though they'd never seen one and neither had I. I always wanted to be an artist, whatever that was, like other chicks want to be stewardesses. I read, I painted, I thought.

(*Rolling Stone*, October 1970)

Before this Janis had been a quiet, compliant girl with a promising talent for drawing. Now she began to develop the shell she later described in her 'Turtle Blues'. In the loudest and most aggressive manner she started to become 'one of the boys'.

Aided by an increase in weight and a very bad skin condition, Janis rejected teen-angeldom for the steady company of five boys with whom she drank beer, swore, and did not screw:

> I didn't hate niggers so I was called a nigger-lover. There was nobody like me in Port Arthur. Everybody else was going to drive-ins and drinking Cokes and talking about going across the tracks to go nigger-knocking. Ya know what nigger-knocking is honey? A bunch of kids get in a car with a long two-by-four and go driving fast. When they see a spade on a bicycle or walking, they stick the two-by-four out of the car window and knock him over.

(*Janis Joplin*, Deborah Landau)

Temperamentally very like her mother, Janis clashed head-on with Dorothy, and in early adolescence began mounting the most alienating rebellion she could. As Janis's biographer Myra Friedman points out, rebellious camaraderie was a much simpler matter for the boys. One of the group was a school football star, another the editor of the school paper: while they raised hell on weekends, they could put it down to natural red-bloodedness, and return to school Monday relatively un-tainted and even idolised by their peers. Such behaviour was patently unacceptable in a girl. Janis began to cut classes. She worked at waitress-ing and selling theatre tickets; and she started hanging out at the local coffee lounge and listening, unlike her rock'n'roll contemporaries, to progressive jazz.

In 1960 Janis graduated from high school. She had already been getting sales for her paintings, and the logical academic step was to Lamar College which offered courses in Fine Art. She continued to live at home, but also kept up a relentless pursuit of wildness, and interrupted her first year at Lamar with a trip to Los Angeles where she had an early taste of 'beat' life. When she returned in early 1962, at nineteen years old, Dorothy and Seth experienced the first of their daughter's attempts to return to the fold. She adopted a serious attitude towards study, and made a determined effort to be neat and respectable in her appearance. It lasted about three months. Towards the middle of the year, after a steady acceleration in party life, Janis and her best pal, Jack Smith, drove drunkenly to Austin, Texas. And Janis stayed.

The seeds, and the seediness, that would soon blossom into the Hippie Nation had already been planted in Austin. While the university remained a safe harbour for wealthy young conservatism and conformity, the flavour of alternative San Francisco could be sampled in The Ghetto, a complex of cheap-rent apartment houses. Janis aligned herself with the musical and artistic population around The Ghetto. They all sounded off

about the values enshrined at the university as much as they did about those of the older generation. Unkempt, barefoot, uncommunicative, Janis became a figure of derision on campus. But in her chosen company she was also wearing a disguise; louder and more raucous than anyone else, Janis was developing the talent to alienate even her closest friends.

She drank more whisky than anyone else, she started taking speed, and the only thing that ever stood between her wretchedness and running the streets in a frenzy of speed and liquor was her singing. While many of her contemporaries were into Peter, Paul and Mary, Janis opted for the gutsiness of Odetta or the pure folk tones of Jean Ritchie. At this stage Janis's voice was untouched; powerful and pure when she wanted it to be, Janis was stylistically undecided. Sometimes she played guitar, sometimes autoharp. But she had also heard Leadbelly records and, more importantly, Bessie Smith. At Threadgill's, her regular singing haunt, she gradually began to favour the blues.

Janis quit Austin at the end of 1962. The student body had voted her 'Ugliest Man on Campus' and she was sufficiently devastated to write to Dorothy of her misery. It was a letter filled with feelings of victimisation because of her 'difference', and Dorothy quite rightly feared the deep depression it indicated. Immediately, she tried to contact her daughter, but by the time she managed to speak to the university's Dean of Women, Janis was gone. Her destination was San Francisco, the paradise of stimulants and hallucinogens.

Nurtured through the fifties in cults like those that grew up around James Dean and Elvis, youthpower was unleashed in the sixties and flourished unrestrained for a decade. By now the generation gap separated

184

two distinct codes of living. When Janis got into Seconal there was nothing of the stigma that still attached itself, at the very same time, to Garland's stimulant/depressant habit. For Janis and the hip generation, it would have been uncool *not* to use it. If the fifties had demanded that as one of the boys she would have to drink harder and swear better than any of them, the sixties had her doing dope and then dealing it. Janis wanted to be 'the best', and her models of success were all male. She hustled like them and she bragged like them about sexual exploits that most of her friends regarded as fantasy. At twenty years old Janis was still fighting her low self-esteem. Her own battle mentality seemed to be discounted in her estimation of the reasons for her rejection; she felt she had suffered during her adolescence because of her looks and because she was more intelligent, more sensitive and therefore more alienated from her peers. Her own particularly successful techniques of alienation were not taken into account.

In this mood, San Francisco suited her well, and fired by the various stimuli of that historic environment, the next two years became a blur of speed, dealing and keeping on the move. She made a couple of trips to New York in her coast-to-coast hustling, and she was putting out feelers in all directions. She sang at the Monterey Folk Festival in the summer of 1963, but was still a long way from a definitive style. In this testing period she craved close personal contact. She made out with women (she'd had her first lesbian relationship at the end of high school), she made out with guys; but nothing lasted. Although performing only spasmodically, she began to feel that her only true release would come from her music, without which, she said later, she would have 'done herself in'.

In the summer of 1965, at the age of twenty-three, Janis returned, scared, to Port Arthur. She wanted to get off drugs, and to stay off them. She enrolled immediately at Lamar; again she adopted a very straight, neat appearance, and she told everyone that she was preparing to get married. But within months of her return she started singing again, and this time people really took notice. Janis would get up on the floor of some folk lounge, open the vocal throttle, and blow the audience away with her Bessie-style renditions of the blues. Her passion for the Empress, and the impression her recordings made, was as great in Janis as it had been in Billie Holiday. But Janis was a white woman, and hearing a white woman do the blues like that was what made the audience sit up and listen: the word started to spread. Her fiancé, meanwhile, scarcely materialised at all, and then only to drift away. It wasn't long before Janis moved back to Austin and started singing in earnest. By now the word about 'this chick singer' was white hot, and just as she was about to join her first rock band in Austin she got a call from the San Francisco band, Big Brother and the Holding Company, to join them as lead singer.

Until this time, Janis said that she had felt 'torn apart' by her desire not to conform to her mother's desires, to her hometown mores, indeed to her own image of what a 'good' life was meant to be. Now, with a roaring rough rock band behind her, the music that had always been her release became a positive statement. Her rebellion took shape in performance, and she found that millions had been waiting for just such an expression. Like Garland, like Piaf, Janis quickly became addicted to the stimulus of the large audience:

> '. . . when I sing, I feel, well, like when you're first in love. It's more than sex, I know that. It's that point two people can get to they call love, like when you really touch someone for the first time, but it's gigantic, multiplied by the whole audience. I feel chills, weird feelings slipping all over my body, it's a supreme emotional and physical experience . . . that 40 or 50 minutes I'm out there, that's when it happens for me. It's like a hundred orgasms with somebody you . . . I live for that one hour on stage . . . I *know* no guy ever made me feel as good as an audience . . .'

(*Janis Joplin*, Deborah Landau)

After one year with Big Brother, Janis and the band appeared at the Monterey Pop Festival, June 1967; in January 1968 she made her New York debut, and became international media property. The Monterey performance is on film; it's possible to *see* what audiences were responding to – so much more reliable than the albums, which were never able to reproduce the excitement that was being generated live. How could an audio disc or tape capture the tornado of aggressive erotica that consumed Janis Joplin as she poured the Southern Comfort down her throat and, if she managed not to fall off the stage, let out sounds that no one had heard from a white woman before?

Nevertheless, even while they were still mixing the 'Cheap Thrills' album, it had 'gone gold' on the strength of orders alone. Young white America had been waiting for a no-holds-barred woman performer; now they couldn't get enough of her. Janis was saying it all for a new generation, giving them the image of a woman prepared to go out unprotected, with soul ablaze, giving everything she had to that moment. It had been the same with Bessie, with Billie, with Edith, and with Judy; now it was part of a so-called sexual revolution, and no one had ever seen anything like it before, as Janis described:

> '. . . sometimes they think they're gonna like you and then you get out there and you really damage and offend their femininity. You know "No chick is supposed to stand like *that*". You know, your tits shakin' around and your hair's stringy, and you have no makeup on, and sweat runnin' down your face, and you're comin' up to the microphone, man, and at one point their heads just go click and they

go "Oooooh, no". You get that a lot, it's really far out, when you're standing on stage you can't see the groovy crowd is usually in the back, because they can't afford the seats down front . . . At my concerts most of the chicks are looking for liberation, they think I'm gonna show 'em how to do it, but the ones right in front are always the country club bitches, they always are. It's so *weird* playing to 14 pantie girdles . . !

'. . . and I'm up there singing, I'm going "Cha-cha-boom-quack-quack"; and I look out at the crowd, and these girls have these pinched little smiles on their faces, and I must be an absolute *horror*, man, they've never seen anything like it, and they don't want to again, man! The chick's up there shakin' it all, "How do you like that boys?" and all the boys go "AAAaaargh" and the girls are goin' "Oh my god, she may be able to sing, but she doesn't have to act like that".'

(*Janis*, David Dalton)

Now Janis could invite and encourage the disapproval of the society she'd grown up in; there were enough like-minded spirits to make her very successful without having to rely on the opinion of middle America. It was also obvious that she no longer relied on Big Brother. At the time of recording 'Cheap Thrills', the split was imminent. The band was feeling the sting of being seen as Janis's support; and Janis was by now into heroin.

All of the women in *A Star is Torn* were addicts of some kind. They all drank to excess – Judy Garland and Marilyn Monroe perhaps less than the others – and alcohol no doubt contributed to a general physical debility in all of them except Patsy Cline who died too young to have noticed the long-term effects of her steady intake. In addition, Edith Piaf was addicted to morphine, Judy and Marilyn to uppers and downers, and Billie and Janis to heroin. But theorising about the 'addictive personality', even when lay observation suggests the existence of such a thing, especially amongst those perceived as extroverts, is a distraction. These women were not simply rare cases of a combination of great talent and some genetically determined inclination towards destructive substances. They were addicts because they were not in control of important areas of their lives; many of the events and practices that governed their lives were beyond their understanding, and they were not encouraged to learn more. Even if a drug may have first been taken for legitimate reasons (Piaf's arthritis, Monroe's chronic insomnia), it was convenient to use it thereafter to block out the conflict and confusion. One could say the same for millions of 'ordinary' women. In the case of stars, fame, idolisation, so-called success and the pressures that go with it often exacerbate private feelings of low self-esteem and failure.

187

It was certainly the case with Janis. Her public persona was strong, wild and careless of criticism. If anyone was offended it was their loss, not hers. And this character performed offstage as well as on, as in the prime-time coast-to-coast interview in which her host foolishly asked what she did in her spare time. Janis was succinct: 'Fuck! Ha ha ha ha ha ha haha', and the nation's switchboards went berserk. But she was never secure in her success. At its height she confessed to her manager, Albert Grossman: 'I'm afraid I'm gonna be one of those raucous old drunk ladies out on Skid Row and picking up all the young boys.'

Although Janis is credited as writer on a number of the songs she recorded, she never took her authorship seriously, and denied her abilities by saying she didn't 'write' songs, she just 'made them up'. At that time, many songs were already falling into a group-effort category, with a lyric emerging simply to suit a certain musical feel rather than words having paramount importance per se. And Janis's main attraction was always her live performance: then, lyrics were easily disregarded and often unintelligible in the maelstrom of Joplin at full tilt.

But two of her songs were hits. One, 'Kozmic Blues' (see p. 181) had more in common with Bessie's 'Young Woman Blues' than with the sixties-male version of the deserted, broken hearted woman that she sang about in 'A Woman Left Lonely' or 'One Good Man'. The other was a little ditty which she laughingly described as a 'song of great social and political import':

Oh Lord, won't you buy me a Mercedes Benz
My friends all drive Porsches
I must make amends
Worked hard all my lifetime
No help from my friends
Oh Lord, won't you buy me a Mercedes Benz

Oh Lord, won't you buy me a colour TV
'Dialling for Dollars' is waiting for me
I wait for delivery each day until three
So Lord, won't you buy me a colour TV

Oh Lord, won't you buy me a night on the town
I'm counting on you Lord, please don't let me down
Prove that you love me, and buy the next round
Oh Lord, won't you buy me a night on the town

('Mercedes Benz', Joplin)

As for the trappings of fame and fortune and what they did for the actuality of life, Janis hit the nail on the head when she described life on the road:

'. . . reality is cold dressing rooms. Lousy food, sitting alone in motel rooms having to watch TV; stewardesses and people on airplanes treating you like a freak, lousy halls and bad sound, playing for people out there in Kokomo who just look at you, at your outsides, like curious. Guys on the road at least have girls they can pick up, but who are the boys who come to see me – thirteen year olds, man.'

(*Janis Joplin*, Deborah Landau)

In a heroin high, nothing touched her at all. She called 1969 the year of the Kozmic Blues.

In the first half of 1968, her concerts with Big Brother were fetching about $4,500 a gig; in March 1969, Janis took in $30,000 for one weekend at the Winterland. By comparison to male superstars of the time, she did not spend lavishly. She bought a house in Larkspur, a quiet town not far from San Francisco, and the famous customised psychedelic Porsche; but apart from anniversary gifts to friends and the occasional assistance to those in trouble ($20,000 for the defence of a friend on a serious criminal charge), colleagues considered her 'tight'. She kept meticulous accounts. No doubt the cost of the habit was omitted.

Her pick-up band remained just that. More professional than Big Brother ever was or intended to be, they never captured the old wildness. In April she toured Europe, and in the third week played London's Royal Albert Hall. She had asked Dorothy, somewhat mollified by her daughter's success, to accompany her: she politely refused. In May Janis found herself on the cover of *Newsweek*, and in June she was so heavily into heroin that the recording sessions for the 'Kozmic Blues' album were a fiasco. Judy Garland died on the 22nd of that month, and the summer of 1969 saw hippiedom's finest hour, Woodstock. Two years before Janis had stolen the limelight at Monterey; now, at twenty-six, she was so stoned that she blew the performance at Woodstock completely. By December, friends were trying hard to get her off the drug. At the end of the year she played her last gig with the Kozmic Blues Band.

In her short biography of Janis, Deborah Landau talks about Janis's fate as a woman destined not to succeed as a human being but only as a sex symbol, the 'right' or the 'wrong' kind. Given only the choice of 'vestal virgin or sensuous whore', how much freedom did she actually have in opting for the latter? Janis proved that a female rock singer did not have to conform to the sweet stereotype of past female performers, but she had to assume the persona of the whore in order to do it. The construction of a shell of some kind had been noticed early on by Country Joe McDonald, Janis's lover during the first months with Big Brother in San Francisco:

'. . . sexism killed her. Everybody wanted this sexy chick who sang really sexy and had a lot of energy. She didn't have the kind of

American Beautiful Woman face – she had big bones . . . She was hard only because she was made hard . . . because she was defensive . . . she was competing with a homecoming queen.

'But I think she was just beginning to realise that the homecoming thing was bullshit, and she didn't have to be that at all.

'. . . And people kept saying one of the things about her was that she was just "one of the guys". That she was trying to be one of the guys. But that's a real sexist bullshit trip, 'cause that was fuckin' her head around, one of the guys. She was one of the women. She was strong, groovy woman. Smart, you know? But she got fucked around . . .'

(*Janis Joplin*, Deborah Landau)

If sexism killed Janis it was because she broke the rules of rock society and had to pay the price; but before she did, she unveiled Pearl, her final and most convincing persona. In 1970 Pearl, the archetypal tart with the heart of gold, and with feathers, pearls, glitter and even wilder abandon than before, became Janis's alter ego. Pearl was not just an extension of what she'd been doing all along, but a complete identity which actually allowed another quieter, quite conservative Janis (the one who had twice run home to set life clean and right) to function and make plans with a freedom previously denied her.

It was no coincidence that Janis counted among her idols Bessie Smith, Zelda Fitzgerald – and Mae West. Mae's public image was a prototype for Pearl; funny, witty, in control of love, sex and business. Yet Mae, in a rare interview in *Ms* magazine in February 1984, said enough to show that her image was just that – something which she manufactured and controlled. Unlike Janis's schizoid reality, Mae held all the trump cards for survival in her time. She talked about her absolute devotion to her mother:

> 'I was always more like my father than my mother, more like a man. My mother took wonderful care of me, but as I grew up, it was as though I became her mother and she was my child. I wanted to take care of her and spoil her the way she had done for me!'

She said that the only great love affair of her life began when she was five, and that was with the stage. As for men, she always made the one she was with feel like a hero, but she never craved 'just one'; it was always she who ended the affair. She never sought her identity through a man:

> 'I always put my money into my own projects, something I was doing or something I could see. Money is sexy for men, but people don't find it feminine for a woman to talk about it. So you don't have to talk about it, just have it. The real security is yourself. You know you can do it, and they can't ever take that away from you.'

In that interview Mae spoke as a woman who had beaten the world of men and money at its own game. It was reminiscent of Sophie Tucker; where Mae used sex, Sophie had used fat. The last of the Red Hot Mommas was always her own boss, her own business manager, and her husbands were, according to her biographer, 'disposable merchandise'.

Retrogressive as these tactics may now seem in the light of contemporary feminist thought, for Mae and Soph' they were at the very least modes of survival that women like Judy and Marilyn were unable to call on. Nor could Janis. At the very time she was deliberately using Mae as a model for Pearl, concentrating her strength and resilience in that character, she was privately turning back to a model that Dorothy and Port Arthur had shown her. Her talk about really wanting a split-level bungalow and a couple of kids might have been taken ironically had it not been for the fact that that was precisely the direction she was taking in the last year of her life. In the end she was, unlike Mae and Sophie, still defining herself in terms of a norm she aspired to but had simply failed to achieve. She spoke as if success had actually spoiled her chance at the good life:

> 'I can't quit to become someone's old lady, 'cause I've had it so big . . . most women's lives are beautiful because they are dedicated to a man. I need him too, a big lolling, loving, touching, beautiful man, but it can't touch, it can't touch hitting the stage at full-tilt boogie.'

> (*Janis*, David Dalton)

What she was saying had infinitely more in common with Piaf and Garland than with her heroine, Mae West.

In April 1970 Janis formed the Full Tilt Boogie Band. Now, in the most promising musical collaboration to date, Janis/Pearl had a performing context. The efforts of Janis's friends had succeeded, and she was off heroin. She had vacationed in Rio, found a new lover, and was feeling optimistic. But Pearl was hitting the bottle in a big way. It was obvious that as Janis cleaned up her own act for Janis, she abrogated all responsibility for Pearl, the whore, who hung out in bars, partied day and night and generally took on all the worst aspects that had once been just part of Janis. This schizoid existence was reflected in her moods. Pearl – and her colleagues – were delighted with the new album and confident of its success: Janis was depressed about her career. Bad concerts were getting bad notices and, unknown to her, concert bookers had started to cancel dates. *Janis* began to opt out again. She returned to Larkspur with plans to marry Seth Morgan. Characteristically, having made a firm step towards securing a different kind of future, Janis relaxed, and went back onto heroin.

On 18 September Jimi Hendrix died of an overdose, and Janis plunged into severe depression. On Thursday 1 October in Los Angeles, in actions which were either typical of her continuing state of ambivalence about her future prospects or the greatest betrayal of an unconscious belief that she was 'better dead than wed', Janis read over her pre-marital agreement and also signed her will. On Saturday she called City Hall, presumably about the marriage licence. That same day a deal of extremely pure heroin was procured for her. At approximately 1 a.m. the next morning, after an easy night of cruising and a few drinks, one of the Full Tilt boys saw Janis home to the Landmark Hotel. Within an hour on Sunday morning, 4 October 1970, Janis died of an overdose.

Set in the context of show business biography, especially in the era of sex, drugs and rock'n'roll that spawned a death list of sixties heroes like Brian Jones, Jimi Hendrix, Jim Morrison, Brian Epstein, Phil Ochs, Keith Moon and Lenny Bruce, to name the most obvious, it is all too easy to see Janis as another casualty of the times. Set in the context of a history of premature deaths amongst unique women singers, it isn't so simple. That she died so young, younger than the others, *is* perhaps explicable in terms of the youth culture that swam in a sea of dangerous drugs – but even that isn't enough. If all the above male casualties, including Jimi (who, given the double-barrelled exploitation he suffered as a black man in show business, had most reason), took on a course of positive excess which eventually killed them, Janis's case simply was different. It hadn't really changed since Marie Lloyd's day; a woman could *do* what a man could, but she certainly couldn't get away with it without being branded. And none of these women escaped that branding without it taking a considerable toll of their self-esteem.

Still in 1970, the year that saw the publication in the United States of Kate Millett's *Sexual Politics*, Shulamith Firestone's *The Dialectic of Sex*, and *Sisterhood is Powerful* edited by Robin Morgan, a woman like Janis was not able to avail herself of the feminist tools which might yield a solution to the unfair demands on a woman in such a society. Janis had been aware ever since high school that her best chance was to go with the guys if she wasn't going to be lumbered with the terminal boredom and aesthetic suicide of the feminine stereotype; she also knew there was a price to pay for that decision.

For those eagerly awaiting Janis's next album, waiting to see where she/Pearl would go next, her death at twenty-seven was a profound shock. In the end, the image of liberation was a shallow one; Pearl was still deeply rooted in female stereotype. Retrospectively the sadness lay in the fact that she died at a time when a new wave of feminism was just about to liberate many more women in all areas of entertainment over the next decade. Suddenly there would be the possibility of increasing self-determination, and subsequently stronger and more independent music and performance, even in rock'n'roll, without the necessity of the various 'shells' that Janis and her predecessors since Marie Lloyd had constructed.

But the women in *A Star is Torn* had missed out, Janis had missed out, and it was both a confirmation of that view, and an even greater shock, to find the process reiterated yet again for another generation, some thirteen years after Janis's death.

n the few weeks between the transfer of the show *A Star is Torn* from the end of its London run to a return season in Australia, Karen Carpenter died – of heart failure as the apparent result of nine years' anorexia nervosa. She was included, briefly, via a chorus of 'Close To You' in the show's finale. Yet people failed to make connections. What did the saccharine sweetness of The Carpenters have to do with Janis screaming '. . . felt just like a ball and chain . . .' or Judy's tormented '. . . alone, by myself, from now on . . .'? Bette Midler had won an Oscar nomination for her in-all-but-name portrayal of Janis in *The Rose*; she had also attended an Emmy awards presentation wearing a 45rpm record on her head as a hat: 'Miss Karen gave it to me,' she quipped, and the audience howled with laughter. Janis, on the one hand, was a heroine; Miss Karen was a joke. Now the joke was dead too.

And yet, given the thirteen years that separated their deaths, and the shift in society during those years that had forced rebellion underground and rendered it unfashionable, it isn't difficult to see that if heroin was the response of the sixties, anorexia was the response of the late seventies and eighties. By different methods, both Janis and Karen were rebelling against the conformity of middle-class America, and both revolts ended in death. That Richard Carpenter referred specifically to Janis Joplin's death as the turning point away from hard drugs in his soft pop scene indicates just how much pressure Karen must have been under not to take a similar road. Still, she needed *some* way out of her cloying surroundings.

In Karen's case, the possession of her life and body was as clear as in Garland's. The Carpenter parents were said to be well-meaning but authoritarian, mother Agnes in particular. She ruled the duo with constant moral and ethical guidance, and Karen was professionally glued to her brother and his musical judgement. When something vital seemed to be missing from the pinnacle of her thirty-year-old daughter's success, mother Agnes manoeuvred Karen's marriage, just as Judy Garland had

195

been handed over from mother to studio to husband. Like Judy, Karen never had a chance to test her own self-sufficiency. In both cases rebellion went underground, and self-reliance never surfaced.

While alcoholism is still regarded as vaguely disgusting and abnormal in women, as was Judy and Janis's general 'lack of control', the most insidious aspect of anorexia is that it actually manifests itself as something which is initially advantageous. Because the stereotype of desirability is currently a gauntly thin woman, the anorexic can disguise her personal rebellion by becoming, she believes, more attractive. And for a while that is true. It's the perfect option in an era when the kinds of freedom known to a previous generation of teenagers are no longer viable: classes are to be attended, not dropped out of; the future is no longer full of peace, love and rainbows; buckling down is the order of the day. The anorexic rebel has every appearance of a well-behaved compliant and increasingly attractive young woman; at the same time she is slowly beginning to kill herself in an attempt to exercise control over the one thing she feels is truly hers, and truly within her power.

By 1983 it was possible to believe that things were getting better. The feminist promise of the seventies was slowly being fulfilled: there were more women in rock – some mixed their own sound, produced their own albums, had a hand in their own management. Superstars like Streisand were their own boss; Dolly Parton ran her business and went on the road while her husband stayed home and minded the farm. Chrissie Hynde had a kid and still strutted front and centre with the best of them. Yet none of those possibilities seemed to reach Karen Carpenter who had been dying for nine years.

The year of her death was also the year that Bizet's *Carmen* came out of copyright and immediately went into multiple productions on stage and screen. Few could have predicted the continuing success of its theme. The classic tale of the predator temptress who must die for her ball-crushing sins was still depressingly potent. On Broadway, the smash-hit was *Dreamgirls*, in which a woman deprived of career and her female companions by a two-timing hustler sang a first-half closer of undying fidelity to the punk, and had the house in tears of ecstasy and empathy. 1983 also saw two new stage shows about Marilyn Monroe. The London *Marilyn* was born of Mailer out of misogyny, with Marilyn a self-absorbed advertisement for sex, her only deep and lasting affair being with a prancing preening character called . . . Camera. Broadway's *Marilyn: An American Fable* poured irony on irony by using junior veteran Christi Coombs (1,450 performances of *Annie*) to slay the audience with a ballad about 'following my star'. As Christi hugged her teddy bear and sang her little heart out, it's unlikely that she had been adequately prepared either for the slamming the show got when it opened, or for the sudden cessation of her role as young Marilyn, when it folded almost without trace.

The signs of promise and progress in the early seventies seemed to disappear into the thin air of recession and reaction. Why should further casualties be surprising then, when, despite isolated advances, the old lies were being perpetuated as grandly as ever? In 1984 Esther Phillips died. The natural successor to the line from Bessie to Billie to Dinah, 'Little Esther' had first made the big time in 1963. Later, her cover version of Dinah's 'What A Diff'rence a Day Makes' was a hit revival. At the end of 1980 she looked great, and despite an old heroin habit, she was said to be clean. Yet she died without reaching forty.

Meanwhile Nina Simone was playing Ronnie Scott's in London, to a whole new generation. Many of us began listening to Nina Simone when we were young and wanted to identify. She wrote 'Mississippi Goddam' in 1963, and as the songs of the white sympathisers in the Black Rights movement, Joan Baez, Bob Dylan, Phil Ochs, drew attention to the issues and the music that grew out of it, so Nina Simone was discovered on record. Her interpretation of songs like 'Pirate Jenny', 'I Think It's Gonna Rain Today', 'Everyone's Gone To The Moon' and originals like 'Four Women', made the Simone records a unique experience. Her rare piano and vocal style used otherwise innocuous songs to convey the sense of outrage and protest that pervaded North America in the mid-sixties.

Her first Australian tour was around 1973. There were rumours of 'unreliability' and 'difficulty'. The concerts were very different from the albums and expectations. Fans were 'disappointed' by what she did and did not give. But even then the general feeling was one of concern because the recordings had already given so much. When the album 'It Is

Over' appeared, many thought she meant it as more than merely a song title. After that, the infrequent press reports noted 'bad' concerts, walkouts, tantrums: the kind of reportage that picks at the scab but makes no attempt to examine the wound underneath.

To most outward appearances, Nina Simone is a living example of the kind of performers who populate this book. It is not possible to listen to her sing lyrics like

Every time I look into this hellhole I'm in . . .

or

Quelle pain, quelle pain, quelle pain . . .

or

Let that love be of a different kind
I'm so tired of the same old thing . . .

and not be aware of the pain opening up on stage. Indeed, when questioned about the searing grief and isolation that many of her lyrics and ad libs reveal, her brother-manager Sam Waymon confirmed (in a respectfully noncommittal way) that it would be correct to assume that these were heart-felt statements.

If Phyl Garland, in his *Sound of Soul*, is correct and Nina was born in the mid-thirties, then she is already doing better than most of the women in this book. Her body looks healthy, the skin glowing on arms and shoulders; but there is a rigidity of movement and fixed gaze ahead, an inability to remember which song is next, or the name of one of her musicians, that raises doubts and fears for her physical state. The old followers were frankly nonplussed by the huge success of her 1984–85 London dates. This was not the Simone genius of the albums: neither the voice nor the piano technique were there. But it *was* a performance, and it *did* drive the crowd wild. The 'legend in her own time' syndrome was at work, with audiences applauding her life, her courage in the face of discrimination and exploitation, and a compelling performance. And some of the audience were as predatory as those who had followed Garland or Joplin: one young man sees her guided out onto the stage at the beginning of the set and wriggles ecstatically. 'Oh! Is she *out* of it!' he gasps.

Nina Simone has had in common with the women in this book a history of male mismanagement. She took on a husband-manager, and the breakdown of the marriage also saw a breakdown of her professional support system. The logical step was to turn to a male member of the family, in this case her younger brother Sam, who had begun his musical education in church with Nina and their mother, and had toured with her before. Sam as manager in 1984 was not only organising her work, chasing pirate record royalties, trying to redress the imbalance she had experienced at the hands of the white-dominated record and entertainment industry, but also accompanying her onstage when required.

They set up two keyboards opposite each other, and during the set Sam Waymon's face was a study in total encouragement. From the first song of the set, in which she thanks God for a brother who loves her, to a soulful duet in 'Let it be Me', it is obvious that in this particular performance Nina Simone has commended herself into his hands. And for his part, he was saying a lot of the right things about giving her enough time off for rest (in Guinea with her friend Miriam Makeba), for writing her autobiography (*Lady Noire: Between The Keys*); giving her the space to breathe as he tried to tread the fine line between brother who loves her but doesn't *know* her completely, and manager who demands discipline and professionalism.

Only time will tell whether his concern is enough. Whatever her state, people will continue to make money out of Nina Simone. But when Sam Waymon expresses his regret that it is still necessary for a man to help a woman in this business, it must be said that it's not quite true any more. There are women who have snatched the controls of self-determination and, by having a controlling financial and managerial interest in their careers, have matched the boys at their own game. But secondly, and more importantly, his assertion ignores the fact that the game itself is being reappraised and rejected by millions of women. For many, if the game created by men, played out in a patriarchal society, and still overwhelmingly run by men, means that a few women succeed spectacularly, most are done over and rejected, and a few suffer and die, then the game is not worth playing. The determination of feminism to view events as personal-political has produced an unwillingness to accept the inevitability of female suffering, whether in show business or any other business, or at the most personal and private level, simply because that *is* woman's lot in the way of the world.

Without reappraisal of this kind, the line of extraordinary, talented, famous women who go down under unnecessary pressures will continue in exactly the same way as the line of ordinary, extraordinary, unpublicised women. Whether one works for change or not depends entirely on a gut reaction, an intellectual reaction or total indifference to the pain and death of other human beings. That too is something taught by society at large. The industrialised nations are encouraged to be indifferent to the pain and death of vast numbers of human beings in other nations, as well as to the less fortunate in their own countries. To be unmoved by the suffering and death of a Garland or a Monroe is only part of the learning process that will gloss over what may happen to Nina Simone, Lena Zavaroni, Debbie Byrne, or Christi Coombs at the hands of this show business, and that allowed actress Eva Mottley to despair and die with barely a ripple on the smooth surface of the television success with which she had so recently been associated in the drama series 'Widows'.

The ideological tools are there for the establishment of women's independence, fulfilment and survival. But as the media further trivialise feminism in a general period of social backlash and retrenchment, it is no wonder that young women turn again to heroin in a repetition of the hopelessness that Janis Joplin perceived in her Kozmic Blues:

> 'The Kozmic Blues doesn't exist, unless you have nothing. Kozmic Blues to me means . . . I remember when I was a kid they told me "Oh, you're unhappy because you're going through adolescence, as soon as you get to be grown up everything's going to be cool." I really believed that, you know. Or, as soon as you grow up and meet the right man; or – if only I could get laid, if only I could get a little bread together, everything will be alright. And then one day I finally realised it ain't all right, and it ain't ever going to be all right, there's always something going wrong . . . You'd never touch that fuckin' carrot, man, and that's what the Kozmic Blues are, 'cause you know you ain't never going to get it.'

(*Janis*, David Dalton)

Janis's solution to this despair was to rage herself out; Karen, for whom rage was not allowed, starved herself to death in the same kind of knowledge that something was wrong and would always be wrong with what was being offered to her. Feminism has developed in some women the kinds of strengths necessary to recognise those wrongs and to ignore the carrots still being used to keep us moving along old and ultimately unrewarding paths. Until those strengths can be effectively passed on to all women, sung and unsung, unnecessary tragedies will continue to occur. In the end, the solution to this despair must lie in re-assessment and, perhaps, rejection. The women in *A Star is Torn* were among the most celebrated figures of their times, and it has been the response of other women to emulate that success, or to envy it. But if their lives and deaths can be used as indicators, it would seem that the glittering prizes of that most glittering profession, show business, were at the very least inadequate, and more realistically, treacherous and illusory. The talent to entertain *is* something to be admired, sought out, and nurtured; but the hype, lies, empty idolatry, overwork, deceit, cruelty, exploitation, and the dangerously schizoid behaviour those things have produced, particularly in women entertainers, together present a shameful aspect of our popular culture. Like so many aspects of our profit-hungry society, the condition is not immutable; and the new wave of feminism has helped to mark ways for change. By learning to cherish what is truly dear – the woman, the talent, the energy – and to reject the false goals daily shoved in front of all of us – fame, fabulous wealth, in a word, stardom – we could still have our singers, and have them healthier, happier and longer.

Select Bibliography

Biographies and autobiographies of the principal women, in chronological order of subject

Farson, Daniel, *Marie Lloyd and Music Hall*, London, Tom Stacey, 1972

Jacob, Naomi, *Our Marie*, London, Hutchinson, 1936

MacQueen-Pope, W., *Queen of the Music Halls*, London, Oldbourne

Albertson, Chris, *Bessie*, New York, Stein & Day, 1972; Wellingborough, Patrick Stephens, 1983 – with bibliography and select discography

Maxwell, Gilbert, *Helen Morgan: Her Life and Legend*, New York, Hawthorn Books, 1974

Farmer, Frances, *Will There Really Be A Morning?*, New York, Dell, 1972; London, Allison & Busby, 1973

Chilton, John, *Billie's Blues*, London, Quartet, 1975; New York, Stein & Day, 1975 – extensive bibliography including magazines and newspapers

Holiday, Billie and Dufty, William, *Lady Sings the Blues* (Barrie & Jenkins, 1958), London, Sphere Books, 1973

Widgery, David, 'Billie Holiday – The Woman Who Moved the World', *The Wire*, Issue 7, 1984

Berteaut, Simone, *Piaf*, London, W.H. Allen, 1970; Harmondsworth, Penguin, 1973

Crosland, Margaret, *Piaf*, London, Hodder & Stoughton, 1985 – complete discography and filmography

Grimault, Dominique and Mahe, Patrick, *Piaf and Cerdan*, London, W.H. Allen, 1984

Lange, Monique (trans. Woodward, Richard S.), *Piaf*, London, W.H. Allen, 1981; New York, Seaver Books, 1983

Piaf, Edith (trans. Owen, Peter), *The Wheel of Fortune: The Autobiography of Edith Piaf*, Denville, Dimension Books, 1965

Carey, Gary, *Judy Holliday: An Intimate Life Story*, New York, Putnam, 1982; London, Robson Books, 1983

Alexander, Shana, *Talking Woman*, *Judy Garland*, p.25, New York, Dell, 1976

Dahl, David and Kehoe, Barry, *Young Judy*, London, Hart, Davis & MacGibbon, 1975

Deans, Mickey and Pinchot, Ann, *Weep No More My Lady*, London, W.H. Allen, 1972; London, Granada, 1973

Edwards, Anne, *Judy Garland*, London, Corgi Books, 1974

Frank, Gerold, *Judy*, London, W.H. Allen, 1975

Harnetz, Aljean, *The Making of the Wizard of Oz*, New York, Knopf, 1981

Minnelli, Vincente and Arce, Hector, *I Remember It Well*, New York, Doubleday, 1974

Morella, J. and Epstein, Edward Z., *The Films and Career of Judy Garland*, London, Leslie Frewin, 1969; New York, Citadel, 1969 – complete filmography

Spada, James and Swenson, Karen, *Judy and Liza*, London, Sidgwick & Jackson, 1983; New York, Doubleday, 1983

Smith, Lorna, *Judy – With Love*, London, Robert Hale & Co., 1975

Susann, Jacqueline, *Valley of the Dolls*, London, Corgi Books, 1966; New York, Bantam, 1981

Torme, Mel, *The Other Side of the Rainbow – With Judy on the Night Patrol*, New York, William Morrow & Co., 1970

Anderson, Janice, *Marilyn Monroe*, London, W.H. Smith, 1983; New York, Crescent Books, 1983

Guiles, Fred Lawrence, *Norma Jean*, London, Granada, 1985 – good filmography

Hembus, Joe, *Marilyn: The Destruction of an American Dream*, London, Tandem, 1973

Mailer, Norman, *Marilyn: A Biography*, London, Hodder & Stoughton, 1973

Miller, Arthur, *After the Fall*, New York, Viking, 1964; Harmondsworth, Penguin, 1968

Monroe, Marilyn, *My Story*, New York, Stein & Day, 1974

Murray, Eunice and Shade, Rose, *Marilyn: The Last Months*, New York, Pyramid Books, 1975

Rosten, Norman, *Marilyn: A Very Personal Story*, London, Millington, 1967

Spada, James and Zeno, George, *Monroe: Her Life In Pictures*, London, Sidgwick & Jackson, 1982

Stern, Bert, *The Last Sitting*, London, Orbis, 1982

Summers, Anthony, *Goddess: The Secret Lives of Marilyn Monroe*, London, Gollancz, 1985; New York, Macmillan, 1985

Weatherby, W.J., *Conversations with Marilyn*, New York, Ballantine, 1976; London, Sphere, 1977

Nassour Ellis, *Patsy Cline: An Intimate Biography*, New York, Tower Books, 1981 – with discography

Dalton, David, *Janis*, London, Calder, Boyars & Neal, 1972; New York, Simon & Schuster, 1972

Friedman, Myra, *Buried Alive: The Biography of Janis Joplin*, New York, William Morrow, 1973; London, Plexus, 1984

Landau, Deborah, *Janis Joplin: Her Life and Times*, New York, Warner Paperback, 1971 – includes select discography

Other Women

Annan, Gabriele, 'Girl from Berlin – Marlene Dietrich', *New York Review of Books*, 14 February 1985

Brooks, Louise, *Lulu in Hollywood*, London, Hamish Hamilton, 1982; New York, Knopf, 1982

Burgess, Muriel and Keene, Tommy, *Gracie Fields*, London, W.H. Allen, 1970

Clarke, Jane and Simmonds, Diana, *Move Over Misconceptions: Doris Day Re-appraised*, London, British Film Institute, 1980

Freedland, Michael, *Sophie: The Sophie Tucker Story*, London, The Woburn Press, 1978; Totowa, Biblio Distributors, 1978

Garland, Phyl, *The Sound of Soul*, Chapter 5, 'Nina Simone, High Priestess of Soul', Chicago, Henry Regnery Co., 1969

Haney, Lynne, *Naked at the Feast: The Biography of Josephine Baker*, London, Robson Books, 1981

Higham, Charles, *Marlene: The Life of Marlene Dietrich*, New York, W.W. Norton & Co., 1977

Horne, Lena and Schickel, Richard, *Lena*, New York, Doubleday, 1965

Hotchner, A.E., *Doris Day: Her Own Story*, London, W.H. Allen, 1976

Lynn, Loretta and Vecsey, George, *The Coalminer's Daughter*, London, Granada 1976; New York, Warner Books, 1977

Morley, Sheridan, *Gertrude Lawrence*, London, Weidenfeld & Nicolson, 1981; New York, McGraw-Hill, 1981

O'Day, Anita and Eels, George, *High Times, Hard Times*, London, Corgi Books, 1981

Stassinopoulos, Arianna, *Maria Callas*, London, Hamlyn, 1981; New York, Ballantine, 1982

Warren, Doug, *Betty Grable: The Reluctant Movie Queen*, London, Robson Books, 1982

Waters, Ethel and Samuel, Charles, *His Eye Is On the Sparrow*, New York, Doubleday, 1950; London, Greenwood Press, 1978

The Men

Aftel, Mandy, *Death of a Rolling Stone: The Brian Jones Story*, London, Sidgwick & Jackson, 1982; New York, Delilah Books, 1982

Bosworth, Patricia, *Montgomery Clift*, London, Sidgwick & Jackson, 1979; New York, Bantam Books, 1979

Bryden-Brown, J., *J. O'K: The Official Johnny O'Keefe Story*, Sydney, Doubleday, 1982

Caress, Jay, *Hank Williams: Country Music's Tragic King*, New York, Stein & Day, 1981

Dalton, David, *James Dean: The Mutant King*, London, Plexus, 1983; New York, St Martin's Press, 1983

Eliot, Marc, *Death of a Rebel: The Life of Phil Ochs*, New York, Doubleday, 1979

Flippo, Chet, *Your Cheatin' Heart: Hank Williams*, New York, Simon & Schuster, 1972; London, Eel Pie Publications, 1982

Fisher, Eddie, *Eddie: My Life, My Loves*, London, W.H. Allen, 1981; New York, Harper & Row, 1981

Flynn, Errol, *My Wicked, Wicked Ways*, Pan Books, 1959; New York, Buccaneer Books, 1976

Goldman, Albert, *Ladies and Gentlemen, Lenny Bruce!*, New York, Ballantine, 1971

Guiles, Fred Lawrence, *Tyrone Power: The Last Idol*, London, Granada, 1980; New York, Berkley Publications, 1980

Hopkins, Jerry, *Hit and Run: The Jimi Hendrix Story*, New York, Perigi Books, 1983

Hopkins, Jerry and Sugarman, Danny, *No One Gets Out of Here Alive* (Jim Morrison), London, Plexus, 1980; New York, Warner Books, 1980

Rooney, Mickey, *I.E. An Autobiography*, New York, Putnam, 1965

Russell, Ross, *Bird Lives*, London, Quartet, 1973

Shulman, Irving, *Valentino*, New York, Simon & Schuster, 1968; London, Leslie Frewin, 1968

Collective Biographies

Bogle, Donald, *Brown Sugar: 80 Years of America's Black Female Superstars*, New York, Harmony Books, 1980

Brown, Peter Harry and Brown, Pamela Ann, *The MGM Girls: Behind The Velvet Curtain*, New York, St Martin's Press, 1983; London, Harrap, 1984

Dahl, Linda, *Stormy Weather: The Music and Lives of a Century of Jazz Women*, London, Quartet, 1984; New York, Pantheon, 1984

Handy, Antoinette D., *Black Women in American Bands and Orchestras*, New Jersey, The Scarecrow Press, 1981

Jones, Leroi, *Blues People*, New York, William Morrow, 1963

Korda, Michael, *Charmed Lives: A Family Romance*, Harmondsworth, Penguin, 1979; New York, Random House, 1979

Matson, Katinka, *Short Lives*, New York, Quill Paperbacks, 1980; London, Pan Books, 1981

Mordden, Ethan, *Movie Star: A Look at the Women Who Made Hollywood*, New York, St Martin's Press, 1983

Pavletich, Aida, *Sirens of Song: The Popular Female Vocalist in America*, New York, Doubleday, 1980

Placksin, Sally, *American Women in Jazz: 1900 to the Present*, Wide View Books, 1982

Stelzer, Dick, *The Star Treatment*, New York, Bobbs Merrill Co., 1977

Steward, Sue and Garratt, Sheryl, *Signed, Sealed and Delivered: True Life Stories of Women in Pop*, London, Pluto Press, 1984; Boston, South End Press, 1984

Music, Entertainment and Movies

Backus, Rob, *Fire Music: A Political History of Jazz*, Chicago, Vanguard Books, Emancipation, Black Graphics International, 1976

Bushy, Roy, *British Music Hall: An Illustrated Who's Who from 1850 to the Present Day*, London, Paul Elek, 1976

British Film Institute, *Star Signs: Papers from a Weekend Workshop*, London, 1982

Carey, Gary, *All the Stars in Heaven: The Story of Louis B. Mayer and MGM*, London, Robson Books, 1982

Crowther, Bosley, *Hollywood Rajah: The Life and Times of Louis B. Mayer*, New York, Dell, 1960

Dyer, Richard, *Stars*, London, British Film Institute, 1979; Champaign, University of Illinois Press, 1979

Gussow, Mel, *Darryl F. Zanuck: 'Don't Say Yes Till I've Finished Talking'*, New York, Da Capo Press, 1971

Harker, Dave, *One for the Money: Politics and Popular Song*, London, Hutchinson, 1980

Haskell, Molly, *From Reverence to Rape: The Treatment of Women in Movies*, New York, Penguin, 1974

Hentoff, Nat and Shapiro, Nat, *Hear Me Talkin' to Ya: The Story of Jazz By the Men Who Made It*, New York, Penguin, 1962

Huston, John, *An Open Book*, London, Macmillan, 1981; New York, Ballantine, 1981

Kaplan, E. Ann (ed), *Women in Film Noir*, London, British Film Institute, 1978; Champaign, University of Illinois Press, 1980

Kay, Karyn and Peary, Gerald (eds), *Women and the Cinema: A Critical Anthology*, Toronto/Vancouver, Irwin & Co., 1977; New York, Dutton, 1977

Leslie, Peter, *A Hard Act to Follow: A Music Hall Review*, New York, Paddington Press, 1978

Navasky, Victor, *Naming Names: Historical Perspectives*, New York, Viking, 1980; London, John Calder, 1982

Oakley, Giles, *The Devil's Music: A History of the Blues*, London, BBC, 1976; New York, Harcourt Brace Jovanovich, 1978

Palmer, Robert, *Deep Blues*, London, Macmillan, (Papermac), 1981; New York, Viking, 1981

Roddick, Nick, *A New Deal in Entertainment: Warner Brothers in the 1930s*, London, British Film Institute, 1983

Sampson, Henry T., *Blacks in Blackface*, New Jersey, Scarecrow Press, 1980

Schary, Dore, *Heydays*, New York, Berkley, 1981

Schiffman, Jack, *Uptown: The Story of Harlem's Apollo Theatre*, New York, Cowles Book Co., 1971

Selznick, Irene Mayer, *A Private View*, London, Weidenfeld & Nicolson, 1983; New York, Knopf, 1983

Southern, Eileen, *The Music of Black Americans: A History*, New York, W.W. Norton & Co., 1983

Talbot, David and Zheutlin, Barbara, *Creative Differences: Profiles of Hollywood Dissidents*, New York, South End Press, 1978

Walker, Alexander, *The Celluloid Sacrifice: Aspects of Sex in the Movies*, London, Michael Joseph, 1966

Walker, Alexander, *Stardom: The Hollywood Phenomenon*, Harmondsworth, Penguin, 1974

Feminism, Politics and Society

Anderson, Jervis, *Harlem: The Great Black Way 1900–1950*, London, Orbis, 1982

Banks, Olive, *Faces of Feminism: A Study of Feminism As a Social Movement*, Oxford, Martin Robertson, 1981; New York, St Martin's Press, 1981

Banner, Lois, W., *Women in Modern America: A Brief History*, Harcourt Brace Jovanovich, 1974

Bauer, Jan, *Alcoholism and Women: The Background and the Psychology*, Toronto, Inner City Books, 1982

Cliff, Tony, *Class Struggle and Women's Liberation 1640 to the Present*, London, Bookmarks, 1984

Eichenbaum, Louise and Orbach, Susie, *Outside In, Inside Out*, Harmondsworth, Penguin, 1982

Eisenstein, Hester, *Contemporary Feminist Thought*, London/Australia, Allen and Unwin, (Unwin Paperbacks), 1984; New York, G.K. Hall, 1984

Friday, Nancy, *My Mother, Myself*, New York, de la Corte, 1977; London, Fontana, 1979

Frieze, Irene H., Parsons, Jacquelynne E., Johnson, Paula B., Ruble, Diane and Zellman, Gail L., *Women and Sex Roles: A Social, Psychological Perspective*, New York, Norton & Co., 1980

Harley, Sharon and Terborg-Penn, Rosalyn (eds), *The Afro-American Woman: Struggles and Images*, New York, Associated Faculty Press, 1978

Hull, Loria, Scott, Patricia Bell and Smith, Barbara (eds), *All the Women Are White, All the Blacks Are Men, But Some of Us Are Brave*, New York, The Feminist Press, 1982

Jacobson, Bobbie, *The Ladykillers: Why Smoking Is a Feminist Issue*, London, Pluto Press, 1981; New York, Continuum, 1982

Keohane, Nannerl, Rosaldo, Michele Z. and Gelpi, Barbara C. (eds), *Feminist Theory: A Critique of Ideology*, Brighton, Harvester, 1982; Chicago, University of Chicago Press, 1983

Loewenberg, James and Bogin, Ruth, *Black Women in Nineteenth-Century Life*, Philadelphia, Pennsylvania University Press, 1976

MacLeod, Sheila, *The Art of Starvation*, London, Virago Press, 1981; New York, Schocken Books, 1983

McConville, Brigid, *Women Under the Influence: Alcoholism and Its Impact*, London, Virago Press, 1983; New York, Schocken Books, 1985

Marable, Manning, *How Capitalism Underdeveloped Black America*, Boston, South End Press, 1982; London, Pluto Press, 1983

Mitchell, Juliet, *Psychoanalysis and Feminism*, Harmondsworth, Penguin, 1974; New York, Random House, 1975

Mitchell, Juliet, *Women, The Longest Revolution*, London, Virago Press, 1984; New York, Pantheon, 1985

Nicholson, Joyce, *The Heartache of Motherhood*, London, Sheldon Press, 1983

Orbach, Susie, *Fat is a Feminist Issue*, London, Hamlyn Paperbacks, 1978; New York, Berkley, 1982

Rich, Adrienne, *On Lies, Secrets and Silence: Selected Prose 1966–78*, London, Virago Press, 1980; New York, W.W. Norton, 1979

Roebuck, Janet, *The Making of English Society from 1850*, London, Routledge & Kegan Paul, 1973; Boston, Routledge & Kegan Paul, 1983

Weeks, Jeffrey, *Sex, Politics and Society: The Regulation of Sexuality Since 1800*, London, Longman, 1981

Index